AMERICA'S MASS MEDIA MERCHANTS

AMERICA'S MASS MEDIA MERCHANTS

WILLIAM H. READ

THE JOHNS HOPKINS UNIVERSITY PRESS
Baltimore and London

This book has been brought to publication
with the generous assistance of
the Andrew W. Mellon Foundation.

The Johns Hopkins University Press, Baltimore, Maryland 21218
The Johns Hopkins Press Ltd., London

Library of Congress Catalog Card Number 76–17231
ISBN 0–8018–1851–6

Library of Congress Cataloging in Publication data
will be found on the last printed page of this book.

For my wife, Dot

CONTENTS

ACKNOWLEDGMENTS

Without the encouragement and assistance of Samuel P. Huntington, Associate Director of Harvard's Center for International Affairs, this book would not have been written.

While I was a Fellow of the Center (1972–73) he advised me to undertake a preliminary study of transnational mass media, and when a grant by the Rockefeller Foundation enabled the Center to expand its work on transnational processes, he arranged for me to remain at the Center for a second academic year to write this book.

I am also grateful to three other members of the Center for International Affairs: Professor Raymond Vernon and Professor Joseph S. Nye, Jr., who read parts of my manuscript and offered their comments, and Peter Jacobsohn who edited my drafts.

I wish also to thank Professors Anthony G. Oettinger, Ithiel de Sola Pool, and W. Phillips Davison for their suggestions and comments.

Besides an abundance of available intellectual talent, I had strong support, too, from my employer, the U.S. Information Agency and its broadcast arm, the Voice of America, who extended my leave; my typist, Amy Gazin, who was cheerful throughout; and my wife, Dot, who endured my ups and downs and odd work hours.

AMERICA'S MASS MEDIA MERCHANTS

AMERICA'S TRANSNATIONAL MASS MEDIA

ransnational mass media is a label for a little explored yet intriguing post-World War II phenomenon—the expansion of private American mass media abroad. Just as other U.S. institutions have thoroughly established themselves in foreign countries—prominent among them being the armed forces, multinational corporations, and banks—so too have the American print and visual industries. In the vanguard of this development are a few mass media merchants whose activities are sanctioned by the freedom of information principle proclaimed by the United Nations in 1948. Today, however, it is doubtful that the greatly enlarged U.N. membership still accepts that principle. Indeed, so often is it violated that one publication routinely keeps "a running record of bannings, confiscations, excisions, and other steps taken by government authority to prevent people from reading" its magazine. Who are America's mass media merchants? Why have they weighed anchor rather than remain content with successful domestic businesses? And what's at stake in their being caught up in the intensifying demand for a new world order?

THE TUBE AND
THE TIMES WORLDWIDE

This book could have been entitled *All the News That's Fit to Print in the Americas, Europe, Africa, Asia, and Australia,* or it might have been called *"Hawaii Five-O": A TV Favorite in Half the Countries of the World.* But this volume is about more than just the exported information of one newspaper, the *New York Times,* or foreign sales of a single television series. It is about them and eight other leading American mass media that, in pursuit of additional income, are pervasively disseminated in foreign *markets,* a word not always to be used interchangeably with countries. For although these media do, in some instances, define the areas in which they so widely circulate abroad as

1

countries, their inclinations are to disregard international borders whenever and wherever doing so facilitates distribution of their goods.

This commerce is, therefore, more accurately labeled transnational than international. It is related to the essential issue of world order during the final quarter of the twentieth century, namely, whether the U.S.-championed and dominated Western system of international order will remain sufficiently adaptable or whether it will need to be radically reordered. The necessity for change, whether by adaptive transformation or radical reformation, is universally agreed upon, yet neither the process nor the outcome is clear. A stumbling block for both is the conundrum of these times—modernization with its homogenizing effects weighed against an equally strong traditional desire to preserve diverse cultures and national identities. The issue— whether all people should become alike in the interests of peaceful progress—remains arguable. The result is that the extent to which agreement seems to be emerging, that global political and economic interdependence need to be accepted, is not matched by a simultane- ous commitment to pay a cultural price for it. Is this proposition truly self-contradictory, or is there an alternative?

In the end, this book, whose chief purpose is to identify and detail a significant transnational phenomenon bearing on this question, reads the available evidence as saying that commercial American mass media are tools of accommodation in a world being at once integrated by modern technology and fragmented by the pursuit of diversity. A world of *dualisms* exists in which, for instance, the international readership of *Time*, consisting of a twenty-five million-person global information elite,[1] has, at the same time, members who are prominent national decision-makers in a hundred different countries. America's foremost weekly newsmagazine offers but one of many accommodating, albeit sometimes controversial, dualisms breaching gaps between two tiers—the social integration and segregation of humankind.

To some critics of the current world order, the real issue goes be- yond forms of accommodation, for they contend that commercial American mass media circulate abroad as just another part of an inequitable system that must be fundamentally reordered. But skepti- cal Americans wonder whether a system other than their preference for an open international marketplace, with its pressures on sellers as well as buyers, really would be better, and if so, for whom?

Even before asking that question, however, should not the present system itself be scrutinized? This question provides a starting point for the author, who foresees, indeed invites, that the result of the revela- tion of the extent to which American mass media have penetrated foreign societies with market strategies may make the reader thirst for more answers than this book offers. Nonetheless, even the risks of an inexhaustible analysis of this little studied yet fascinating form of communications seem worthwhile, because already commercial American mass media are permeating human activity on an unprecedented global scale.

That the U.S. is a traditional and giant trading country is no surprise to anyone. But seldom do we think of media as being among America's biggest exports. The sale of Boeing Aircraft to China, wheat to Russia, and the multinational corporate structures of IBM and ITT were prominent symbols of American trade in the quarter century after World War II. To these can be added news services, some magazines, films, and TV programs.

The evidence is there plainly for all to see, although the casual observer, like a foreign tourist, might mistakenly think these media are for the convenience of Americans abroad. Far from it. The prime consumers, those whom U.S. media merchants seek to inform and entertain, are non-Americans. These media reach every corner of the world, ranging from near-saturation of the English-speaking Canadian provinces to restricted penetration of communist-ruled countries. So pervasive is the foreign dissemination of American commercial mass media that if one word must be chosen to describe this phenomenon it is, inescapably, *ubiquitous*.

Consider the following:

—Two hundred leading newspapers outside the United States were subscribing to either the *New York Times* or the *Washington Post-Los Angeles Times* supplementary news services by 1973. Among them was an influential "American in Paris," the *International Herald Tribune*, the world's only truly international newspaper.

—United Press International, one of America's two world news agencies (The Associated Press is the other), boasted in its 1973 annual report that UPI stories were being translated into forty-eight languages.

—In the magazine field, *Reader's Digest* has attained the astronomical foreign circulation of 12 million copies a month. Meanwhile, *Time* and *Newsweek*, perhaps inspired by, certainly not unmindful of, *RD's* extraordinary success abroad, have launched specially edited foreign editions.

—The trailblazing success of American movies and film makers abroad has been capitalized upon by the offspring of Hollywood, telefilm producers, who derive a vital portion of their incomes from foreign sales. Exports of what may be called the U.S. visual industry amounted to $335 million in 1973, double the figure of two decades earlier, according to the U.S. Commerce Department.[2]

The international commerce in mass media, insofar as U.S. merchants are concerned, is dominated by a handful of organizations that also hold commanding positions in the American domestic market. For reasons that are somewhat arbitrary, the list of the media considered in this book is restricted to eight print media and two visual. They are:

PRINT

The Associated Press (AP)
United Press International (UPI)
The New York Times News Service
The Washington Post-Los Angeles Times News Service
International Herald Tribune (IHT)
Time
Newsweek
Reader's Digest (RD)

VISUAL

Motion Pictures
Telefilms

Other U.S. media are abroad, too, but AP and UPI are America's only general news agencies and by definition have substantial worldwide operations. The six other media were selected because each met the test of being substantially involved in foreign markets. By "substantial" is meant that they have sizeable distribution (both numerically and geographically) as opposed to random distribution of their messages abroad, that they have significant revenue-seeking interests in foreign operations, and that they are considered influential in foreign countries.

It would perhaps be possible to compile a more structured and detailed list of criteria whereby one could say with greater precision whether any mass media organization was engaged in substantial foreign operations. This would be an overly finicky process akin to categorizing all large vessels in such a way that some coastal freighters would be considered ocean-going ships and others river boats. The focus here is on mass media supertankers that clearly meet the aforesaid criteria of size, finance, and influence. The list presented here, therefore, is more one of consensus than division. The organizations listed can be called, unquestionably, world merchants, both for the stated objective reasons and a subjective one as well—each has a global self-image.[3]

Thus the prime focus here is on the short list of commercial mass communications organizations which have been identified as having three attributes—worldwide dissemination, a substantial financial stake abroad, and significant foreign impact. They are America's leading mass media merchants.[4]

THE CONTROVERSIAL QUESTION: WHY?

Why did these organizations—the news services, some magazines, and the motion picture and television program industrialists—become world traders instead of simply staying at home and doing business there? Was there some compelling reason to go abroad, or some happenstance, or some design, or fate? And why is this curious phenomenon so predominantly an American one?

Rarely have these questions been asked, which seems unfortunate, for the global distribution of American mass media suggests global impact of some consequence. There are signs, however, that this topic no longer is a sleeping giant.

Communist countries, of course, have long criticized Western, especially American, media for their successful international circulation, but such outcries often are dismissed as being tinged with, if not wholly motivated by, envy. But what once was exclusively an issue between East-West cold warriors has turned into a source of North-South tension and even a sore point in bilateral relations with the United States' best friend, Canada. Whereas Moscow propagandists and their fellow travelers once were alone in charging that the spread of imperialism's private media was detrimental to foreign countries, there emerged in the late 1960s a chorus of other criticisms such as the Third World's complaint of "cultural imperialism" and the Canadian nationalists' charge that their country's legitimate quest to firmly establish a Canadian identity was being stifled by the media barons of Manhattan and Hollywood.

The old notion that the world might be a better place to live in if mass communications linked its inhabitants has been challenged by the very fact that a new degree of global linkage has been accomplished by American mass media. This fact apparently disturbs an overwhelming majority of the nations of the world as evidenced by United Nations debates, begun in 1966, on direct broadcasting by satellite. Although the U.S. did not have the technical means to bounce television signals off satellites *directly* into homes abroad, the possibility of that happening some day was sufficient incentive to build an anti-American coalition at the U.N. made up of communist, less-developed, and small—like Canada—powers, who want regulations of some kind to govern international telecasting using satellites. Arguing against restrictions, U.S. delegates to the world organization cited the free flow of information principle as embodied in the two decades-old United Nations Declaration on Human Rights. But the argument fell on deaf ears as most of the delegates were mindful that under that principle the world casually had come to "Love Lucy" without advance consideration of the cultural impact of that globally popular American television program.

The tensions and challenges growing out of the foreign circulation of American mass media give a sense of urgency to the need for understanding this phenomenon. Although the field of international communications *still* is dominated by studies of either communications policies or media in other countries, which in effect means that much of the so-called *international* literature actually is within a *national* context, a few analytical steps have been taken in response to the controversies stirred up by America's mass communications commodities. The little that so far has been published on the subject has been generally of the media-fault-finding variety. For instance, the *Journal of Communications,* acknowledging that "the most pervasive—and the least studied—form of international communications is the world trade in canned images and sounds," printed three articles with the overall heading, "Cultural Exchange—or Invasion?"[5] The trio of authors unanimously found the U.S. visual industry to be an invader of foreign countries with most of the negative aspects the word connotes.

Essentially, the critics have sounded a cultural alarm, warning that more harm than good results from the worldwide spread of American TV programs, movies, and their media brethren, which, it is argued, have gone abroad for purely selfish commercial reasons as well as to strengthen America's post-World War II economic and political hegemony in the world. The merchants are pictured as greedy capitalists, ingeniously forcing their banal, value-loaded, American products upon unsuspecting, hapless victims abroad who ingest these culturally inappropriate wares to the delight of Washington, which, after all, has championed this development as being in the national interest of an internationally powerful United States.

But is all of this so? For a moment, let's defer the cultural impact question, which will be discussed at length later, and focus now on the reasons why American mass media, more so than the print or visual media of other countries, have spread worldwide.

One explanation that can be dispensed with fairly quickly is the assertion that private American media fully collaborated with post-World War II U.S. government to achieve this end. While there are shreds of evidence to suggest this near-conspiracy theory, the great body of information supports the opposite view. American movies and news agencies, the leading mass media at the end of the war, had gone abroad before the conflict. While prewar America was in a period of self-imposed political isolation, the big U.S. motion picture companies and both the Associated Press and United Press[6] were active in foreign countries. As early as the mid-1920s, U.S. film makers were producing an estimated 90 percent of the movies shown abroad.[7] As for the news agencies, AP severed its ties with the European news cartel in 1934 and then began independent foreign service, something its chief competitor, United Press, already was doing so successfully that by the outbreak of World War II in 1939, UP was directly serving 486 newspapers in fifty-two foreign countries.[8]

After the war, if the media were indeed allied with the government to preserve a dominant U.S. position abroad, they apparently were not always deemed reliable allies. By 1953, for instance, the motion picture industry had come under such sharp attack for selling America short abroad that the industry was vigorously defending itself against charges of "handing over victory in the world's ideological struggle to the Kremlin on a celluloid platter."[9] The news agencies were, it seems, at least inadequate to the supposed task of supporting the government's foreign policies as evidenced by the decision of the U.S. Information Agency (USIA) to operate its own news service around the world.

Finally, by the early 1970s, the government's own foreign information organization began to view the private media as competitors abroad, or if not that, then at a minimum, not very useful to the business of government. The U.S. Senate Foreign Relations Committee used the very word "competition" after taking a look at the situation in 1973. "As the number of private information sources has increased," a Committee report said, "USIA personnel have gradually come to see themselves as being in 'competition' with these other sources—in an effort to 'balance the distortions' produced by the normal flow of news and communications."[10] James Keogh, the director of the information agency who, as a former executive editor of *Time*, had firsthand knowledge of the private media, did not go that far, at least on record. But writing in the *Foreign Service Journal*, Keogh said, "The news media have no desire to be the platform for official statements or explanations of U.S. policy. Replying to foreign critics of the United States is not their job," he wrote.[11]

So the collaboration case in foreign relations as the basis for the expansion of American mass media outside the United States cannot be made satisfactorily if all the evidence is weighed. This is not to say that American political power at the end of the last world war was of no benefit to mass media exporters. Certainly, by championing an open international system it was a facilitator. Countries dependent on U.S. military power for their security and economic benevolence for their well-being had to think twice before courting the displeasure of Washington by forbidding entry to American mass media. Moreover, the U.S. government aided its private media merchants by successfully advocating that the press freedom amendment of the U.S. Constitution be given international expression in the "free flow" principle of the U.N. Declaration on Human Rights. The document had the effect of bestowing legitimacy on American mass media operations in foreign countries.

The noncollaboration case also does not claim that American mass media abroad have been of no benefit to the U.S. government, for certainly they have in terms of presence and credibility, USIA Director Keogh's opinion notwithstanding. But a theory that purports to explain the growth of U.S. private media abroad *only* as a direct consequence of a continuing and reinforcing condominium of foreign interests existing always between Washington officialdom and the mass communications industry fails to account for the media's extensive pre-World War II overseas activity and considerable postwar disharmony between Washington and private mass communicators.

One example of political considerations alone motivating the expansion of an American mass medium into a foreign market had an ironic twist. In 1958 the patriotic publisher of *Reader's Digest*, DeWitt Wallace, launched the magazine's first foreign language edition, Spanish for Latin America, in an attempt to counter Axis influence in the hemisphere. He was willing to accept an anticipated financial loss in furtherance of his political goal. The results were that the Spanish language edition of *Reader's Digest* was an instant, *profitable* success in Latin America, and soon became the single most popular magazine in that region. As for the intended political impact, that could not be so easily measured as the economic results. Curiously enough, *RD* had slipped through the back door of Latin America and to its surprise soon became a welcomed permanent resident after arriving as an uninvited visitor.

The histories of the other American media abroad all have backdoor stories and underlying economic motivations, too. United Press began foreign operations because it faced a cartel to which the Associated Press belonged (but which AP abandoned when UP did well on its own overseas). Neither began as a world news agency, but their mutual competition led them down the same global path. Other back entrances have been through random foreign exports that mounted so as to inspire corporate interest in foreign markets as sales at home began to level off.

Whatever these media back doors to the world market were, the amazing thing has been the success to which they led. While the mass media of some other countries also circulate outside their borders, no other single nation does anywhere near the volume of international mass communications business as the United States. The two world wars suggest a reason for this, the explanation being that in spite of the devastation after both wars the U.S. communications industry was still fully functioning abroad. But there are flaws in this narrow explanation, too. German film makers, for instance, were going strong only a few years after World War I. And Canada, whose wartime fortunes were on a par with the United States, always has been a big importer and not much of an exporter of mass media products.

What Germany and Canada lacked, respectively, were widespread cultural compatibility abroad and a sufficiently large domestic communications base from which to export. Each country has one but not the other. The United States has both. But to understand why American commercial media have reached around the world, it is not enough to merely cite the combination of commercial incentive and U.S. political power. Behind that is the large, communications-intensive American society with its penchant for innovation and an emigrant-given preference for media with transnational cultural contents.

The domestic base of American media is not only critical in terms of large population and ocean-to-ocean size, but also because it has been a proving ground for market strategies. The basic skills and expertise that are so useful when expanding into various foreign markets have been largely acquired within the United States, which is not so much a single national market as a complex of submarkets. As Ben H. Bagdikian, a noted journalism critic, has pointed out,[12] mass communications in the United States has traditionally been imbued with a strong sense of localism. The trick of a few major mass media organizations has been to blend the local operations into countrywide schemes. The talent developed in doing this was subsequently applied abroad.

This is clearly the case with the news agencies that provide their services to newspapers and broadcast stations throughout the U.S. and in so doing have mastered the ability to provide common material to all, regional material to some, and specific material to any subscriber. Local newspapers in America, despite some well-publicized big city closures, are thriving partly because they participate in this efficient news system.

Less apparent is the local connection of so-called national television and magazines. But the connection is there. The television networks actually own but a few stations themselves, seven being the statutory limit. Their programs, however, are distributed through hundreds of local affiliated stations whose owners are extravagantly courted by both the networks and independent producers who depend on the local stations to broadcast their programs. The major trick in the magazine field is to acquire a large readership across the country with the same appealing copy and pictures and then deliver that audience to advertisers either as a whole or—and this is the local connection—subdivided into geographic (regional and metropolitan) or demographic (income, occupation, age, sex, etc.) editions. Advertisements in *Time*, for instance, can be targeted to readers in the Southwestern United States, Northern California, the Atlanta metropolitan area, or to businessmen or college students, representing just a few of *Time*'s domestic advertising editions.

In support of this localized or fragmented market approach in the United States, each mass communications organization has a flexible nationwide distribution system usually coupled with local representatives and production facilities as needed. The end result is what Americans call national mass media, even though these media's special strength—a strength that has served them well abroad, too—is their ability to cater to local markets.

Besides their locally oriented operational style, American mass media organizations have entered the international marketplace with bountiful resources derived from a communications-intense native society. No country in the world values communications more than Americans, as evidenced by the fact that a single carrier, American Telephone and Telegraph, is the biggest of U.S. big businesses, having twice the assets of General Motors. Other equally impressive statistics attest to this as well: Americans consume more than four times as much newsprint as do the Japanese, runners-up in world consumption; there are more radios than people in the U.S.; nearly half the world's telephones belong to Americans; and untold billions of dollars worth of TV sets have been purchased by Americans.[13] Furthermore, futuristic communications notions like electronic mail and cordless telephones already have become realities in the United States with the development of telecopiers and bellboy phones.

Hence the mass media that have gone abroad from the U.S. are attached not only to parent organizations that offer them resources and rights, but in turn they are linked to a dynamic U.S. communications complex out of which, for instance, came communications satellites which further enlarged the capabilities of the mass media flow around the world.

Satellite communications are but a single example of the inventiveness and/or innovativeness that has been a hallmark of American industry. It is not an exaggeration to assert that all the concepts, techniques, and technology of commercial mass communications either have been developed or first exploited in the United States. In the communications field the United States has had an abundance of individual pioneers like Bell and Edison, a passion for research and development, and an instinct to borrow and copy. There is an innovative urge among American mass communicators that is reinforced by their quest for a competitive edge. In looking through the annual reports of U.S. mass communications organizations one is constantly reminded of this.

UPI's 1973 report, for instance, told of its going from the telegraph to the electronic age with the introduction of a computerized international information storage and retrieval system that features interconnected computers in New York, Brussels, and Hong Kong.[14] Beyond that, UPI also claimed to have made "innovations in [its] news report" and announced that an exclusively designed, ultramodern newspicture receiver was in the works. All this was proudly disclosed before the UPI report noted that one of its Vietnam war photographers had won a Pulitzer Prize. That innovation takes precedence over journalistic excellence within a news agency is not odd; it is reflective of priorities.

Finally, the domestic base is blessed, at least insofar as the development of mass media is concerned, with two major centers, New York and Southern California. A megalopolis is a fruitful environment for mass media because supercities attract creative talent and provide media organizations with supporting infrastructure and test audiences. The advantages of having two mass media centers is America's alone among those countries that distribute significant amounts of mass media abroad—there is only one London in Britain, one Paris in France, one Mexico City in Mexico, one Moscow in the Soviet Union, and one Tokyo in Japan.

The other important factor in understanding why American mass media have done so well abroad is content. Because the infancy of these media coincided with the great turn-of-the-century migrations to the United States, they have had an innate quality of transnationalism. In order to reach the masses, the media had to appeal to the babel that had invaded New York, Chicago, St. Louis, Pittsburgh, Cincinnati, and other cities. Their universal messages had to transcend imported cultural barriers and embody widely accepted values. The movies accomplished this task first with upbeat, optimistic stories that characteristically had happy endings. Central to this approach was the star system that stressed individuals (not classes), personal achievement, and social mobility (for whites). The overall theme was, by and large, that the good life was for everyone.

Print media in America were acquiring less parochial qualities at about the same time. Biases and opinions in news stories gave way to factual reporting as publishers both attempted to broaden their circulation base among an increasingly literate population and began to rely ever more on news agencies that had to neutralize their copy so as to make it acceptable to many editors.

In sum, American mass media during the first third of the twentieth century invested themselves with a bland ideology compatible with various cultures. Thus they were being well prepared, albeit unwittingly so, to venture into foreign countries. Moreover, the response to the culturally variable audience the mass media initially faced at home was a harbinger of adaptability that has characterized the more successful American media abroad. As we shall see, none of these media have themselves been unaffected after moving into the world marketplace. Each has adapted itself more or less to foreign conditions just as they once learned to change their character at home.

There is, in fact, a discernible cycle of adjustments that begins after random exporting grows to a threshold level of generating meaningful income. At that point, the media merchant usually becomes a *national exporter*, meaning that sales in foreign markets are actively sought but the character of the organization remains essentially American. The American owners and employees are the same and the products they sell abroad are merely spin-offs of their domestic business. The New York Times News Service fits this description. The second stage is that of a *multinational* media organization, that is, one whose once wholly American character has been diluted, perhaps by adding foreign employees, or tailoring material for foreign audiences, or both. *Newsweek*'s international edition, one-half different from the domestic magazine and with a staff of eight non-American columnists, is a multinational one. The third, and last stage, is *international control* by which is meant that essential responsibility for the medium is shared by representatives of two or more countries. Hollywood film-makers, originally national exporters, then multinationals, eventually shared their control in numerous movie productions in deals termed coparticipations. Popular during the 1960s, especially in Britain and Italy, the formula basically provided that Hollywood's big studios financed and handled the worldwide distribution of otherwise foreign-made movies.

WITHIN A NEW WORLD ENVIRONMENT

Another way of examining this phenomenon is from the perspective of the audience. Let's imagine for a moment that a non-American was curious, in a general sense, about the way his country would develop domestically. What this imaginary character wants, in other words, is a glimpse of future society in his homeland. His curiosity might be satisfied by picking up copies of *Time* and *Newsweek* at his local newsstand, assuming he lives in a non-communist country, and by spending some time watching American television programs broadcast by a local station. Among other things, these media will offer him a look at life in the United States, a highly developed country that is on the brink of moving into a post-industrial age.[15] In a sense the future of America will be the future of the world, unless, of course, history no longer repeats itself and the basic progress of nations from subsistence rural agricultural economies to interdependent urban industrial ones is broken. Political systems notwithstanding, this has been, and seems likely to continue to be, the organizational direction of humankind in quest of improving our comforts, curing our ailments, enlarging our knowledge, becoming more mobile, and so forth. Clearly the current pacesetter in more of these fields than any other country is the United States, whose pathbreaking achievements (dubious though some may be) are replicated elsewhere. So, to the extent that U.S. mass media mirror American society, the curious foreigner who consumes these media can see seeds of future world trends and their implications for his own country.

He also may depend on some of these media to bring more than just insights into what has been called "the American way of life." Through U.S. news media, news agencies especially, the individual can monitor activities in third-world countries. What he knows about a coup in a distant land or new legislation in a nearby one may come via

AP and UPI. New York, because it is the headquarters of these two news services, can be as much a window-on-the-world for a non-American as for an American.

Moreover, the non-American also at times can find segments of his own society reflected in an essentially American mass media outlet such as one of the twenty-five foreign national editions of *Reader's Digest*, each of which publishes material on local as well as American and international affairs.

The foreigner who consumes some of the vast outpouring of American mass media typically is near the top of the social ladder in his own country and some in almost all countries of the world belong to what might be called an international information elite.

Researchers for the U.S. government have concluded that much of the U.S. media merchandise is received by an elite who, regardless of their geographic location, share a similar, rich fund of common experience, knowledge, ideas, ways of thinking, and approaches to dealing with contemporary problems.[16] There are, of course, other significant factors besides information that transcend national, cultural, or social differences—higher education, particularly in the technical sciences, for example. Conflicting with such transnational factors are entrenched traditional barriers to world community, language for instance, that remain and separate the multitudes of mankind. Nevertheless, now as never before cross-border bonds are being forged among the elites of national societies.

Increasingly, what they have in common is the ability to understand English and similar frames of reference about an agenda of world affairs and modern social organization. The former facilitates some direct or retailed media exports, such as *Time* and *Newsweek*, which are not translated but, by way of illustration, are readable in English by an estimated three-quarters of the elite West German population, one-quarter of the influential citizens of Lebanon, and nearly all of Indonesia's top crust of society. These findings were contained in a U.S. Information Agency survey which also found that "on the average as many as 15–30 percent" of selected elite audiences in non-communist nations read *Time*.[17]

These audiences, it should be emphasized, are few in number (*Time*'s international circulation in 1973 was 1,300,000),[18] but the importance of reaching this type of reader should not be underrated since exposure to media, as demonstrated by Dr. Elihu Katz in his classic study "The Two-step Flow of Communications,"[19] is greater among opinion leaders.

So when American media play an agenda setting role globally, the effect can be to assign the degree to which international attention is focused on an issue. The energy crisis during the winter of 1973–74 dramatically demonstrated what can happen. When the Arabs temporarily turned off the oil, the whole world acted like a single short-term market, because of instantaneous news coverage reaching people everywhere nearly simultaneously.

The cited U.S. Information Agency research concludes that the world's "information elites" have "roughly similar clusters of interests" beyond their parochial concerns.[20] The principal one identified by the government researchers has been international affairs, including economics. Another, albeit smaller, cluster can be labeled social issues. Comparatively low interest was found for information about art and popular culture. The directions of this, as yet inconclusive, research indicates a preference for substantially useful information related to the two-tiered world discussed earlier: global interdependence in politics and economics balanced against global diversity in cultural preferences.

Private research by *Newsweek* led to the same findings, which prompted creation of a half-same, half-different international edition of the American news magazine in January 1973. With the global information elite audience in mind, *Newsweek* asserted that its new international role was to provide an "understanding of events taking place far beyond the borders" of its readers' countries, because such information is needed by "corporate decision-makers and government leaders of the world."

Obviously such audiences are elite not only in their information tastes, but in education, income, and other demographic characteristics as well. A typical member could be described as a 37-year-old non-American, who has attended either a university or technical school, probably is now a business executive earning $13,386 a year, which enables him to own a car, buy life insurance, and occasionally travel to foreign countries. That happens to be a composite profile of a person who either subscribes to or buys at a newsstand outside the United States a copy of *Newsweek*'s chief competitor, *Time*.[21]

A salient feature of these transnational elite audiences is that they sit atop indigenous societies that are, in the main, highly nationalistic. This is no more a paradox, however, than the nobility of the Middle Ages who were the embodiment of state sovereignty but whose social life styles were more attuned to foreign courts than domestic village life. But unlike the Middle Ages, there are now bonds among lower classes, too, created by indirect or wholesale American media exports that seep into the social fabric of many nations. For example: the global U.S. news services are purchased by several thousand foreign mass media outlets and are also distributed to several hundred various national news agencies; Hollywood's bit of the something-for-everyone approach of either making movies for many different audience types or banal TV shows with common low tastes concludes with wide distribution abroad—and these films may be seen even by illiterates, of course.

America's transnational mass media, which so extensively circulate around the world, are in fact but one current in a large river of intangible world commerce originated in the United States. Just as mass media within the U.S. were said to be part of a communications-intensive society, so it can also be said that when exported they are related to, not isolated from, the exponential growth in information movement between the United States and other countries. That movement has made the inhabitants of the world more sensitive to each other than ever before and created a sense that we live in a new world environment. Almost overnight the centuries-old practice of neighborly gossip about happenings in the next village has been replaced in the modern world by dinner table talk of events in far distant lands. Suddenly we have more abundant information about an earthquake in Guatemala than about a death next door. And the trend is for even more world compactness.

In 1965 communications satellites provided very limited trans-atlantic service among five countries. By 1972, nearly unlimited service was available among forty-nine countries worldwide.[22] This meant that our most technologically advanced communications system had expanded to a point where computers an ocean apart were able to exchange the equivalent of 70,000 words per minute; compact, desk-top facsimile transceivers added an electronic age dimension to the old adage "a picture is worth a thousand words"; inter-continental direct telephone dialing became a reality; and the world literally has watched some television events as they occurred, the Olympics, for instance.

Travel statistics are another indicator of rapidly expanding information movement.

	1931	1950	1972[23]
U.S. Travelers Abroad	430,000	670,000	7,200,000
Foreign Travelers in U.S.	230,000	500,000	3,000,000

Most of these travelers are curious, fun-seeking tourists. But even they are information carriers, rarely hesitant to tell foreign acquaintances about life back home. More abundant carriers are travelers like businessmen who go abroad with heads full of new ideas and attaché cases crammed with supporting documentation. They, not infrequently, are parts of organizations with very sophisticated means of information transferal.

At J. Walter Thompson, a giant American advertising agency, a process termed "syndication of experience" has been designed to systematize the information flow among its U.S. and foreign offices. The once casual intra-agency exchange of proofs and storyboards has been giving way to a highly structured approach which has been described by a J. Walter Thompson executive this way:

. . . a report is put together which includes a briefing document on the marketplace which lists the products that are competitive to those of our clients, lists advertising budgets, sales, market shares, a brief history of the economic environment and legislative environment in which the business goes on. This document would include representative examples of both print and broadcast activities and would also include sales promotion. The material is forwarded to a central location where it is coordinated, printed and distributed. And perhaps the most sophsticated of all these advertising exchange programs will begin to take place in 1974 when we hope to have videotape cassette capabilities throughout the world. This will enable us to have an even more meaningful exchange of advertising. . . .[24]

In sum, there can be no doubt that the means of international information exchange has grown enormously since World War II and much of the content has become increasingly complex. The question that naturally arises is: What is the impact of all this?

The adman's likely reply is that for him the impact either is more or less successful advertising campaigns, which in turn are a component of profit/loss figures for his clients. But that, of course, is a narrow, self-serving view. A different evaluation might be made by a foreign politician who considers American advertising in his country detrimental because he believes it creates popular desires that cannot be satisfied.

Even a non-commercial activity like the State Department's exchange of persons program can be seen from more than a single perspective. Convinced that "person-to-person diplomacy" is "a human contribution to the structure of peace,"[25] the U.S. Government operates a program that between 1949 and 1972 gave international travel grants to 148,848 persons. The majority (60 percent) were scholars, the rest were so-called "international visitors" drawn mainly from elite groups. While this program well may be diplomatically advantageous to the United States, it also can be argued that the exchange of scholars may foster an undesired brain drain.

All this—the exchange of persons, the adman's videotape cassettes, the statistics on travel and satellite communication, and much more— is part of an enormous and complex transnational circulation of information and ideas that is a growing process, and *a process in which American mass media are heavily involved.*

The process gives rise to new sociological expressions, such as Global Village, and it confronts politicians with a new issue which might be called *informational sovereignty versus free flow of information.*

Just, it seems, as the world was beginning to get a grip on the traditional nation-state system, there has emerged so-called transnational activity that is reshaping the global environment. Détente with communist countries coincides with an economic crisis in the West. And while discussion of the former divides along rehearsed lines, the latter baffles even the experts. Governments understand military-security matters, but not the workings of multinational corporations. Looking back, one sees that the first half of this century was dominated by war or the threat of war as states carved up the international landscape and delineated it with frontiers. The second half of the century, however, has witnessed a nascent development characterized by activity that has a high disregard for borders, indeed territory itself. The growth of non-governmental international organizations, the worldwide flow of scientific knowledge, and the spread of private banks with their networks of foreign offices are parts of this phenomenon. So, too, are some of America's major mass media organizations.

The term transnational has been employed to label this phenomenon, although its dictionary definition of "going beyond national boundaries of solely national interests"[26] may fall within the purview of common usage of the word international. Indeed some critics argue that transnational and international have synonymous meanings or that the former is in reality but a part of the latter. Here is grist for the mill of semanticists, but it is of small value in understanding these media. The purpose of referring to the foreign activities of some American mass media organizations as transnational is to emphasize that they belong to an enlarging assortment of enterprises that are engaged in significant foreign operations that are apart from the more traditional conduct of international affairs.

ACCESS TO AND SUCCESS
IN THE GLOBAL MARKETPLACE

The world is our market, say America's leading commercial mass media merchants. They invariably express pride in being able to say that their products are sold worldwide, or on every continent, or in nearly every country. They suffer from what has been called having-flags-on-the-map syndrome, from exaggerating the potential of foreign markets, and from simply having global intentions of doing business literally everywhere.

But in practice they operate on the principle of fragmentation. They recognize, or soon learn to, that the world is cut up into pieces and they attempt to market their wares among some of the divisions, the most profitable of which by far are the industrialized Western countries. There are two forces that bring about fragmentation. In one category are natural barriers like rivers and mountains and artificial borders created by politicians and armies. The other category is composed of less precise dividers, less precise because they are related to changeable human conditions. Thus humankind is separated by language, education, and other social and cultural factors of which income is the most important to the media merchant.

It is the nature of mass media that they, like religions, frequently are an imperfect fit for better defined territorial divisions. Such imperfections can breed tensions between national territorial forces (governments) and transnational forces (external mass media). Indeed, there is a growing controversy abroad over U.S. media, which will be covered in more depth shortly. Here suffice it to restate that a characteristic attitude of media merchants is to operate abroad without regard to national boundaries insofar as possible, while the strong predilection of governments is toward inviolate frontiers.

It is not that the merchants seek confrontations with governments; rather, they try to eschew restrictions on their abilities to fulfill media desires of various aggregations of foreigners, a notion their detractors dismiss, alleging that the merchants create those needs and/or secure their positions with imperialist tactics. The nature of the situation is revealed in an examination of two crucial aspects of international marketing: access and success. Both access to foreign countries and successful sales once admitted are regulated by four interacting factors of which politics and economics generally dominate questions of entry, while social and cultural conditions tend to be more decisive with respect to whether the merchants' business succeeds.

Politically, Americans step into the international arena holding to the philosophy of free flow of information. While the principle contained in the United Nations Universal Declaration on Human Rights that "everyone has the right to . . . impart information and ideas through any media and regardless of frontiers" may not be on the tip of every merchant's tongue, nonetheless, it is an ingrained American belief. But political barriers also check an American flow of information to a third of humankind living in communist countries. And, occasionally even some U.S. allies, albeit of the authoritarian variety, practice censorship against American media. Economically, Americans seek an open marketplace but frequently they face discriminatory taxes, quotas, and similar economic restrictions. Occasionally, a country may be open, but a thriving local industry, like that producing TV programs in Japan, may be very competitive.

Once local access is gained the merchant still has to sell to the indigenous consumer, who must have both a taste for what is being offered and the ability to buy. Neither condition always exists. For instance, if the most populous market in the world, China, tomorrow lifted all barriers preventing the internal dissemination of foreign mass media, the decision hardly would be a boon for, to choose one medium, *Time*. After all, the cultural barrier of language alone would be formidable, not to mention that because of China's economically backward status few Chinese could afford to pay the overseas price of a dollar or more for a copy of *Time*, nor would many advertisers be interested in buying space in the newsmagazine reaching the relatively poor Chinese market.

So each market has a distinct, indeed unique set of political, economic, social, and cultural factors that collectively act as gatekeepers, regulating its intake and acceptance of American mass media. For their part the media merchants, despite much talk, indeed boasting, about their worldwide sales, normally concentrate on marketing their wares in a few places abroad: Canada, Western Europe, Japan, Australia, and to some extent Latin America. Each, of course, has its own peculiarities.

Neighboring Canada, whose indigenous mass media industry is comparatively much smaller than that of the U.S. and has minimal checks, is so accessible that American mass media merchants consider Canada a special market, a hybrid more domestic than foreign. In distant Japan, culture is a durable barrier and it is reinforced by a large economy capable of supporting a major indigenous communications industry that can satisfy the mass media appetites of most Japanese.

Japan and Canada are political friends of the United States and both have prosperous, educated populations. But culturally, the former is isolated from the U.S. and the latter's anglophobe population integrated with it. The former is an economic giant; the latter is a small economic power. Those are fundamental reasons why American mass media have saturated the English Canadian market and barely dented the much larger Japanese one. There are, of course, other variables of which geography is not the least. Nevertheless, culture and economics, not politics and social conditions, are basic to understanding why *Time* magazine once sold ten times more copies in Canada (480,000) than in Japan (47,000), or why *Reader's Digest*, which reaches Japanese (and French Canadians) in their native language, has a circulation three times larger in Canada (1,510,948) than in Japan (585,030).[27] The disparity holds true in broadcasting, too. Canada imports more than one-third of its television programs, while Japan imports only a few percent.[28]

There is nothing unique about all this, as is shown in the striking similarity between the wide West German media bridge to its lingual southern neighbors and the heavy flow of American media into Canada. The following can be equally said about both the German-Austrian/Switzerland and American-Canadian relationships: the former are six to ten times larger than the latter; radio and television broadcasts by the former greatly spill over into the latter, who also import more than a quarter of their TV programs mainly from their bigger neighbors; substantial quantities of print media flow from the former to the latter, indeed in both Austria and Canada there are local editions of German and American magazines, respectively; finally, the flow from the smaller countries to the larger ones is, in comparison, much less.

This one-way flow pattern results from an identical set of factors—Germany and the United States have open political and economic access to their smaller neighbors who, for their part, are culturally and socially homogeneous with their bigger neighbors. Thus a firm foundation for cross-border media penetration exists.

SUMMARY

In summary, ten of America's leading commercial mass media organizations have traveled abroad as part of a huge transnational flow of communications, ignoring international borders whenever doing so seemed both feasible and desirable. This controversial commerce fosters the spread of dualisms, creating, for instance, a global informa-

21

tion elite whose members are also prominent persons in their own countries, while at the same time it further induces leading U.S. mass media corporations to become multinational.

Conditions that affect the global flow of commercial mass media—a fascinating phenomenon dominated by Americans and contributing to a new world environment—are the abilities and inclinations of merchants to sell their media commodities in foreign markets where demands for their wares are governed by four interacting factors: political and economic considerations, which tend to have greater influence on the question of foreign market access, and social and cultural factors, which, if entry is gained, tend to have greater influence on successful acceptance by foreign audiences.

Everyone acknowledges that we live in a contracting world where human beings, though countries and continents apart, are ever increasingly sensitive to each other. America's mass media merchants, for better or for worse, function to make that so.

AMERICA'S
VISUAL MEDIA
MERCHANTS

ovember evenings are warm in tropical Malaysia. So it was no surprise during an overnight stay in 1972, in the pleasant, medium-sized city of Ipoh, to see a cluster of people at the opposite end of a long, partially open veranda of the Station Hotel, one of those impressive but outdated relics of British colonialism. As I strolled toward them I was first amused, then fascinated, and finally shocked. My amusement was the discovery that the ever growing worldwide habit of TV viewing had taken hold in this enchanting country too. My fascination was the audience—far different from A.C. Nielsen's profile of typical American viewers. There was the hotel porter, a dark-skinned South Asian whose ancestors no doubt traveled from India to Malaysia at the behest of their British lords; the room clerk, a Cantonese member of one of the many overseas Chinese communities that dot the rim of Asia; and a youthful Malay who, judging by his short, faded-white coat, was either a room boy or an apprentice waiter playing hooky from the hotel restaurant. My shock was cultural, for the program that held the rapt attention of this multi-ethnic group was "Marcus Welby, MD," a Hollywood produced *telefilm* series dramatizing the trials and tribulations of an American family doctor.

THE GLOBAL FLOW
OF AMERICAN TV PROGRAMS

The flow of American television programs around the world is nothing short of incredible. So widespread is their global distribution that it is much easier to list those countries that have TV systems (a handful of countries have yet to make the investment) but broadcast no U.S. programs. According to Dr. Tapio Varis, a Finnish researcher, who published in 1973 the first useful inventory on the worldwide trafficking of TV programs,[1] there were five: Mainland China, North Korea, North Vietnam, Albania, and Mongolia. Everywhere else, in more than 100 countries—republican and monarchic, communist and cap-

italist, industrial and agrarian—made-in-America programs are telecast at least occasionally, and in many cases daily.

One of the most successful American programs was "Bonanza"
which, while topping the rating charts during its peak years in the
United States, was also seen by tens of millions of foreigners. In 1972,
NBC estimated that the weekly world audience for that popular
western was 350 million viewers. Latins, Asians, Europeans, even a few
Africans were fans. They saw the Cartwright family ride the ranges of
the Ponderosa and heard Ben and his sons speak, through the art of
dubbing, in a variety of native languages. The Cartwrights, said NBC
proudly, "can truly be described as the first TV family of the world."

"Bonanza," like numerous other TV westerns, has disappeared from
the American network schedule but, of course, there is never a programming void. As the wave of westerns receded a new wave of detective programs came into vogue in the United States and these shows
too were offered abroad. Among the most popular has been "Hawaii
Five-O," a police-action adventure series set in the exotic Hawaiian
Islands, which in 1972 was being sold in fifty-six countries.[2]

The determinants for the export bill of fare are past and present
programs produced for the American market. In effect, any U.S. TV
show preserved on film is a potential export and nearly every such
program is available for a price from a distributor. The bulk of U.S.
programming sold abroad is entertainment—drama, adventure, mystery, detective, westerns, cartoons, and TV movies. A trend toward
apolitical documentaries and educational programs also has developed. Comedy, although available, runs into cultural barriers, while
newsfilm, once a major export, has dropped low on the export list for
reasons that will be explained later. In sum, foreign TV stations can
buy anything from 223 vintage episodes of Danny Thomas's hit series
of the 1950s, "Make Room for Daddy," to recent network one-time
"specials." Even shows that are disasters in the U.S. like the ill-fated
"Tim Conway Show," which CBS cancelled after a brief thirteen-week
American run, are offered for sale abroad.

How much programming all this amounts to no one really knows,
although Varis, in his pioneering study on the international flow of
TV programming, estimated that U.S. exports annually amounted to
between 100,000 and 200,000 hours. The exporters themselves say they
do not know the total number of hours, simply because their measuring stick is financial, not temporal. Sources within the U.S. telefilm
industry, when asked about the 100,000 to 200,000 hour estimate,
tended to neither accept nor dispute it. When pressed, a usual response was, "Sounds like a good ballpark figure."

On the other hand, industry insiders more readily agreed, if only casually, with Varis's findings that the distribution of the total number of hours of TV dramas, westerns, detectives, and the rest that are exported from the United States, flow in roughly equal thirds to television stations in Europe, Asia, and Latin America. On a strictly percentage-of-total-hours worldwide calculation, the flow to the United States' North American neighbor, Canada, and to the Middle East and Africa is small. In the Canadian case, however, every hour is financially golden, whereas the Mediterranean region generates "change," as some merchants refer to not quite inconsequential business, and Black Africa is fiscally hardly worth their effort.

These provide hints why the American exporters have reacted rather passively to an examination of their business as measured by sixty-minute multiples. For them, it is a purely academic exercise of little relevance to the commercial world in which programming for television is sold. The volume of revenue, or more precisely the return on investment, not the number of hours, is what counts for a major distributor like Viacom or a giant producer-distributor like MCA-TV. Furthermore, their world is meaningful in terms of who are the best-paying customers, not where those buyers are located, except to the extent that a program can be "bicycled" through a cluster of countries. For example, a single telefilm dubbed in Spanish frequently is sold throughout Central America on the understanding that after the first country televises the program, the same film print is then shipped to the second and so on until every participating country in this so-called bicycling arrangement has broadcast the program. Bicycling is necessary, the distributors say, because license fees in some countries are so low (less than $100) that the fee collected from just one country would hardly cover the cost of the actual celluloid film, much less production costs or even overhead expenses plus a bit of profit.

Costa Rica, El Salvador, Guatemala, and Honduras pale in importance to the exporters in comparison to the big four—Canada, Britain, Japan, and Australia; little matter how many hours of American programs are shipped to those Central American countries or what percent of some grand hourly total they represent. One sale to the Canadian Broadcasting Company (CBC) or the British Broadcasting Company (BBC) dwarfs even the most lucrative deal imaginable with Televisora de Costa Rica or Radio y Television Hondurena. If a programming trend seems to be developing in Tokyo or Sydney, it would command priority attention at several posh Park Avenue offices in New York, while the vagaries of TV in San Salvador or Guatemala City would be, at best, of passing interest.

25

To an American who distributes television shows abroad, a map of the world long would have most prominently featured Canada, Britain, Japan, and Australia. For years these four were not the icing on the export cake; they were the cake itself. The situation, according to industry sources, started changing during the mid-1970s when, for instance, Japanese stations were buying American movies but not any program series. How much of the big four's importance to U.S. telefilm exporters has diminished as these countries have become more program self-sufficient is difficult to assess, but as late as 1971 they were accounting for about two-thirds of the industry's foreign sales. The other third was largely in sales to Brazil, France and West Germany. After them the income earned abroad was near the inconsequential level.

For the year 1971, when the Exporters' Association estimated that foreign revenues totaled $85 million, TV Guide calculated that figure broke down as follows:[3]

Canada	$16.5 million	19%
Australia	$15.0 million	18%
Japan	$14.5 million	17%
United Kingdom	$10.0 million	12%
Other Countries	$29.0 million	34%
Total	$85.0 million	100%

For an American distributor that markets its TV program wares in 100 foreign countries, but earns two-thirds of its foreign income in just 4 countries, those 4 are of paramount importance even if they import only a tiny fraction of the aggregated program hours.

Both measuring devices—program-hours-exported and income earned from foreign sales—are useful, but nonetheless inadequate, means of examining the worldwide flow of American TV shows. The principal drawback is that neither tells us anything about the audience. Who watches is just as significant as what is shipped to where. Counting program hours can be as misleading as the charade American broadcasters play with the U.S. Federal Communications Commission at license renewal time. It is then that the amount of time the broadcasters have devoted to certain program types, religious for instance, are considered, but without weighing the fact that church programs normally are aired on Sunday mornings when audiences are miniscule. Similarly, publicly available gross revenue figures reveal little about the audiences who view American TV exports. It is not inconceivable that the same program in both Canada and Japan would have been seen by more Canadians although they are five times fewer in number than the Japanese. American professional football, for instance, has been as popular with Canadian TV audiences as in the United States. But in Japan, where U.S. football games have been seen on a delayed edited basis in a slack viewing period, televised American football was an oddity and had low audience ratings.

Unfortunately, there has not yet been sufficient, uniform, and reliable data collected in order to do detailed audience analysis studies of American television programming in international distribution. So an examination of the global flow of these programs is circumscribed. Nevertheless, the fiscal and temporal data that is available sheds revealing illumination on this fascinating aspect of international commerce.

Varis's study on the flow of TV programs between nations featured a table (see Table 1) giving percentages of imported versus domestic

TABLE 1: Television Programming
1970–1971
(in percentages)

Country/Television Station	Imported	Domestic
Canada/CBC*	34	66
Canada/RC*	46	54
United States/16 commercial*	1	99
United States/18 noncommercial*	2	98
Argentina/Canal 9	10	90
Argentina/Canal 11	30	70
Chile*	55	45
Colombia	34	66
Dominican Republic/Canal 3/9	50	50
Guatemala*	84	16
Mexico/Telesistema	39	61
Uruguay*	62	38
West Germany/ARD	23	77
West Germany/ZDF	30	70
Finland	40	60
France	9	91
Iceland	67	33
Ireland	54	46
Italy	13	87
Netherlands	23	77
Norway	39	61
Portugal	35	65
Sweden	33	67
Switzerland/Deutsch*	24	76
United Kingdom/BBC	12	88
United Kingdom/TV*	13	87
Bulgaria	45	55
German Democratic Republic	32	68

TABLE 1: Television Programming (*continued*)
1970–1971
(*in percentages*)

Country / Television Station	Imported	Domestic
Hungary	40	60
Poland	17	83
Rumania	27	73
Soviet Union/Cent. 1st*	5	95
Soviet Union/Estonia	12	88
Yugoslavia/Beograd	18	82
Australia	57	43
People's Republic of China/Shanghai*	1	99
Republic of China/Enterprise	22	78
Hong Kong/RTV & HK-TVB (English)*	40	60
Hong Kong/RTV & HK-TVB (Chinese)*	31	69
Japan/NHK General	4	96
Japan/NHK Educational	1	99
Japan/Commercial Stations	10	90
Republic of Korea/Tong-yang	31	69
Malaysia	71	29
New Zealand*	75	25
Pakistan	35	65
Philippines/ABC, CBV	29	71
Singapore*	78	22
Thailand/Army TV*	18	82
Dubai	72	28
Iraq	52	48
Israel	55	45
Kuwait	56	44
Lebanon/Telibor	40	60
Saudi Arabia/Riyadh TV*	31	69
Saudi Arabia/Aramco TV*	100	0
United Arab Republic	41	49
Yemen*	57	43
Ghana*	27	73
Uganda*	19	81
Zambia*	64	36

* This data is based on sample week(s): all other figures are based on the full year 1970–1971. Repeats are included.

Source: Tapio Varis, *International Inventory of Television Programme Structure and the Flow of TV Programmes Between Nations* (Tampere, Finland: University of Tampere, No. 20/1973). Reprinted with permission.

programs in a broad sampling of television outlets around the world. The percentage of imported programs was not, unfortunately, broken down into country of origin (a task, no doubt, beyond the scope of the study). Nevertheless, because Varis found that American exports were at least five times larger than Britain's, the second leading exporter, and because he wrote of "the American hegemony in the world TV markets," the impression formed was that the words "imported" and "made-in-America" were approximately synonymous. This would probably be true if one accepts his high estimate of 200,000 hours of exported American programs in 1970; ten times more than British exports in the same year. More realistic, however, appears to be his conclusion that, "in Western Europe . . . American-produced programs account for about half of all imported programs, and from *15 to 20 percent of total transmission time*" (emphasis added).[4] Still, that is an impressive amount and one cannot help but wonder just how many American shows are seen outside Western Europe in countries where the percentage of imports exceeds domestic production.[5]

More than anything else, the import/export statistics in table 1 suggest that a gross imbalance has existed in the international flow of television programming. Major exporters are minor importers and vice versa; hence the world's runaway exporting leader, the United States, imported only 1 percent of its commercially shown programs and 2 percent of the shows screened by the Public Broadcasting Service. Britain, which Varis reported in the number two exporting position, was importing only 12 percent by the BBC and 13 percent by The International Television Authority (ITA), the commerical service. And France, in third place with 9,010 hours exported by its national TV system, ORTF, in 1971, imported a mere 9 percent in the same year.

The conclusion, then, is that the principal flow is from the big to the small. That is, a few rich, industrialized, Western countries have been the chief program suppliers and all other countries have been more or less consumers. Admittedly, this conclusion is generalized and overstated. It overlooks, as Varis did not, that there are significant regional production-export centers—Mexico City for Spanish-speaking Latin America or Beirut and Cairo for the Arab-speaking world, for instance. But the thrust of the study is clear: an imbalanced pattern has developed that has given rise to cries of cultural imperialism.

The other measuring stick, a financial one, does not contradict the conclusion of an imbalanced global flow of television programming, but available fiscal data does suggest that the nature of the imbalance may be different than that implied in import/domestic program hour percentages.

Very little credible financial data actually has been made public since this is the most sensitive area in the highly competitive business of selling television programs. The two basic sources are yearly estimates of gross revenues made by the Motion Picture Export Association of America and *Variety*'s annual publication of "global prices for

TV films." (See table 2.) Total Foreign Syndication Sales by the American TV Industry.[6]

TABLE 2: Global Prices for TV Films

	Price Range Half-Hour Episode		Price Range Feature Film	
CANADA				
CBC	$2,500–	$4,000	$3,500–	$12,000
CBC (French Net)	2,000–	3,500	4,500–	5,500
CTV Network	1,500–	2,000	5,000–	10,000
LATIN AMERICA & CARIBBEAN				
Argentina	500–	800	1,600–	3,500
Bermuda	25–	40	90–	150
Brazil	1,400–	2,000	4,500–	7,500
Chile	65–	70	350–	400
Colombia	190–	200	700–	1,000
Costa Rica	35–	45	170–	180
Dominican Republic	50–	60	225–	250
Ecuador	40–	70	150–	200
El Salvador	35–	40	150–	175
Guatemala	50–	55	175–	200
Haiti	20–	25	75–	100
Honduras	25–	30	75–	125
Jamaica	30–	35	90–	100
Mexico	700–	850	800–	1,400
Netherlands Antilles	25–	30	90–	100
Nicaragua	25–	35	150–	200
Panama	45–	55	150–	175
Peru	115–	130	700–	800
Puerto Rico	500–	600	3,000–	3,750
Trinidad & Tobago	30–	35	60–	100
Uruguay	75–	85	350–	550
Venezuela	500–	600	2,000–	3,500
WESTERN EUROPE				
Austria	375–	400	1,400–	1,800
Belgium	400–	600	1,200–	2,000
Denmark	200–	250	1,000–	1,200
Finland	250–	350	1,000–	1,200
France	2,700–	3,000	7,000–	8,000
West Germany	3,000–	3,500	11,000–	16,000
	(undubbed)		(dubbed)	
Gibraltar	26–	35	75–	125
Greece	110–	140	400–	600
Ireland	70–	75	275–	300
Italy	600–	900	6,000–	8,000
Luxembourg	160–	200	175–	225
Malta		28	no sales	
Monaco		130	130–	175
Netherlands	550–	575		1,850
Norway	150–	175	300–	450
Portugal	150–	200		500

	Price Range Half-Hour Episode		Price Range Feature Film	
Spain		460	2,800–	3,100
Sweden	400–	500	1,400–	1,600
Switzerland	150–	210	900–	1,500
United Kingdom	3,500–	4,200	18,000–	30,000
EASTERN EUROPE				
Bulgaria	45–	100	no sales	
Czechoslovakia	150–	250	1,000–	1,500
East Germany	350–	400	1,500–	1,800
Hungary	100–	160	400–	600
Poland	150–	200	400–	600
Rumania	150–	200	200–	300
USSR	120–	300	*6,000–	8,000
Yugoslavia	75–	90	200–	450
NEAR EAST AND SOUTH ASIA				
Cyprus	30–	35	100–	150
India	no sales		no sales	
Iran	100–	110	350–	500
Iraq	100–	125	200–	250
Israel	75–	200		***500
Kuwait	60–	90	250–	350
Lebanon	50–	60	200–	250
Saudi Arabia	60–	70	250–	350
Syria	50–	70	90–	120
UAR-Egypt	150–	170	400–	800
AFRICA				
Algeria	90–	100	no sales	
Kenya	25–	30	no sales	
Nigeria	35–	40	80–	110
Rhodesia	no sales		no sales	
Uganda	25–	30	no sales	
Zambia		50		100
FAR EAST				
Australia		**	12,000–	30,000
Hong Kong	60–	75	200–	400
Japan	3,000–	3,500	15,000–	40,000
South Korea	50–	80	250–	350
Singapore	50–	60	175–	200
Malaysia	50–	60	175–	200
New Zealand		297	700–	900
Philippines	150–	250	500–	900
Ryukyu Islands (Okinawa)	50–	60	100–	125
Taiwan (Formosa)	50–	60	150–	250
Thailand	100–	175	500–	800

* USSR: Dollar sales very rare and prices unsettled; still seeking barter deals.

** Australia: Telefilm sales in Australia are made under various arrangements.

*** Israel: Few American sales of features.

Source: *Variety*, 9 January 1974. Reprinted with permission.

Year	Total Foreign Syndication Sales
1963	$ 66,000,000
1964	70,000,000
1965	76,000,000
1966	60,000,000
1967	78,000,000
1968	95,000,000
1969	99,000,000
1970	97,000,000
1971	85,000,000
1972	93,000,000
1973	130,000,000

The Motion Picture Export Association, whose members include Allied Artists, Avco Embassy, Columbia, MGM, Paramount, 20th Century-Fox, United Artists, Universal Pictures, and Warner Brothers —all producing TV shows as well as theatrical movies—provided the foreign syndication sales figures with the explanation that the figures are "relatively reliable estimates of the total annual sales volume of American television producers/distributors." *Variety*'s price list is thought to be uneven, for the simple reason that in the competitive and arcane world of American TV, financial information is closely held.

At first glance, the sales volumes and price list reflect two realities: first, despite some ups and downs over a decade, the business of exporting American television programs has not grown much and, second, many countries buy shows at bargain basement prices. From 1963 to 1973, the volume of sales doubled from $66 to $130 million, but in real-dollar terms, that is, discounting inflation, it represents an unspectacular performance. The second factor helps explain the first; even though television experienced a worldwide expansionary boom during the 1960s, with stations going on the air in practically every country, many of the newcomers were poor men in a rich man's business. Natural market forces kept prices down, so far down that Haiti's paying as little as $20 for a half-hour episode of an American TV show that cost tens of thousands of dollars to produce is nothing short of preposterous. Yet that is what *Variety* reported as the lowest foreign fee. Moreover, thirty-five countries were spending under $100 per program which is barely an improvement when one considers that "Bonanza" was produced at a cost of $250,000 per program.

No wonder, then, that American distributors focused on the big four—Britain, Canada, Japan, and Australia—plus West Germany, France, and Brazil. That was where the money was—not a few dollars, or even a couple of hundred, but thousands of dollars could be earned per program sale which in turn amounted to millions annually. Just one thirteen-week series sold in each of those seven countries alone could generate more than a quarter million dollars in gross revenues, or between 20 and 30 percent of the producers net income. The money was there because substantial numbers of viewers were there, too.

Again, data on foreign viewers, ratings of particular programs abroad, and other indicators of who watches imported programming have yet to be systematically compiled and published. But the United Nations does provide figures on the number of television sets in the countries of the world and from these figures one can at least get a solid notion of potential audiences. The overwhelming number of potential viewers for American television programs outside the United States are in Britain, Canada, Japan, Australia, West Germany, France and Brazil. These are, of course, the countries which have accounted for more than two-thirds of the foreign income earned by American TV program exports.

As Figure 1 shows, the seven countries most profitable for U.S. TV exportations plus the U.S. itself (where, of course, the programs are screened originally) all together had 178,984,000 of the world's 247,000,000 television receivers, or about two-thirds of the 1971 total. When the high number of sets in the Soviet Union, which has been generally closed to American imports for political reasons, is deducted from the remaining one-third, the result shows that the rest of the world has only 28,716,000 television sets or approximately 11.6 percent of the total sets in the world. (See Figure 2.)

The implication of this finding is significant for it suggests that the basic global flow of television programming is among *eight* rich countries because those eight have most of the receivers and in turn the largest audiences. The principal stream, to be sure, is from the U.S. to the other seven. On the other hand, there is evidence that, even though the import figures for the U.S. are near fractional size, the huge American viewing market (93 million receivers), characterized by the easiest television accessibility in the world (one set for almost every two Americans), suggest that even one and two percent import figures are not quite so inconsequential as they may seem at first. In terms of audience, American exposure for a single import program is potentially far more rewarding than, for instance, exposure of a single U.S. telefilm in *all* the countries of the Third World. And, as a foreign

33

PROFILE: EIGHT-COUNTRY TELEFILM MARKET

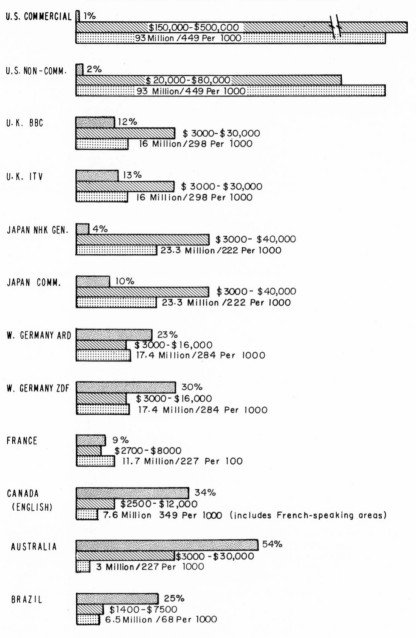

U.S. COMMERCIAL — 1% — $150,000-$500,000 — 93 Million/449 Per 1000

U.S. NON-COMM. — 2% — $20,000-$80,000 — 93 Million/449 Per 1000

U.K. BBC — 12% — $3000-$30,000 — 16 Million/298 Per 1000

U.K. ITV — 13% — $3000-$30,000 — 16 Million/298 Per 1000

JAPAN NHK GEN. — 4% — $3000-$40,000 — 23.3 Million/222 Per 1000

JAPAN COMM. — 10% — $3000-$40,000 — 23.3 Million/222 Per 1000

W. GERMANY ARD — 23% — $3000-$16,000 — 17.4 Million/284 Per 1000

W. GERMANY ZDF — 30% — $3000-$16,000 — 17.4 Million/284 Per 1000

FRANCE — 9% — $2700-$8000 — 11.7 Million/227 Per 100

CANADA (ENGLISH) — 34% — $2500-$12,000 — 7.6 Million 349 Per 1000 (includes French-speaking areas)

AUSTRALIA — 54% — $3000-$30,000 — 3 Million/227 Per 1000

BRAZIL — 25% — $1400-$7500 — 6.5 Million/68 Per 1000

FIGURE 1: Profile: Eight-Country Telefilm Market

34

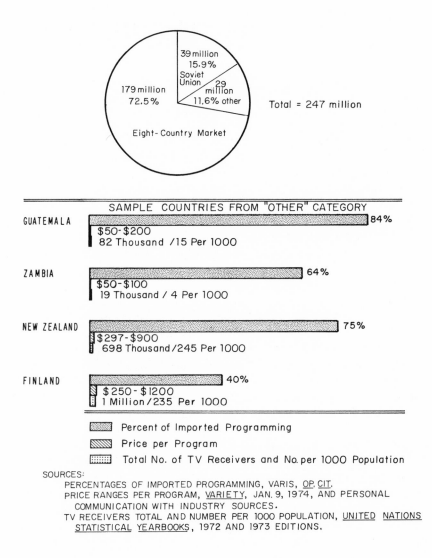

Total = 247 million

SAMPLE COUNTRIES FROM "OTHER" CATEGORY

GUATEMALA
84%
$50-$200
82 Thousand /15 Per 1000

ZAMBIA
64%
$50-$100
19 Thousand / 4 Per 1000

NEW ZEALAND
75%
$297-$900
698 Thousand /245 Per 1000

FINLAND
40%
$250-$1200
1 Million /235 Per 1000

Percent of Imported Programming

Price per Program

Total No. of TV Receivers and No. per 1000 Population

SOURCES:
PERCENTAGES OF IMPORTED PROGRAMMING, VARIS, OP. CIT.
PRICE RANGES PER PROGRAM, VARIETY, JAN. 9, 1974, AND PERSONAL
COMMUNICATION WITH INDUSTRY SOURCES.
TV RECEIVERS TOTAL AND NUMBER PER 1000 POPULATION, UNITED NATIONS
STATISTICAL YEARBOOKS, 1972 AND 1973 EDITIONS.

FIGURE 2: Number of TV Receivers in the World

producer like Britain's Sir Lew Grade has understood so well, selling programs, such as the action-adventure series "The Persuaders" and "The Saint," in the United States pays off handsomely.

It is contended here, then, that the international flow of TV programs can better be appreciated by looking at not only import/domestic program hour percentages and sales figures, but also by attempting to grapple with the most important dimension—the viewers who, although often ignored or sometimes even forgotten, play a crucial role.

To the extent that the U.N. statistics on both the global distribution of TV sets and their numbers per thousand inhabitants are accurate, we have a good idea who the bulk of viewers have been for exported American TV programs: Britons, Canadians, Japanese, Australians, West Germans, Frenchmen, and Brazilians.

That Guatemala has imported 84 percent of its television programs, paying as little as $50 per show, or that Zambia has gotten 64 percent of its shows abroad at costs not exceeding $100 is not unimportant, but it falls outside the mainstream when one considers that Guatemala has only 82,000 TV sets or 15 per 1000 citizens and that the figures for Zambia are even lower, 19,000 or 4 per 1000 citizens. It can be argued that such statistics reflect a high degree of dependency on foreign sources. That is true. But it is equally true for well advanced countries like New Zealand and Finland that were importing 75 and 40 percent, respectively, apparently because neither of these economically developed but small countries could afford many local productions. Furthermore, there is the question of who is dependent—certainly not the masses of the developing world, for they, unlike the elites who rule, are without enough money to buy an expensive TV set. Finally, an imbalance in the flow of TV programs has existed; but do either New Zealand or Finland have the resources, not just capital but sufficient creative talent, too, to redress it? Can a Zambia or a Guatemala even consider attempting to create a two-way flow (the latter not incidentally being primarily TV program dependent on Mexico)?

But the basic imbalance has been between the U.S. and its seven major foreign trading partners. And those relationships already have begun to adjust. The clearest evidence of adjustment is that the U.S. telefilm exporting business has been characterized by stability, rather than rapid growth, while the British industry has led a competitive charge. Varis found that in 1971–72 the BBC *alone* shipped an estimated 6000 program hours to the U.S. Meanwhile commercial British television production companies have been doing even more business around the world, so much so that on 16 April 1975, *Variety* reported, "Brit. Catching U.S. In O'Seas Sales Race."[7] The story said that if movies were excluded, Britain's international telefilm sales were running at about $50 million a year, or nearly matching that of the U.S.

MOVIES:
TV'S RELUCTANT PARENT

Perhaps because television killed "Hollywood: The Motion Picture Capital of the World," theatrical films and telefilms are somehow considered to be parts of separate industries. Of course the days when, as legend has it, even the word "television" was forbidden to be spoken within the confines of a major Hollywood studio obviously have passed as evidenced by the later use of those facilities to make TV program series. Universal Pictures, for instance, under the ownership of MCA has become healthier than ever. Yet a notion of division has persisted.

The argument has been presented in the following manner: production is substantially different—TV has time limitations and deadlines unlike movies; the distribution systems are not comparable, especially in the end where the viewer sits at *home* to watch TV, not in a public theater, hence TV is a much more sensitive medium; and last, but of the greatest importance to the people who control and operate either medium, the financial structures are inherently different—TV has depended on consumer investment in sets and advertising revenue, whereas the basic formula for movies is film rentals to theater owners who sell tickets.

All of this is true. Nevertheless, there is much more, at least in the minds of the audiences, that links, indeed melds, the two. Not only has television allowed audiences to see many of the same performers work in both film and TV, but it has also made more movies available to Americans than have the theaters. The 1966 TV showing of *The Bridge on the River Kwai* drew an estimated 60 million Americans to their sets and touched off a wave of "Big Picture" exposure on the tube. Then the short form, "made-for-TV" movie vogue began, which was nothing more than reworking Hollywood's old assembly line "B" picture format. At the same time, all the original "B" movies have continued to be televised on the much joked about "late shows." All things considered, from an audience viewpoint, an evening in front of the box is not much different, except for the location, from the earlier era of an evening at the movies: a contemporary television package of the evening news, a game show, a series or two, and then a TV movie is remarkably similar to a neighborhood movie theater fare circa 1930s when audiences were offered newsreels, contests, shorts, and a feature film.

Furthermore, the younger medium has borrowed wholesale from the older: co-stars in the new medium are called guests, but, different though the title may be, the performers serve the same function; television begins its Saturdays with children's programming just as the neighborhood theaters once catered to the same movie audience, same day, same time, and so on. The point is that TV undermined movies not because the new medium was different, but because it did the same thing better. TV provided more convenience and more banal entertainment to greater viewing masses.

There is, then, a visual industry whose parts, motion pictures and television, are more analogous to cars and trucks than to, say, boats and airplanes. In other words, to understand American television, including foreign circulation of its programs, one must look at the movies, too, for they are to TV as parent is to child—the parent in this case was perhaps a more notable globetrotter than its offspring.

It may be noted that an earlier observer of the visual industry thought the kinship between American movies and TV to be more like husband and wife. Leo Bogart has written that "The marriage of Hollywood and television may be illustrated by the findings of a Sindlinger survey. During the week of March 1957," Bogart has recounted, "27% of the adult and teen-aged public spent a grand total of 138,200,000 hours attending movies. But in the same period, a like proportion (24%) . . . spent a total of 276,500,000 hours watching movies on television."[8]

In the following pages, which trace the development of the U.S. motion picture industry and its extension abroad, the central theme is that the American movie was a commercial, visual embodiment of a transnational popular culture. Movies began to fade when the commercial cultural torch was passed to (perhaps "snatched by" is better) television and, almost simultaneously, foreign motion picture makers proliferated, some subsequently to shed nationalism in favor of what they called an international, but what is more appropriately termed a transnational, style. In its heyday, however, the American movie was the most convenient and the most controversial mass medium of entertainment and its impact at home and abroad was enormous. So too with its successor, American television.

FROM EDISON
TO INCE

Great inventions are generally of two types: The first is characterized by scientists who labor to achieve a much-desired breakthrough that, if achieved, is predicted to have a significant impact on humankind; the other is either happenstance or even, if consciously pursued, not deemed initially to be of much consequence. The atomic bomb belongs in the first category and Edison's Kinetoscope in the second.

When, in October of 1889, Thomas A. Edison built his peep-show machine that used George Eastman's newly available "roller photography," Edison could not have appreciated that someday several hundred million customers a week would almost religiously troup to tens of thousands of motion picture theaters around the world to see movies. Five years would elapse before the Kinetoscope would even emerge from a near-forgotten corner of the inventor's workshop to offer, on 14 April 1894, to the paying public their first taste of a new medium. The Kinetoscope Parlor on New York's Broadway opened with a bank of machines into which one customer at a time could peek and see bits of vaudeville acts, boxing matches and other trivia. From glimpses of dancing girls and prizefighters, the software of the emerging visual industry developed in the wake of hardware. The process occurred on both sides of the Atlantic, the Kinetoscope having been introduced into England and France. Robert W. Paul, unrestricted since Edison had failed to take out a patent in Britain, reproduced in England a version of the Kinetoscope that initially depended on the Edison studio in New Jersey for films. Exporting of motion pictures from the United States had gotten an early start. In France, the Lumière brothers, inspired by an imported Kinetoscope, built the Cinematographe from which the universal word "cinema" was derived. Their system encompassed both camera and projector. Paul later on was forced to invent a camera after Edison's business manager cut off the flow of films to England in an attempt to regain control of the foreign market. On the eve of the twentieth century, the fledgling motion picture industry already was troublesomely international in scope.

In the United States, the big screen was followed by the screen story. *The Life of an American Fireman*, in which a sleeping fire chief dreams he saved a child's life, was the forerunner for *The Great Train Robbery*, the 1903 classic that generally is regarded as the first motion picture story. Two years later, John P. Harris was charging five cents to see this picture at his Nickelodeon in Pittsburgh. The combination of a screen play and an inexpensive theater was a historic union that started the motion picture industry's first boom.

America was filling up with non-English speaking immigrants at the turn of the century and for entertainment they flooded into the nickelodeons that appeared suddenly like spring flowers in the polyglot cities of the country. Within a year of the first opening in Pittsburgh, nearly 5000 nickel theaters[9] were operating to fulfill the entertainment desires of foreign-born workers who had arrived in America unable to read newspapers or understand vaudeville jokes. Unlike Europe where the infant film industry aimed at more sophisticated audiences, movies in America were finding their greatest acceptance at the lower end of the social ladder where masses of newcomers were clustered.

From this base, movies would evolve as the people's medium, a medium that at its inception had to have a *multicultural appeal* to be successfully attractive and that, as its emigrant audience merged into America's burgeoning middle class, would tag along to a position of exalted national and international prominence.

To understand how the American film industry grew to once dizzying heights, one must first appreciate that the fate of film was intertwined, initially, through the institution of the nickelodeon, with white American workers, most of whom were born abroad. The history of American film, although distorted by excessive attention paid to classic social and art films, in reality is an integral part of the "American Dream"—the social melting pot notion of upward economic mobility into the middle class. Meanwhile, elite Americans (the wealthy and intelligentsia) kept the "legitimate" theater alive; the already bourgeois were to accept the movies once script quality improved; and forgotten Americans (Blacks and Indians) relied on traditional forms of entertainment. The motion picture was well suited to serve its recently-off-the-boat audience for it was then a silent medium —no need to understand English, just watch a simple story unfold through a novel technique and be entertained for a nickel. It was an enjoyable diversion.

In Europe, however, film had not sought the masses, but its "higher brow" development there was not to be unimportant. From the continent came a suggestion of a new direction for America.

By 1910, motion pictures in the United States were reaching a saturation level after only two decades. Clearly something new was required if the industry was to prosper beyond a cheap visual entertainment level. The industry got a double shot in the arm: features and stars.

Two men share responsibility for the introduction of feature films to the American screen. Adolph Zukor, a Hungarian immigrant who had gotten financially involved in exhibition through an investment in a penny arcade, imported from France *Queen Elizabeth*, a four-reel feature film with Sarah Bernhardt as the Queen. It was Zukor, incidentally, who first classified pictures as A and B. A few years later in 1915, D. W. Griffith independently produced in the U.S. his classic, *The Birth of a Nation*. The feature had arrived not only because of Zukor's importing initiative and Griffith's talent, but also because the power of the Motion Picture Patents Company had been broken. The company had represented the major manufacturers of cameras and films. Naturally, only the manufacturers' films were allowed to be shown on their equipment and since equipment rentals were more profitable, film quality suffered until the monopoly was broken.

The feature film emerged as technological improvements helped transform motion pictures from a flickering novelty that entertained mobs to a more respectable, certainly more profitable, medium. There were, according to one estimate, "ten thousand theaters playing to a nationwide audience of ten million weekly, they were doing a greater volume of business by 1910 than all the legitimate theaters, variety halls, dime museums, lecture bureaus, concert-halls, circuses and street carnivals combined."[10] Among the reasons for this extraordinary phenomenon were the "Little Mary" films which debuted in 1909 and popularized the star system.

Mary Pickford, born Gladys Smith in Toronto, began her show business career at age five on the Canadian stage. Said to be ambitious, tenacious, and shrewd, she arrived on Broadway as a teen-ager. There, producer David Belasco re-christened her and gave her a part in a play. When the play closed, she went downtown and took a summer job with the Biograph movie company. D. W. Griffith cast her in *The Lonely Villa* and thus started Mary Pickford on the road to becoming both "America's Sweetheart" and the blooming motion picture industry's first star.

The speed with which the star system was established and its importance to the young industry is dramatically revealed by the rise of Charlie Chaplin. He left vaudeville in 1913 to play slapstick comedy roles in films being produced by Mack Sennett at his Keystone studios in Hollywood. Chaplin earned between $125 and $250 a week playing such roles as a minister in *The Pilgrim* and a policeman in *Easy Street* before his first appearance as a tramp in *Kid Auto Races at Venice* (California). Soon he was to be the richest tramp in the world. The role Chaplin had created, accidentally according to some accounts, was such a box office success that in 1915, just two years after coming to Hollywood, he signed a contract to make twelve comedies a year at a weekly salary of $10,000 plus a $150,000 bonus. British Empire rights were, in turn, sold for $670,000, the full amount of Chaplin's fabulous pay. The deal underscored just how big the transoceanic motion picture business was becoming.

Henceforth, the star was to be supreme, for the star was a personal link with the movie-going masses. Stars embodied American dreams and values and, since America in the early twentieth century was a land of many cultures, their appeal was easily exportable. While film makers abroad were pioneering new techniques and perfecting the craft, American producers and their performing idols approached motion pictures differently. In the words of one of the brightest of the early stars, Douglas Fairbanks, "The art of the screen is almost purely emotional."[11] It was this philosophy that led people of various backgrounds to share cultural experiences vicariously through the stars. This concept is well-illustrated by the western, a motion picture form to which William S. Hart, another early popular performer, made a significant contribution. In his book *Movies: The History of an Art and an Institution*, Richard Schickel recalls that "Hart's major creation was his screen character—the good-bad man [who] has had a limitless appeal. . . ."[12]

The global ascendancy of the American motion picture during the second decade of the century was not due solely to the combination of feature films with their stars finding ever increasing acceptance. In Europe, the First World War erupted, forcing the shutdown of most studios; a notable exception were studios in Germany. The war, movie historian Ramsaye has written, "delivered the screens of the world to the American product. That product," he said, "was almost automatically attuned to a diverse world market by reason of the foreign heritages from many lands of both the initial film audiences and the producers which their patronage encouraged. The American motion picture, born to serve a vast polyglottic patronage was born international in its own home market." So, Ramsaye continued, "It took the world's screens without opposition and with few problems of adjustment." The result was that American movies "came to occupy something like 80 percent of the world's screen time."[13]

The American film makers flourished during the war at the expense of the English, French, and Italians. German film makers, on the other hand, prospered, for the war had closed off their country to most foreign films, and at the end of the conflict a vigorous motion picture industry was rooted in Berlin. The German boom lasted less than a score of years, however, for the Nazis, once in power, clipped the industry's wings and corrupted its soul.

With the American position as the world's film leader firmly established, partially as a by-product of World War I, Hollywood was to be further strengthened with the acquisition of more foreign talent. Chaplin was followed by a parade of English performers who attained fame in America and the gifted Ernst Lubitsch was the first in a wave of German directors to cross the Atlantic. Even from small Sweden, where film making had come alive during the war, there was a talent loss to the magnetic U.S., notably actress Greta Garbo and director Victor Seastrom.

Thus, while it was premature to speak of an internationalized film industry in which persons of different nationalities shared control, it was already possible, following World War I, to characterize the American film industry as multinational in personnel. The impact of what might be called a "talent drain" from Europe was to reinforce the vitality of American movies as a multicultural medium and simultaneously to weaken potential foreign competition.

From Edison's Kinetoscope to nickelodeons to Mary Pickford to *The Birth of a Nation* to the impact of World War I, there had evolved two major directions for movies. At the beginning of the "roaring twenties" this meant, in practice, "formula films" for a middle class enlarged by upwardly mobile immigrants and artistic motion pictures for more sophisticated audiences. The former was of greater economic importance for both the home and export markets.

In a brief career cut short by a fatal heart attack in 1924, Thomas Ince was the first film maker to couple what were to be called American production values with a hierarchical organizational structure. The formula proved successful into the television era in both American and foreign markets. Ince, in other words, fathered the style of American film making that later giants, like Darryl F. Zanuck and David O. Selznick were to adopt when running Hollywood's famous big studios, and faceless TV impressarios subsequently employed.

Like D. W. Griffith, Ince had an indifferent acting career on the stage before transferring to film as a director for Biograph. Later, he, with Griffith and Mack Sennett, formed the partnership of Triangle Productions, where in 1916 and 1917 Ince had a prodigious output of sixty pictures a year. Triangle, a vertically integrated company that produced movies for exhibition in its own luxury theaters at the then exorbitant price of $2 for a best-in-the-house seat, conceived the idea of the double feature. What the audience got was a Griffith picture, which favored the narrative form of storytelling, and an Ince production, which emphasized the dramatic form. Sandwiched between was a short Keystone Comedy produced by Sennett. Triangle went financially bust, but its double billing experiment is memorable for having juxtaposed the contrasting styles of Griffith, who critics since have loved for his moralizing, sentimentality, and even poetry, and Ince, who courted audiences with western melodramas, conflict, and action.

While Griffith's plots tended to wander, Ince's storylines were tight-knit. His films were produced under tight supervision; none of the "off the cuff" shooting in vogue then with most other directors was allowed. Ince, in fact, was more a producer than director. His method was to develop in close consultation with writers, shooting scripts which he insisted that his subordinate directors adhere to. Thus, he ensured continuity at the outset and avoided the danger of wandering that infected Griffith's films. In addition, Ince was a master editor, cutting and splicing until the film as he conceived it was completed. On a baseball team, Ince would have been manager, lead-off hitter, and clean-up batter. "He was instrumental in setting the great American screen style," according to Schickel who also credits Ince with making an unsurpassed contribution to "the creation of a *viable, commercial style*" (emphasis added).[14]

D. W. Griffith certainly was the artistic pioneer of American motion pictures, but Thomas Ince provided the formula that both endeared movies to the middle class and so abundantly fulfilled their desires that the screen became a pervasive form of expression. "After 1919," wrote Lewis Jacobs, another movie historian, "motion pictures with rare exceptions . . . were made to please the middle class."[15] For every Chaplin comedy or *Ben Hur* remembered as a classic of the Griffith era, there were scores of formula films produced by the disciples of Ince. The mainstream was not to be found in the "rare exceptions," but in the "viable, commercial style" that pleased audiences at home and abroad.

FROM SPEAKING STARS
TO SHRINKING SCREENS

The history of the American motion picture in the two-decade period between 1926 and 1946 is like a long, eventful, roller coaster ride: silent pictures gave way to "talkies" in 1926 which led to a 1929 zenith in movie attendance; world depression triggered an attendance drop-off in the 1930s, yet the movies served as a popular retreat or escape for citizens weary of harsh economic realities; on the eve of the Second World War, the screen was approaching its former high; America's entry into the war curtailed Hollywood's activities and turned film-makers into willing, if not very good, propagandists; at war's end, Hollywood was on the upswing and insensitive to the coming of television, which would deflate the motion picture industry just as films had once pricked vaudeville's balloon. During this roller coaster ride, Hollywood was truly to become "The Motion Picture Capital of the World."

The movies were a perfect medium for America in the lively 1920s for they, true to Ince's formula, could cater to what historian Jacobs described as a "national craving for thrills, excitement, escape, and experience." Movie screens fulfilled these desires so well that Jacobs found that "by 1926 the United States had 20,000 theatres, attended by 100 million Americans weekly."[16] "Life is worth living" was a national sentiment that movies marvelously echoed with sound after the 1926 marriage of electronic recording and reproduction equipment with film. Theaters were wired for sound so audiences could hear the stars talk and, at the celebrated outset, sing. Warner Brothers, which had led the charge to conquer silent pictures, in 1928 produced, with great success, *The Jazz Singer*, starring Al Jolson. The next year, box office receipts totaled an unbelievable $1 billion on an estimated weekly attendance of 110 million.[17] To keep America's love affair with the movies going strong and to stabilize production, the costly star system was manipulated with publicity.

But events outside the producers' control were to affect the industry beyond anyone's ability to regain the 1929 record attendance peak, even though the potential audience would mushroom with the nation's population growth. Hollywood's first setback was the Depression. Financially, the industry had flown too high, with fabulous fees paid to stars, extravagant production costs, and tremendous distribution and exhibition overhead. As unemployment lines lengthened, movie queues shortened and the industry responded with belt-tightening and promotion. Meanwhile, the industry again had sparked the wrath of reformers and clergy for lax adherence to its own clean-up promises. Pressured by the National Legion of Decency, an organization formed by the country's Catholic bishops, a Production Code that had been promulgated earlier on a voluntary adherence basis was given teeth; beginning in 1934 violators ran the risk of a $25,000 fine. With attendance off one-third, compliance seemed wise, not only to avoid a stiff fine but also to forestall any potential religious boycott of the box office.

As if twin troubles at home were not enough, the American film industry was suffering problems abroad, too. Since the end of World War I, American movies had circulated overseas freely, an easy process when films were silent. But, by the thirties, nationalistic barriers were going up in Soviet Russia, Germany, Italy, and even Britain. Bans, revenue restrictions, and quotas were among the devices being employed; practices that were later to be used against American television programs. In Japan, U.S. movies were allowed entry but not without a special purpose: they attracted audiences who were then also shown government propaganda films.

Much of the evidence relating to the distribution and impact of American films prior to the Second World War is indirect, but nonetheless there is little doubt that Hollywood's films had gained a significant place in foreign societies. One can only guess at the size of the total foreign audience, keeping in mind that even recorded estimates of weekly domestic audiences were nothing more than that, estimates. But the popularity of American films abroad was beyond question.

Besides nationalistic barriers, however, there were other indicators of American films' popularity and influence abroad. For example, one student of Hollywood in the 1930s, Louise Tanner, reports that "the State Department worried over America's reputation as projected by film versions of *The Grapes of Wrath* and *Tobacco Road*." Furthermore, according to Tanner, "When *Beau Geste* was refilmed in 1939, the villains were given Russian names because the export market to Russia was small. When *Idiot's Delight* was produced by Hollywood, to avoid offending any ethnic group (at home or abroad) it was set in a mythical country whose inhabitants spoke Esperanto."[18] From World War II came tales that included the finding of a Shirley Temple snapshot on the body of a dead Japanese sniper and discovery of a picture gallery of Hollywood stars in Anne Frank's room. Additionally, whenever another talented foreigner, like the superb British director Alfred Hitchcock, arrived in southern California the event served to underscore the international importance of the American film industry and of Hollywood as the mecca of filmmaking.

During the 1930s, when America was depressed not only economically but spiritually as well, movies provided a convenient form of escape, even though movie-goers were forced by economic necessity to visit theaters less frequently. Declining attendance stimulated some new directions; for instance, Mickey Mouse moved up to star billing. Although Mickey was an animated star, he was nonetheless part of a movie trend that diverted the country's attention from social realities.

War clouds were gathering over Europe, soup kitchens were feeding America's hungry, and Hollywood was producing musicals, melo-dramas, adventure stories, and westerns. The movies had become, what Louise Tanner termed, "The Celluloid Safety Valve."[19] Only occasionally was the spellbinding effect of the escapist movies broken. By the end of the decade, both the country and the film business were on a strong upswing with attendance figures climbing toward the record high of 1929. The improving situation was fine with just about everyone and film makers who dared inject a bit of realism risked becoming sensationally controversial, as Charlie Chaplin found out.

Chaplin personally financed a $2 million production intended to arouse American public opinion against fascism. Using comedy, his production *The Great Dictator* spoofed Hitler and Mussolini and then, to ensure that the message was clear, Chaplin capped the picture with a four-minute speech in which he charged that "Brutes have risen to power," and he passionately pleaded, "Soldiers! In the name of democracy, let us unite!" Both Axis sympathizers and pacifists at-tempted to prevent the film from reaching the screen, but it did on 15 October 1940. Some critics branded Chaplin a propagandist. In-deed, he was one; but he was not alone for long. Militant movies emerged so that by the time America entered the war in December 1941 Hollywood's offerings already had included *A Yank in the R.A.F.* and *International Squadron*, both of which portrayed as heroes Amer-ican pilots who had joined Britain's embattled Royal Air Force. The forerunner of these films had been a 1939 feature, *Confessions of a Nazi Spy*. The movie drew a German diplomatic protest and was banned by South American countries that had come under Axis influ-ence. Within three years of that breakthrough, Hollywood went from complacency to fervent, patriotic war-time production.

The war years were not to be, however, a glorious period for the American motion picture industry. Despite a commitment to do its part, Hollywood's contribution to the war effort was mediocre. Al-though film was acknowledged to be an influential mass medium, Hollywood's power in this respect had come as an unconsciously sought result of producing pictures that satisfied mass audiences and thus were commercially successful. Charged with the objective of de-liberately trying to influence audiences, instead of merely exchanging a few hours of screen entertainment for the price of admission, Holly-wood was out of its element. Film makers knew how to entertain, not how to propagandize. Inane films like *The Tank Called John*, *Blondie for Victory*, and *A Yank in Libya* were the principal fare, only occa-sionally interspersed with a masterpiece such as Alfred Hitchcock's

Lifeboat, an allegory of world shipwreck. Meanwhile, the production mill also cranked out a steady diet of entertainment films.

In a review of "World War II and the American film," Lewis Jacobs noted that Hollywood devoted only a third of its wartime output of more than 1,700 movies to war themes and of these only "a small number . . . sharply reflected the varied aspects of war and heightened our understanding of it at that moment."[20]

During the war, movie attendance naturally had declined in the United States. With war's end, however, the motion picture industry quickly renewed its social contract with an adoring public and the upswing of the late 1930s, temporarily snapped by the war, was repeated. Movies circa 1946–47 were about as popular as in prewar days. Moreover, the international outlook was promising. Many foreign studios were closed, some reduced to war-wrecked rubble. But foreign markets, save those coming under communist domination, were accessible. What Hollywood's movie tycoons saw was a *world* motion picture market, with tens of thousands of theaters hosting a weekly audience of several hundred million.

And in that world market, the American movie industry, acting through its agent, the Motion Picture Export Association, was king. The Association negotiated film trade agreements with foreign governments and it negotiated from a position of strength. When, for instance, no satisfactory distribution agreement with Spain could be reached, Hollywood responded with a three-year boycott of the Spanish market. The early postwar commanding position of the American movie around the world can be appreciated statistically: in 1945 the U.S. exported 179 films to Britain or more than four times the number the British produced themselves that year, in 1946 the Italian market opened to an avalanche of 600 American movie imports, in 1947 as India struggled to independence it imported 264 Hollywood films, and so on.[21]

At home, meanwhile, other ominous statistics were being recorded. The manufacturing output in the United States of tiny screen television sets had jumped from 6500 in 1946 to 179,000 in 1947.[22]

INTERNATIONALIZED MOVIES

Paging through back issues of *Variety*, the U.S. entertainment industry's daily record, the reader is repeatedly reminded that the postwar American film business has had its ups and downs and that by the late

1950s it became appropriate to refer to an internationally controlled film industry. Accordingly, in April 1958, *Variety* published its first annual international film report to coincide with the Cannes film festival. That first edition was launched with a sobering headline: "Hollywood Fighting an Uphill Battle for, at least, the Status Quo."[23]

As television began sweeping through the United States during the 1950s, leaving the American motion picture industry crippled and groggy at home, the situation abroad was initially far brighter, for the day of the TV set in foreign living rooms was yet to come. So the decline in domestic film business was being offset in foreign markets, with film rentals abroad accounting for an ever increasing percentage of the American producers' total income. But the new balance could not and did not last long. Adjustments were required, for the impact of American television was forcing movie production cutbacks.

Fewer pictures produced meant two things. First, the oligopolistic American film industry was shrinking below the optimal size that had enabled Hollywood to dominate the world film market. A shrunken industry, however, no longer could benefit from economies of scale. Second, while foreign demand for movies initially held strong in the absence of TV abroad, Hollywood was unable to fully satisfy that demand. Foreign film makers had a grand opportunity to exploit. And they did, backed up by resurrection of prewar nationalistic protection devices, such as film import quotas. In response, the Americans, in effect, followed the old adage, "If you can't beat 'em, join 'em."

The concept gave rise to an internationalized film industry. No longer would the major American film companies continue as almighty, vertically integrated enterprises producing, distributing, and exhibiting movies. Start-to-finish operational control was to give way to a truly international motion picture industry in which Americans were partners.

The first blow suffered by the integrated film companies actually was thrown neither by television nor would-be foreign competitors. Uncle Sam was the villain, at least a villain in the eyes of the MGM lion and his film making mates. MGM was a very rich company during the postwar 1940s when it was one of seven major motion picture companies, with their Hollywood studios turning out on an average more than one completed movie a day. The primary audience for these films was variously estimated at between 60 and 90 million American theater-goers who weekly filled the circuits of MGM and its competitors. For their efforts, the "majors," as the seven big companies that controlled four-fifths of the American film industry were called, shared profits that by 1949 totaled over $200 million.

Profits of such a high order were possible not only because MGM, Columbia, Paramount, Warner Brothers, Universal, United Artists, and 20th Century Fox produced movies, but also because their films either were peddled in packages on theater circuits or shown in company-owned theaters. The chain of owned outlets for MGM films, for instance, were all the Loew's theaters. The system of selling movies in batches was called "block-booking," which meant that if a nonchain exhibitor wished to obtain a film with a very popular star, the exhibitor was required also to rent less desirable movies at the same time as part of a package.

The U.S. Department of Justice examined these arrangements, considered them to be violations of antitrust law, went to court and, despite mighty roaring by the MGM Lion and his friends, by 1950 had forced the divorce of producers and theater owners, and in the process the additionally profitable system of "block-booking" fell victim, as well. Unaffected, of course, were foreign theaters controlled by the "majors" abroad. But what had been lost at home was never to be recaptured abroad. MGM, according to an annual stockholders report, was operating a mere 33 theaters abroad in 1972. Another company, 20th Century Fox, still had a string of 123 theaters abroad as late as 1973. Nearly all were in Australia and New Zealand, remote countries from the United States where William Fox, among the earliest American exhibitors, had gotten into the movie making business only because as an independent theater owner he couldn't get films from the old Motion Picture Patents Company monopoly.

The industry was bitter about the federal government's fateful legal action. The businessmen who controlled Hollywood have been inclined to mark the court's final divestiture order as the day when the ball of string that bound up "The Film Capital" began to unravel. On the other hand, the court order to sell off theater chains could not have come at a better time for the industry. In coming years, television was to drain many of those theaters of their audiences, but at the time of divestiture the movie business was still good. The Palaces and Grands were saleable items at handsome prices. It would be for the new owners to tear them down a few years hence and convert the ground on which they stood into parking lots.

The years of decline brought on by TV and foreign competition were naturally beset with recriminations, with outspoken members of the artistic community offering their own explanations. Hollywood fell, some said, because the greedy businessmen and their cohort producers abused and blacklisted some of the best, genuine talent.

Speaking as an abused writer, Ben Hecht, certainly one of the most gifted of screenwriters, claimed there were only a handful of producers "who actually were equal or superior to the writers." They were, according to Hecht, David O. Selznick, Sam Goldwyn, Darryl Zanuck, Walter Wanger, and Irving Thalberg. The rest, wrote Hecht in a memorable *Elegy for Wonderland,* were "not bright. They were as slow-witted and unprofessional toward making up a story as stockbrokers might be, or bus drivers."[24]

The blacklist is among the most sordid stories to come out of an industry that has had an outsized share of offbeat tales. The story begins in 1947, when a fear of communism crept into the social fabric of America and the response of some righteous U.S. Congressmen was to investigate Hollywood, searching for the infected victims of this alleged new menace. The overly sensitive motion picture industry—sensitive not, perhaps, to having communists in its midst, but rather to any potential adverse public reaction that might precipitate a decrease in box office receipts—was alarmed. Late in 1947, the industry's top brass huddled at New York's leading hotel and there issued what was to be called the Waldorf Declaration. Hollywood pledged publicly not to employ anyone considered politically dangerous. The industry's official spokesman, Eric Johnson, acknowledged that the policy had risks of hurting innocent people and stifling creativity. Nonetheless, the decision was firm, and under constant pressure from the American Legion, which backed up its avid anticommunist position with threats of movie boycotts by the Legion's huge membership, the policy stood for more than a decade.

Nobody knows how many people were blacklisted, for the system was very informal. At least 212 individuals were affected, for their names turned up in one way or another in the Congressional investigations. That the careers of creative, innocent persons were destroyed is well-documented,[25] but the effect of the blacklist on the film industry is less certain.

Hollywood's success, after all, essentially was due to an economic formula of producing films with banal, not innovative, plots. What motivated producers later to breach the dreaded blacklist was the same motivation that imposed it in the first place and, in fact, that had always motivated just about everything in Hollywood: box office success. By 1960, the risk of offending the American Legion had to be balanced against the quest to revive a badly slumping industry with box office smashes. Otto Preminger took a bold step when he hired blacklisted writer, Dalton Trumbo, to write the script for *Exodus.* The American Legion boycotted the film but with little impact, which meant that a colony of underground blacklisted artists could drop their aliases and false fronts that had allowed them, more or less, to keep working.

To argue that Hollywood never should have adopted the blacklist policy makes moral sense, but probably not good business sense. To argue that the policy impaired creativity may be valid, but only to very limited degree. Without the blacklist, anticommunist group pressure may well have reinforced the TV-induced decline in theater attendance, thus felling Hollywood's house of cards even sooner.

Looking back, it was neither trust busting by the federal government, nor abuse of creative talent by inane producers, nor uncourageous bending to ideological politics that killed Hollywood. Television was the villain, for it alone created new economic realities that were to have worldwide implications for the American motion picture industry.

International control of the American motion picture industry came about during the decades of the 1950s and 1960s. International control does not mean that other countries joined in making movies for the world market, although that was true, too. For example, a randomly selected edition of *Variety* (15 January 1975) contained eleven reviews of international films: they were nationally identified as British (1), Italian (2), Spanish (1), Hong Kong (1), Australian (1), American (3), Italian-French (1), and Thai (1). These are movies produced for foreign distribution. But only the Italian-French coproduction is an internationalized movie in the sense that representatives of two (or more) countries shared responsibility for making it. The others, if more information were available, about, for instance, financing, might be put in the internationalized category as well.

There is no universally accepted method for determining the nationality of a motion picture. Audiences probably judge according to the origins of the principal actors, some academicians use the nationality of the director, and so on. Not surprisingly, in an age when casts frequently are multinational, filming is done in a half-dozen countries, and the final product is distributed worldwide, American motion picture executives look at the accounting ledger. Their criterion for judgement rests on the answer to the question: Who invested—that is, who stands to profit or lose? In this book, the critical consideration is control. When two or more representatives of different countries share control over the product, then it is deemed an internationalized movie. Control, to the dismay of many artists, is a word that belongs to the business side of the motion picture industry. Below the rank of producer, the term cannot be applied. To understand this, one may recall that Chaplin *financed* and *produced* his provocative picture, *The Great Dictator*. Chaplin explained his unorthodox technique this way: "What have I worked for all my life . . . if not to gain the independence to make my own pictures as I like? . . ."[26] The erosion of the power of the major Hollywood studios was someday to enable other stars to control their own pictures the same way—Kirk Douglas's production about the Thracian slave turned insurrectionist, *Spartacus*, for example.

The steps the American motion picture industry took on the road to international control, a process which went beyond coproductions, were a high level of exporting, followed by multinational film making —a process that exceeded in scope earlier migrations of foreign talent to Southern California.

At the outset of the modern, or post-World War II, era, the American motion picture industry could be characterized as being a national exporter. Indeed, the U.S. during the second half of the 1940s was *the* exporting country in the world insofar as films were concerned. A total of 622 movies were released in the United States in 1950[27]; virtually all were available for export and most, no doubt, were sent abroad inasmuch as U.S.-produced movies then occupied something like three-fourths or more of the world's screen time.[28]

But by 1955, the impact of television had cut the number of pictures produced in the U.S. to 305, fewer than half as many only five years earlier. With output sharply off at the main source, Europe's recuperating national movie industries had a golden opportunity to fill the gaps, at least those in their own markets.

The U.S. motion picture industry, not unlike other large American businesses, responded by becoming multinational. When this occurred cannot be said with precision, but the reality was indirectly attested to by Eric Johnson, president of the U.S. Exporters' Association, who was quoted by *Variety* on 19 April 1958, as calling for an end to national restrictions to be replaced by an international system of motion picture *interdependence*. While Johnson was principally concerned with pitching the theme—that the "free world's films must be free to travel"—by which he meant quotas and other barriers abroad to American films should be lifted, he also was acknowledging that the American industry was being reshaped.

On one hand, the U.S. industry did not have the clout abroad it once had. For example, negotiations with Argentina resulted in the American exporters agreeing to reduce the number of movies sent to Argentina from 387 in 1957 to 200 in 1958. On the other hand, foreign movie imports to the U.S. soared in earning power: with Brigette

Bardot's sexy French films leading the charge, imports earned nearly $42 million in the American market in 1958, up almost threefold from the previous year.[29]

This is not to suggest that Americans were doing badly abroad: they weren't, as is evidenced by the following figures: in a twelve-month period during 1957–58, 232 American films were shown in Germany compared to 130 German-made films; Austria in 1958 screened 214 American films plus 114 German and 21 of its own; British theaters the same year showed 235 American films versus 105 local productions; Italian screens devoted that year 55.2 percent of their time to American movies and 32.6 percent to Italy's own films.[30] But the monopoly American film makers once enjoyed both at home and overseas was being successfully challenged. To meet that challenge, some enterprising Americans pursued novel approaches and in the process helped along the multinational process.

An obvious step was to bring foreign talent to the United States. While there was nothing new in this, the size of the inflow was unprecedented. No fewer than seventy-five non-Americans were starring in Hollywood-made motion pictures in 1960.[31] More significant, however, was movement in the other direction—going overseas to make movies. Trade journals published details on studio facilities abroad and gave helpful hints on the vagaries of producing outside the comfortable womb of the fabled Hollywood back lots and sound stages. The multilingual associate producer or director became invaluable. American entrepreneurs like Joseph L. Levine in Rome and Samuel Bronston in Madrid appeared as bold new figures in filmmaking.

Levine's brilliance was to take advantage of lower Italian production costs to make films with American performers. He gave the world a series of *Hercules* mini-spectaculars starring Steve Reeves; they did not delight the critics, but as a less expensive twist on an old Hollywood formula, they were successful at the box office. Bronston discovered that the coffers of the American motion picture companies were missing large amounts of funds from Spain, blocked there by local regulation. These were monies earned by the showing of American pictures in Spain, but which the Spanish government insisted had to be spent within the country. Bronston did just that, by producing a series of spectacular movies filmed outside Madrid. He made the Spanish happy with a film about a national hero, *El Cid*, and he also made himself rich with it and other made-in-Spain movies such as *55 Days at Peking* and *The Fall of the Roman Empire*.

One effect of this increasingly popular form of multinational movie making was to further the development of national film industries.

While Americans financed, organized, and starred in these pictures, the other ingredients—technicians, extras, props, etc.—were provided locally. Meanwhile, at least some American film makers were profiting by this approach, not only because of lower production costs and available capital, but also because their productions skirted import barriers in the host countries.

Booms, such as they were in Europe's postwar film industries, all were to become busts with the local arrival of television. In Britain, for instance, growing popularity of the "telly" precipitated a drop in the number of motion picture productions from 429 in 1958 to 319 in 1962.[32] Another indicator that TV had set back maturing European film industries was a plunge in revenue in the U.S. market. After five years of fantastic export growth in the U.S., the box office receipts for foreign films shown in American theaters declined by $20 million in 1962.[33]

With television ravaging the film business on both sides of the Atlantic, multinational movie makers were forced towards efficiency and, in turn, internationalization. As the 1960s wore on, wistful glances were to be cast at the Soviet Union and Eastern Europe as potential new markets, but in the early years of the decade that part of the world was a political nonstarter for Western films. So too, later on, eyes would be cast on Africa, but countries there were just achieving independence when the crunch hit the European film market and therefore were without immediate market potential for movies.

Since declining business in Europe could not be offset elsewhere, the only response open to film makers was greater efficiency. For Europeans this meant coproductions, for Americans it meant coparticipation. Either way, an internationalized film industry was to emerge during the decade.

The reason that the words coproduction and coparticipation are employed here is that they describe different methods of cooperation. In Europe, coproduction of commercial films is almost invariably based on formal agreements between the governments of the countries involved. For example, a French-British motion picture could be coproduced under an agreement concluded by appropriate government agencies, in this instance the Center National de la Cinematographie for France and the Department of Trade and Industry for Britain. The principal economic purpose of coproduction is to confer double or multiple nationality on a film, enabling it to receive government subsidies or advantages under quota or other restrictive systems. The basic attraction, then, is that in effect, two films are made for the price

55

of one. Cooperative film making outside such agreements is termed co-participation, the practice most often engaged in by Americans, with similar advantages resulting.

Whether coproduced under an interstate agreement or by hand-shaking-cum-contract, films made in the sixties inaugurated the decade of joint picture making in Europe.[34] By 1965, only 34 of 142 French films were wholly indigenous,[35] Hollywood's film making unions were screaming about "runaway" (to foreign countries) productions, and insiders discussed the "new one world of film."[36]

The American contributions to this internationalizing process, beyond stars and a few other key personnel, were money and distribution prowess. The major American studios had capital to finance foreign productions and vast, worldwide networks to market films. The once integrated majors, having lost control over their principal exhibition outlets due to the U.S. Government antitrust action and their in-Hollywood production monopoly by big studios due to television, still were wealthy and had their global distribution nets. What the majors needed in order to profit from those facilities was something worthwhile to distribute. The need gave birth to the notion, "Have Finance Will Travel." The slogan was, however, incomplete, for it should have added, ". . . When Distribution Rights Included."

Levine blazed the trail to Italy and the major American motion pictures companies followed. Their official representative, the Motion Picture Export Association, struck a deal with its Italian counterpart for a package of low interest rate U.S. financing in Italy coupled with American production there and, of course, the majors retained distribution rights outside of Italy. The chief Italian bargainer, Eitel Monaco, championed the agreement as being in the joint interests of the Hollywood major motion picture companies and the Italian film industry.

In England, meanwhile, where the BBC was out in front among Europeans in providing television service, substantial amounts of American capital had begun to flow to the motion picture industry by 1960. How much money was provided is not reliably known, but London was developing as a center for "U.S. interest pictures." In 1969, Jack Valenti, president of the U.S. Exporters' Association, while on a visit to London, was to reveal that American investments in British films were running at $96 million annually because, he said, the "talent is here."[37] Realistically, it was the other way around: the money was there.

Although American investments were being made elsewhere, too (*Variety* reported a total of twenty-four countries in 1962), Italy and

Britain were the most important and of the two, Britain was first. In 1965, the top ten motion pictures in the U.S., that is, the biggest box offices attractions, were:[38]

1. *Mary Poppins* (Hollywood)
2. *The Sound of Music* (Austrian exteriors, Hollywood interiors)
3. *Goldfinger* (British)
4. *My Fair Lady* (Hollywood)
5. *What's New Pussycat* (British-French)
6. *Shenandoah* (U.S., non-Hollywood)
7. *The Sandpiper* (Hollywood)
8. *Father Goose* (U.S., non-Hollywood)
9. *Von Ryan's Express* (Italy)
10. *Yellow Rolls Royce* (British)

In the comparatively still rich American market, foreign-made movies had burst into the big time. Two British, one British-French coproduction, and an Italian film had cracked what was still the world's most lucrative film market, the United States. If *The Sound of Music* is given half credit for scenes filmed in the Alps, the top ten in the United States were 45 percent foreign.

Other big hits in the United States that came from Britain and had been made with American financing were: the Beatles' *A Hard Day's Night, Dr. Strangelove*, a tragi-comedy about Soviet-American nuclear warfare, and a James Bond action-thriller, *From Russia With Love*. With blockbusters like that, the British motion picture industry was in fine shape and it was overly grateful to the "Yanks." The director of the Federation of British Filmmakers went so far as to say that, "American distributors have brought to us more than money and opportunity for worldwide release; they have also brought experience, talent, vigour and imagination."[39] What, of course, he meant was that to get the Americans' coveted money and distribution benefits, the British were making American-styled movies.

Moreover, the Americans were getting something extra in Britain, too: handsome subsidies. Not only did American-financed films escape the British quota requiring theaters to devote at least 30 percent of their screen time to indigenous films, but these movies also reaped, in 1965 alone, $14 million, or something like 80 percent of British government film subsidies that year.

U.S.-financed, British-subsidized, American-styled motion pictures distributed worldwide rejuvenated the business of importing "foreign" films into the United States. The plunge of foreign picture earnings in the U.S. during 1962 quickly turned around, with an extra shot in the arm from U.S. investments in Italian films. In 1963, foreign movies shown in the United States earned $69 million, of which $12.5 million was from American-financed, Italian-made epics.[40] The next year, revenues totaled $71 million of which $50 million was earned by British films, most of which were U.S.-backed, and $9 million by Italian movies of which Levine's Embassy Pictures accounted for about half.[41]

Coparticipation, which was an incipient trend for American motion picture companies at the beginning of the sixties, was the industry's central policy at the end of the decade. Professor Thomas H. Guback, of the University of Illinois, has reported that during that period "American-financed films abroad rose from about 35 percent to 60 percent of the total output of American producers." Professor Guback worried about this development for he wrote in 1973, "Europeans cannot lose control of the economic end of film making and expect to retain autonomy in the cultural or social spheres."[42] His message, in fact, had been grasped already.

BACK TO EXPORTING

By 1970 in England, what was seen as an American raid on the Eady Film Subsidy Fund, came under attack; while in Italy, only a few years after Italians had sought additional U.S. monetary and distribution involvement in their industry, cries of American colonization were being heard. Simultaneously, the global market for films was experiencing a metamorphosis, with the budding of national film industries outside the Western world. Eastern Europe led the way. Even the Soviet Union shifted from "boy loves tractor" and "girl fulfills quota" themes to more artistic films that were exportable, if only in small numbers and for limited audiences. Suddenly, too, or so it seemed, the less affluent countries of the world were following India's lead and developing their own film industries. Turkey, South Korea, Taiwan, Hong Kong, the Philippines, and Brazil were in the movie business. Mexico and Egypt were strengthening their positions in the Spanish- and Arabic-speaking regions of the world, respectively.

As the 1960s drew to a close, a new sense of nationalism was afoot in the world and it was reflected by new directions in the motion picture business. For Americans, the new period was to be one of retrenchment, of going back home and of watching Italy step forward to assume a positon of prominence alongside the U.S. in what was left of the global film business. For the other Europeans bad times had arrived: the British industry fell into the doldrums; Spain attempted to stimulate its troubled industry with a new "order"; and the Germans did no better than to produce a few popular sex films. The countervailing wind of nationalism was not, however, without opportunities, albeit limited ones. In a world tired of big power confrontations, disenchanted with an America that had tarnished its image, and filled with backward yet developing and proud young countries, film had a special relevance. Local films could be a barrier against social homogeneity, by reversing film's previous international role of binding the nations of the world together. National film industries could reinforce indigenous cultural identities. The trend at the outset of the 1970s was toward the nationalistic film; television and an occasional movie of universal appeal would inherit what was left of the global visual industry.

The new era belonged to the producer who knew his home market. Accordingly, France's earlier ratio of coproductions versus local productions reversed itself by 1972 when seventy-one indigenous and forty-nine coproduced films were made.[43] So strong were nationalistic sentiments in Canada, which always had depended on America for its movies and lost its best film talent in migrations to Hollywood, that starting in 1968 subsidies were to be offered to indigenous filmmakers who rarely showed a profit.

The trend was to hold true for America itself, with pictures like Mike Nichols's *The Graduate* leading the way. Some Hollywood veterans were amazed that a film without an established star could do so well. They should have known better, if only because that earlier pacesetter in the rush to go abroad, the savvy Joseph E. Levine, had backed the picture. *The Graduate*, a movie about America's rebellious middle-class youth, inspired not only similar thematic pictures but also was in the vanguard of movies about the home country. Back in the late 1950s, when the major American motion picture companies were shooting ever more abroad, the non-American theme dominated. Oscar winners for best picture, beginning in 1956, were *Around the World in 80 Days, The Bridge on the River Kwai, Gigi,* and *Ben-Hur.* During the internationalized sixties, foreign themes continued strong. But in the seventies, the lawless days of America's own *Bonnie and Clyde* and *Godfather* were to be preferred along with so-called disaster pictures which made Americans wonder how safe were all those jetliners they flew in and skyscrapers they worked in.

The international distribution of motion pictures was not to cease, but the numbers of films in circulation were to be fewer as there evolved a triple-tiered world structure: a handful of worldwide releases, a few regional production centers, and national industries practically everywhere.

The trend was disastrous for what remained of Hollywood's one-time great motion picture studios, because the trend meant nothing less than the fast erosion of their last base of strength, distribution. Suddenly the festering problems of Hollywood had to be faced directly. Twentieth Century Fox on the heels of $15 million profits in 1968 took a whopping $64 million loss the next year and plunged even further in 1970 when Fox accountants wrote a loss of $78 million as the once rich film company atoned for years of decline. The MGM Lion, whose mighty roar was once literally heard around the world through the mammoth worldwide film distribution network of Metro-Goldwyn-Mayer, was forced to look elsewhere for its supper. MGM consolidated its foreign network of ninety-one offices staffed by 2400 employees with Fox in 1972.[44] The decision came just one year after MGM had advertised: "Give Us Your Film—We'll Give You The World."[45] Instead of offering the world to independent filmmakers, MGM interests switched to owning a Las Vegas hotel and expanding further into television program production and marketing which in 1971 included licensing for the first time to the Soviet Union a television series, "Daktari."

Film distribution, when there was something worthwhile to distribute, had been a good business for the majors, for their fees were about one-third of the box office gross for this service. As late as 1969, U.S. distributors earned $25 million in Germany, for instance.[46] But overhead costs were high (critics have contended that they were unnecessarily high due to poor management) and with nationalism in vogue, the laws of economies of scale again were working in reverse against the big companies just as had happened before with production. To be financially viable, the majors felt they must have more business.

They turned to Italy, where motion pictures had made a comeback and were doing well at the box office. The Italian production industry was baited with even more U.S. money, but this time the Americans wanted distribution rights in Italy itself. The reason was simple: the box office gross in Italy was $565 million in 1968, a big pie from which to take a one-third distribution cut.[47] The American's point was not lost on the Italians. In order to free themselves from U.S. domination, the Rome film makers persuaded the Italian State bank, Banca Nazionale del Lavora, a long time patron of the national industry, to provide even more funds. According to *Variety*, BNL poured $39.5 million into Italian film making in 1971, or 48 percent of the industry's total funding that year.[48] As for distribution, two of Italy's motion picture magnates, Rizzoli and DeLaurentis, formed their own distribution company. By 1973, *Variety* would proclaim: "Italy: World Film Power."[49] That fact was all too clear as Italian companies started pulling some of Hollywood's old tricks: directors abandoned style in quest of box office appeal, filming abroad for background effects (even in the U.S.), and making trendy pictures like the offbeat western *Trinity Is My Name*, and even shooting some movies in England with American actors. The clearest of all signs, however, was an appeal from Rome that rang like an echo: now it was the Italian motion picture association saying that foreign markets should be open for their films.[50]

With admissions to Italian theaters running better than 10 million a week in 1972,[51] Rome's busy film industry had a domestic base from which to export, second only to the American market which, by the start of the seventies, was down to a mere 15 million weekly admissions.[52] So, not only was the absolute world supremacy of the American Motion Picture a thing of the past, but the much deteriorated U.S. industry was being crowded by Italian competition.

In a quarter century after World War II, the U.S. motion picture industry had gone nearly full circle—national film exporter, multinational movie maker, international motion picture partner, and then retrenchment toward national exporter. The process, in fact, was less one of rounding a circle than tracing an inward spiral, for the postwar orbit of the American motion picture industry was that of a falling star.

The murder of "Hollywood: The Film Capital of the World" by television no longer is mourned, nor, of course, is the expanded family of nations sorrowful that American motion picture global hegemony has been shattered. Indeed, some have seen a new opportunity for the *theatrical motion picture* which had come to stand "somewhere between the stage play and the television show," as one perceptive observer of the industry put it as early as 1962.[53] With the tyranny of the assembly line gone, producers could cater to more discriminating audiences who numbered somewhere between the tens of thousands willing to purchase expensive tickets for stage presentations and the tens of millions who watched television at home. The new equation at last put American movies at the threshold of a mainstream shift from business to artistry.

The business was to belong to television, which, thirsting for program material, ironically turned to its victim, Hollywood. Not only were movie rights purchased for TV broadcast, but the facilities of the big studios around Los Angeles were converted to television production requirements. Charles Champlin reported in the *Saturday Review* that by the end of 1966 "footage equal to 600 feature films a year"[54] was being cranked out by Hollywood's new made-for-TV mill. The visual industry, Champlin said, was at full employment, even silver screen stars were moving into the new home screen medium to imbue television programs with the same stable mass appeal as the old B movies had.

Ma and Pa Kettle motion pictures no longer played in neighborhood theaters, but the "Beverly Hillbillies" graced TV screens in prime time. America's visual industry merely has transformed its chief means of distribution.

TELEVISION:
AMERICA AND THE WORLD

The rapid growth of television after World War II is an awe-inspiring phenomenon in the history of human kind. Within a quarter century nearly every country in the world had a TV system. This is not to imply, however, that television has become universally available to all peoples of the world. To the contrary, great masses who live in economically backward regions, especially those in rural areas, are without TV. While television antennas can be observed prominently affixed to slum shacks in urbanized centers of Latin America and to lesser extents in Asia and Africa, the penetration of TV in the less developed countries has been well below that of the industrialized countries. China, where a quarter of the human race lives, has a TV system barely beyond the experimental stage and India, with a population of 600 million, is still experimenting with television as the twentieth century enters its final quarter.

In 1975, when the United Nations estimated that for every urban resident in the world there were approximately 1.5 persons living in rural areas,[55] television in the countryside was an embryo. Moreover, roughly half the world's population lived in rural mud huts or their equivalents. So television, whose growth pattern has been one of wealthy nations and urban centers first, poor nations and rural areas last, still had far to reach before it embraced all humankind.

But even if about half of the world's population still could not tune in, governments everywhere welcomed the new medium within a remarkably short time. By 1960, there already were 74 countries with television systems, most in a primitive stage. In the next decade, when television outside the United States experienced its greatest development, that number rose to 134, that is, nearly the entire family of nations had TV in some stage of service.

The U.S. was the mother country for the development of TV. The early strength of American leadership in the field is evidenced by the fact that there were 310 sets in the U.S. for every one thousand Americans by 1960—a density level that only three other countries had reached by 1970. Canada then had 332 sets per thousand citizens, Bermuda 315 sets (many in hotels that catered to American tourists), and Sweden 312. Meanwhile, American set ownership climbed to 412 per thousand, as television viewing of the 1970s became less a family and more an individual activity in the United States.

Since the United States clearly established leadership first in the new field of television, the U.S. was in a strong position to influence the medium as it took hold in many places abroad. To understand that influence, especially as it has been manifested in the heavy flow of American programs to foreign stations, one must look at the origins and development of the U.S. television system itself.

AMERICAN TV: FROM ADOLESCENCE TO MATURITY Metaphorically speaking, television in the United States never was an infant, at least not a babbling baby. Wireless radio was an existing *sound* medium to which an image was added. In other words, radio technology was pushed until the broadcast medium included an electronic picture, too. The importance of this evolution was to cast TV originally in the mold of radio-cum-picture. Suppose for a moment that television had been perfected by motion picture instead of radio technicians. If MGM instead of RCA had pioneered in TV, the American television system likely would have gone off in the direction of viewers paying for shows delivered to them by cable, instead of commercial sponsorship of programs distributed through-the-air. Or suppose television had been an invention of a common communications carrier, Bell Laboratories, for instance. Then the system might have been much like the telephone, with the consumer paying the phone company for the use of its facilities and making separate deals with program producers. Not only are such alternatives feasible, but they have been offered to the American public. That neither pay-TV nor videophone has been widely accepted attests to the strength of the original system of broadcast television which grew out of commercial network radio. Only cable has had some limited success due to broadcast television's inadequate service in sparsely populated and poor TV signal reception areas. So TV arrived as a picture tube implanted in a radio set, not as a miniature home movie theater or an audio-visual phone.

Television's arrival in America actually was tardy, for the technology was available before the Second World War. In 1938, RCA's David Sarnoff informed the Radio Manufacturers' Association that "television in the home is now technically feasible."[56] The thought must have been tantalizing for both speaker and audience. RCA through its subsidiary, the National Broadcasting Company, would be able to both produce and distribute television programs. More importantly, however, RCA and the other radio manufacturers would share in a bonanza if the American public took to buying TV sets with the same eagerness the public had been purchasing radios. Whatever dreams any of the manufacturers may have had then were tempered by the fact that in 1938 the United States had not yet recovered from the long economic depression.

Still, the message was clear: RCA and its business associates intended to put television into the American home. NBC took the lead in programming with telecasts from the 1939 New York World's Fair. Going on the air shortly thereafter were CBS and DuMont. On the eve of America's entry into the Second World War, a half dozen commercial television stations were licensed to operate in the United States, and there were an estimated 10,000 receivers. The war postponed the commercial development of TV, while the electronics industry devoted its energies to military-related production. Across the Atlantic, where technical development of TV was advanced in some European countries, the war would sidetrack television for an even longer period than in the U.S.

After World War II, during the late 1940s, television moved out of the experimental stage and toward a prominent, indeed usually the most prominent, position in the living rooms of American homes. The transition to commercially profitable telecasting was not without some risk. In those early days, the ledger sheets of the TV broadcasters were written in red. CBS President, Frank Stanton, put the financial loss of networks and stations combined at $48 million during the three year period 1948–50.[57] These were years when the first stations were built and organized into networks so that programs of sufficient appeal could be televised to the potential set-buying public.

The method for doing this was to follow the trail of radio, which in America was government-regulated but privately operated. Radio networks expanded their operations into television as did many of the networks' affiliated local stations.

Programming, which in the early years was limited to a few peak viewing hours in the evening (a pattern generally followed when TV first was introduced into foreign countries) came from two sources—the stage and radio. With the networks originating telecasts mainly in New York at the beginning (not until the summer of 1951 did AT&T open the first transcontinental coaxial cable making coast to coast simultaneous television transmission possible), the New York stage was a rich resource. Both what was left of Vaudeville and off-Broadway style plays went before the eye of the television camera. From radio came personalities and programs that the new medium was able to adapt and adopt.

Meanwhile, the sports world, which had embraced radio as a stimulus for bringing fans to the stadium, fought a rearguard action against TV, fearing it would have the opposite effect. Hollywood, of course, would toss the program-hungry new beast nothing more than old (not necessarily vintage) films, for which a few more dollars could be earned when dusted off for sale to TV. For neither sports officials nor film-makers, both of whom were later to throw themselves at the feet of TV, was there anything approaching love at their first sight of television.

The American public, on the other hand, quickly became fascinated with the new medium. For television, postwar America was in a favorable economic and social situation. The country had put the depression of the 1930s behind it; consumer purchasing power was strong. Socially, secondary education had become standard, more leisure time had become available, and the nation's population became concentrated in metropolitan areas. In sum, a large, urban, no longer overworked, middle-class audience was within easy reach of short-range TV signals radiating from the top of New York City's Empire State Building and other big city transmitting facilities.

This audience was introduced to television basically in two ways which, not incidentally, have been another pattern outside the U.S., too. One phase was public viewing—television sets in store windows, special display centers, and the like. Perhaps the most significant place of viewing by potential set buyers was in neighborhood taverns or bars. These were popular gathering places for workingmen, many of whom had recently entered the middle class. The other introductory level was the upper-middle class or wealthy who were the first to acquire television sets for their homes. Their sets provided home entertainment not just for the immediate family, but for relatives and friends as well. Typically, a rich uncle bought a set and then invited his relatives to visit for an evening of television viewing.

TABLE 3: Growth of TV Penetration in Different Segments
of the U.S. Market
1949–1956

From Market Research Corporation reports.

	Sept. 1949	Oct. 1950	July 1951	July 1952	July 1953	July 1954	July 1955	July 1956
U.S. Total	6%	18%	27%	37%	49%	58%	68%	76%
Region								
Northeast	13%	35%	45%	59%	69%	77%	85%	88%
South	1	4	13	17	30	37	54	64
North Central	4	15	27	39	50	61	70	79
Mtn., S.W.	*	3	10	16	31	40	52	62
Pacific	5	19	26	34	47	56	66	76
City Size								
Farm	*	3%	7%	12%	23%	28%	43%	54%
Under 2,500	*	5	9	16	26	41	56	67
2,500 to 50,000	*	9	16	18	31	39	53	65
50,000 to 500,000	*	17	28	37	51	64	75	82
500,000 & over	14%	40	53	69	77	81	87	89
Income								
Upper Fourth	7%	24%	33%	45%	58%	70%	81%	87%
Next Fourth	7	19	32	41	55	63	76	85
Next Fourth	6	18	28	40	50	59	69	76
Lowest Fourth	3	12	18	23	32	41	48	58
Education								
Grade School	4%	16%	23%	31%	43%	51%	62%	70%
High School	7	22	34	45	57	65	75	83
College	6	17	24	38	48	61	73	79
Family Size								
1 & 2 Members	4%	12%	19%	28%	38%	48%	59%	69%
3 Members	6	18	30	41	52	65	73	81
4 & 5 Members	7	22	35	45	58	69	78	85
6 & More Members	6	19	27	39	53	55	66	74
Age of Housewife								
Under 35	8%	23%	36%	44%	58%	65%	75%	82%
35 through 44 Years	8	23	37	48	60	68	74	82
45 Years & Over	3	12	19	28	40	49	61	70
Presence of Children								
5 Years & Under	7%	23%	36%	48%	54%	65%	75%	81%
6 to 12 Years	7	22	35	46	56	65	76	83
13 to 20 Years	6	18	28	39	49	58	71	78
No Children	4	13	21	29	37	50	61	70

* No Data.

Source: Leo Bogart, *The Age of Television* (New York: Frederick Ungar Publishing Co., 1958). Reprinted with permission.

Table 3 reveals the fantastic growth pattern of television in the United States during the period of its greatest expansion (from 6 percent penetration of American homes in 1949 to 76 percent in 1956). The table shows that in 1950, when television started to become popular in America, the largest group of buyers of home sets were upper income men who lived in one of the many major cities of the northeast. They were married to a woman under 45, had several children at home, and were probably high school graduates. While the same group still was at the top six years later, all other possible combinations had narrowed the original gap and no sector lagged in bringing television into their homes. Even a majority of poor, undereducated heads-of-households living on farms in the southwestern part of the U.S. had a home TV set in 1956.

The widespread acceptance of television into the American home in such a short span of years was astonishing. All the more so because the investment was a major three-figure expenditure per family. The total bill for the nation during this expansionary phase has been estimated at $15.6 billion to buy and maintain (electric power usage omitted) 42 million sets.[58] Complete television saturation of the American market, which came a few years later, might have been achieved during this period except that the spread of television had been so rapid the government was forced to "freeze" issuance of new station licenses in order to ensure orderly expansion of the medium.

Leo Bogart, who chronicled American television through the mid-1950s, reported that, "On the evening of 7 March 1955, one out of every two Americans was watching Mary Martin play 'Peter Pan' before television cameras. Never before," he said, "had a single person been seen and heard by so many others at the same time." To Bogart, "the age of television had arrived."

With the new "age" came much change. Most notable were shifts in leisure time activity. With television sets playing in the average American home something like five hours a day, and the average American watching more than two hours of programming each day, less attention obviously was being given to other activities. The litany may be familiar: movie attendance plunged drastically, magazine and book reading declined (not newspapers, though), radio was forced to chart a new course, and scores of minor league baseball teams folded as their once faithful fans stayed home to watch major league games on TV. All this took place before politicians began running media (read television) election campaigns and the U.S. government spent a million dollars trying to ascertain whether violence on television causes antisocial behavior.

Since commercial television in the United States had been fostered by commercial radio, it was not unexpected that program control during the development years of the fifties rested with the same advertisers who had provided much of national radio's programming. The system that brought forth the new visual medium was one in which a sponsor, usually through an advertising agency, purchased network time for the purpose of broadcasting a program produced either by or for the sponsor. Networks, in this arrangement, were something akin to a common communications carrier, although the system had greater complexities than a true common carrier like Western Union or AT&T. The broadcast station owner was licensed by the U.S. Federal Communications Commission to serve the public interest, which meant that program responsibility could not be abandoned or even delegated to just any money-in-hand sponsor for any purpose. If, for example, an advertising agency supplied a program that contained obscenities that were aired, the arm of the law would reach out for the station owner, not the agency. The telephone company, of course, is not held responsible for the actions of obscene callers.

The practice of sponsors buying time and filling it with their own programs in the early years of television was reflected in numerous program titles—"Kraft Theater," "Philco Television Theater," "Alcoa Playhouse," "General Electric Theater," "Colgate Comedy Hour," "Gillette Cavalcade of Sports," "Camel News Caravan." (The titles also indicate one of television's prime program resources: the stage.)

Early critics of the medium fretted over the concentration of program production, especially prime time shows, in the hands of sponsors, or more particularly their surrogates, advertising agencies whose "Madison Avenue" image was generally that of unscrupulous profiteers. Genuine concern about television programming was based on two factors. First, the rapidity with which television had seized the very living rooms of an entire nation allowed little time for thoughtful appraisal of what was happening, much less, time to make orderly social adjustments. Second, the large amounts of money required to sponsor half-hour and hour-long network transmitted programs (nearly a half billion dollars by 1956) were spent by relatively few companies, most of whom used the new medium to encourage purchases of their soaps, cigarettes, cars, packaged foods, and other consumer products. No one doubted the importance of the new medium, but some worried whether television should be given over to hucksters. Apprehensions were reinforced by stories—a natural gas company ordering that a television drama it sponsored about the Nuremberg war crimes trials make no mention of gas being used to exterminate Jews in Nazi Germany, and a network executive who is supposed to have danced to a sponsor's tune in order to convince the client that the network could be trusted to get the rhythm right.

With program production costs ranging from about $2000 for fifteen minutes of daytime soap opera up to $200,000 for a ninety-minute evening spectacular, the dozen or so top sponsors who together accounted for nearly half the network's advertising income could indeed dictate program content and crack the whip that made broadcasters jump, even dance.

Two network executives, however, envisioned alternative production arrangements. Sylvester L. (Pat) Weaver, while president of NBC in the early 1950s, gave television the "magazine concept," with the early morning *Today* and before bedtime *Tonight* shows (a midday women's show, *Home*, was a failure). Not only did NBC produce these shows itself, but the network also sold the shows' commercial time to many different advertisers, just like magazine publishers did. The other innovator was Leonard Goldenson, president of United Paramount Theatres company which acquired the struggling American Broadcasting Company in 1953. Just because the motion picture industry had not invented television did not mean, at least not to Goldenson, that there was no potential for TV in Hollywood. Goldenson, in fact, was motivated to turn in that direction because ABC's tiny network of thirteen affiliated stations was unattractive to major advertisers with their ready-made programs intended for mass audience consumption. Goldenson's initial deal was with Walt Disney who produced for ABC Television a show called *Disneyland* and then an after-school block-buster, *The Mickey Mouse Club*.

The beginning of the end of sponsor-supplied network television programs had begun. When, in the early 1950s, Sylvester and Goldenson pioneered new directions, no one would have forecast that the sponsors' then almighty power over television programming would evaporate in a decade. Sponsors would not abandon the medium, for the reach of television (to an advertiser expressed in terms of two to four dollars a commercial minute per 1000 homes penetrated) was efficient and effective. But a new structure was emerging in which advertisers would *participate* in sponsoring television programs produced by or for the networks, but in either case, they were network, not sponsors' programs.

While the "Age of Television" was an American reality in the mid-1950s, the TV revolution abroad was yet to come. Only Canada, which is so closely tied to the U.S., approached the United States in terms of a proportional number of TV sets. But the new visual medium was stirring considerable interest outside North America. The BBC got a commerical competitor in Britain when the Independent Television Authority was created with passage of the Television Act in 1954. Meanwhile formative systems were underway throughout continental Western Europe, a few East European countries, the Soviet Union, Japan, and a half-dozen Latin American countries.

Public television viewing, an introductory phase experienced a few years earlier in the United States, was popular in these countries. In France there was an institution for it—Tele-Clubs were formed to buy receivers for collective viewing in small provincial towns. Elsewhere TV was making its debut, just as telecasting had in the United States, at international fairs in cities like Jakarta, Bangkok, and Karachi. It was merely to be a matter of time before television was to come of age abroad—frequently with a helping American hand. So television outside North America was at best in early adolescence when American TV was growing into maturity at the close of the 1950s.

In America, the youthful period of television, as seen with *hindsight*, was something more than merely the introduction of a new mass medium. Television, because of its extraordinary acceptance by the American people within a half-dozen years, hastened the social integration of the nation, a process begun several decades earlier by network radio and national magazines. The speed, however, was uncomfortably fast and gave rise to controversy. For instance, traditional politicians complained they had trouble coping with the new medium while civil rights advocates skillfully exploited it.

TV's impact on America was perhaps most clearly revealed in sports, which are cultural activities belonging to the soul of any nation. The national pastime, baseball, under the influence of television, at last lived up to its billing and became national; the Braves moved from Boston to Milwaukee, the Dodgers from Brooklyn to Los Angeles and so on. Professional fooball fell into the loving embrace of the wealthy television networks and was born anew as a national sport. Professional football organized itself like the national networks, with franchises situated carefully around the country in conformity with television markets.

For the *nouveau riche* television organization, however, the new medium was primarily thought to be a money machine. TV offered a giant electronics corporation like RCA multiple business opportunities. RCA manfactured sets that potential customers could first watch in public places, then buy for their homes and finally, supplement with portables for any room—and later the cycle could be repeated with color sets. RCA also manufactured television cameras, transmitters, and other broadcast equipment, again for two cycles (black and white, then color). And, of course, its network, NBC, originated and distributed programming nationally to stations including those that RCA itself owned and operated in five of the best markets—New York, Chicago, Los Angeles, Washington, D.C., and Cleveland. In 1956, just one of the rich television pies from which RCA took a generous slice was NBC's share of $1.2 billion in combined network and station advertising expenditures.

Whatever the medium's often debated social implications were, its economic rewards were indisputably good for those who had gotten in on the ground floor. Mindful of this, Americans began casting more than curious glances abroad toward the end of the 1950s when the domestic system began a transition into maturity and foreign systems showed signs of adolescent vitality.

As the potential of emerging foreign TV markets piqued the interest of American networks, the character of the U.S. system, as has been noted, was itself changing. Essentially, during the late 1950s, control over the big audience evening programs was passing from sponsors to the networks, which in turn embraced film makers as the chief new source for evening prime time television programming. In effect, the networks were divorcing themselves from the New York theater stage and marrying Hollywood's film studios.

The switch had a significant implication for the budding foreign market, because the replacement of live drama on American television with canned film shows meant that the stocks of exportable programming would soar. This was true even after the invention of video tape which made possible the recording of live performances using television cameras.[59]

Pat Weaver's "television as a magazine" concept at NBC contributed to the ascendancy of network program control, but the credit for substituting Hollywood productions for sponsor-supplied shows belonged to ABC's Leonard Goldenson. After contracting with Walt Disney for several television packages, Goldenson persuaded Warner Brothers to produce for ABC-TV a series of programs based on characters in three Warner movies (*King's Row*, *Casablanca*, and *Cheyenne*). At that moment, television as "theater in a box" was doomed by television as "movies for the home screen." Action-adventure TV series, the most saleable American programs abroad, were to become abundant.

Television's move to Hollywood was not, however, prompted by a desire to export more programs. That was, and has remained, of secondary importance to the American TV industry. But in the then young world of television abroad, what the leader did at home was bound to have international side effects. It's instructive, therefore, to examine further how and why the U.S. commercial television business changed.

There was no real fight for program control, although there were to be some unpleasant moments. Both the networks and the advertisers shared a mutual interest in ratings, that is, the number of viewers watching television at a particular time. The advertisers' role changed radically, although their influence on the medium remained, for essentially the business of American broadcasting has been to present programs so that commercial messages could reach large audiences. The advertising community sought change in order to lessen its risks in the ratings game. Their new role as participating sponsors was a scheme by which investments could be made in, say, a half dozen shows instead of being the sole sponsor of a single program. When a single show flopped, it was a disaster to a lone sponsor, especially with skyrocketing production costs (in 1958 an average one-hour variety program cost about $88,000 to produce; in 1971 just one minute of commercial time on Flip Wilson's popular show was billed at $86,000). The prudent advertiser decided that it was better not to have all its eggs in one basket; better to spread its business around because a poorly rated show now and then was tolerable. Along Madison Avenue this new attitude was captured in the expression "$4 Television." Within a price range in which $4 was about average an advertiser could reach 1000 American homes with a commercial message and not have the worry of producing the program that delivered the audience.

Meanwhile along nearby Sixth Avenue in midtown Manhattan where the television networks have their New York headquarters, rating wars were being waged. CBS was the long-reigning champion, having mastered such strategies as "program flow" and "counterprogramming." To play such a game required, of course, complete program control. Otherwise a network would not have been able to "build," as their executives were fond of saying, an evening's schedule that fed audiences from one program into the next or pursued straying viewers with a different format (a variety show, for instance) when the two other competing networks were offering similar program types (westerns, for example). Scheduling, the process of moving programs around like chess pieces on a board divided into half-hour time segments, became arcane, crafty, and indeed, crucial network business.

Its importance rested on the fact that in its mature phase television had blanketed the American market, which was filled with tuned-in viewers. The trick was to get the largest *share* of the available audience especially during the evening hours, which normally peaked at about 81 million viewers at 8:30 P.M.[60] In other words, the audience was there; the question was how it would be divided among the network competitors. The ultimate competition was to win the September-to-May overall season ratings. In his last programming campaign, CBS vice president Mike Dann waged a legendary 100-final-days offensive that caught NBC at the wire. After a disputed photo finish that gave victory to CBS by two-tenths of a single rating point for the 1969–70 season, Dann exclaimed, "This is the happiest day of my life."[61]

The tyranny of ratings and expensive production costs combined to create on television a "vast wasteland," as Newton Minow was to describe the situation in his initial speech as chairman of the Federal Communications Commission during the Kennedy Administration. The "wasteland" developed because higher ratings could be gotten with "Cheyenne" and a bevy of other westerns filmed in Hollywood than with "Studio One" and the other live TV playhouses that had originated from New York. Moreover, film had three other advantages —resale in domestic and foreign syndication, previewing, and, most importantly, lower costs for reaching 1000 homes with one minute of sponsored commercial time.

Initially, syndication, the practice of reselling programs after they have been seen once, sometimes twice, on network television, was a bit of unexpected added profit. But as production costs rose, syndication was *the* profit. Inevitably, syndication sales not only were the margin of profit, but defrayed part of the production costs, as well. For example, in his book on the business of broadcasting,[62] Les Brown recalls that an ambitious young producer, Burt Rosen, set out in 1969 to do a "special" for CBS starring the then very popular, sexy actress, Raquel Welch. Rosen estimated the budget for the program at about $400,000, which was $50,000 over what Coca Cola and Motorola had agreed to pay as sponsors. Only through foreign sales and repeat showings in the United States could the deficit be made up. This was impossible with a live production.

Film also made previewing possible. Not only could a sample, or pilot program, be shown to network executives for evaluation, but to test audiences as well. CBS used something called a Program Analyzer to judge audience reaction. Tourists were invited into a small screening room in New York where "Little Annie," as the analyzer was nicknamed, was housed. There about a dozen viewers conveyed their favorable and adverse reactions to pilot programs by pressing buttons during a screening period. Afterwards they also completed a questionnaire. The other networks employed the services of Audience Studies,

Inc., which ran a more sophisticated operation in Los Angeles, but with the same purpose of attempting to diminish uncertainty. The effectiveness of these systems was questionable because the results of such research are not foolproof. Still, they have been useful tools, if for nothing else than to take some of the mental anguish out of making program decisions. If previewing diminished insecurity among television executives, it also reinforced the position of filmed series that were bought on the basis of an acceptable pilot, not merely the word of a creative producer who could only describe what "live" presentations might look like. With the advent of videotape, few truly live programs have remained on American television. Videotape proved to be both a useful new production tool and a perfect answer for the question, why take a chance?

Finally, there is the matter of the advertiser. As Les Brown has written, "In day-to-day commerce, television is not so much interested in the business of communications as in the business of delivering people to advertisers. People are the merchandise, not the shows. The shows are merely the bait."[63] And, it may be added, filmed shows have become very good bait.

By the beginning of the 1971 American television season in September, half of the prime-time programming on network television was regularly scheduled filmed series provided by the six major Hollywood studios (MGM, Paramount, Screen Gems which is a subsidiary of Columbia Pictures, 20th Century-Fox, Universal which had become part of MCA, and Warner Brothers). So involved had Hollywood become in filming television programs that the industry leader in the early 1970s reported that, "Production and distribution . . . for television exhibition continues to be MCA's largest operation."[64] MCA made block-buster films like *Airport* which, after playing the movie house circuit, were sold for television broadcast. MCA made movies exclusively for television screening. And, importantly, MCA made filmed television series; thirteen hours a week in 1972, or about one-fifth of all network prime time programming. The company's gross revenues from television, including syndication sales abroad, totaled $120 million in 1972, according to MCA's annual report.[65] Because it produced such popular programs as "Ironside," "Kojak," "McCloud," "Columbo," and "Marcus Welby, M.D.," all but the last action-adventure programs, "MCA's products reach[ed] markets virtually everywhere but China and the Soviet Union," the company boasted.

Besides the major Hollywood studios there were minor producers as well. Known as independents they sold first-run film programs to the three American networks and rerun rights to the nearly 700 local

commercial stations in the United States. One of these so-called independents, Metromedia Producers Corporation, had an inch-thick
"promokit" detailing all its film wares.

The voracious program appetite of American television was not
being satisfied by film alone. Weaver's magazine concept blossomed
into an array of "talk" shows, news programs found permanent positions in the "fringe" time slots before and after evening prime time,
soap operas and game shows flourished during the day hours, while
weekend mornings featured children's cartoons followed by sports in
the afternoon. But the evenings, when audiences were largest and the
costs-per-commercial-minute highest, belonged to film.

A few shows would successfully fight the film trend of the 1960s, but
the battle was uphill and defeat sometimes came through an unanticipated new twist. One such factor was demographics, television's
word to describe the quality of the audience. When it was discovered that overall audience size was near constant, networks sought
shares of that audience that were attractive to advertisers. During the
1960s that meant pursuing an 18- to 49-year-old audience who, said
numerous sponsors, were their best customers. The demographics game
was to drive even high-rated programs off the air, such as "Red Skel-
ton's Comedy Hour" (too many pensioners in the audience) and lead
to such inane sales pitches from networks to potential advertisers as,
"Audience of 12 Returning NBC Shows Reveal High Usage of Dry
Dog Food."[66]

Insofar as foreign television was concerned, the American emphasis
on film created huge catalogues of programs that could, potentially, be
sold abroad. And, even though satellites made international "live"
telecasting possible, their high tariffs (transoceanic rates start at $2280
for ten minutes) have limited satellite usage by television to exceptional events.

Film also enables foreign producers to attempt to crack the lucrative
American market. The Japanese had some success with cartoons and
the BBC found the door open at the Public Broadcast Service, a non-
commercial alternative to the much criticized profit-seeking networks.
But only one foreigner seriously tried to wedge himself into the American market—and made it.

Sir Lew Grade, London's master showman, who has been called a
"genius" by one of his enthusiastic underlings, turned out, with some
success, so-called "mid-Atlantic" programs. His concept was to produce
at the Elstree studios of Associated Television Corporation Limited
(ATV), a London based entertainment conglomerate, television programs saleable on both sides of the Atlantic. By producing for both

markets (as opposed to the American practice of producing first and foremost for the U.S. networks, with little advance consideration of foreign syndication), Sir Lew calculated he could meet American network production standards at lower than Hollywood prices. A subsidiary organization, ITC, was the vehicle he used to become the first foreign producer to get regularly scheduled series on an American network (ABC). ITC gave American network viewers "The Persuaders," co-starring Hollywood's own Tony Curtis and Britain's Roger Moore, who earlier had become known in the U.S. on an ITC syndicated show, "The Saint"; Robert Vaughn, another actor who already had starred on American TV, was cast in "The Protectors," and the American actress, Shirley MacLaine, in her own show, "Shirley's World."

These shows were, in fact, just a few of ITC's nearly 100 television programs available for sale outside Britain, most of which, like those in American producers' catalogues, were action-adventures.

Although ITC's slogan was that it "entertains the world," clearly the U.S. market, where by the late 1960s a one-hour prime-time network program commanded from $200,000 up, was the part of the world that most interested Sir Lew. He went so far as to purchase standard American (525-line) television equipment so that ATV/ITC could videotape in London, programming for sale to the U.S. networks, usually either as one-time specials or from the summer season.

Sir Lew's singular success in the American market has been due to the ability of his large organization to produce on the American scale. Furthermore, unlike most other foreign television executives, he operates a commercial company, not a government monopoly. His raison d'être has been the same as that of MCA, not that of the BBC or Japan's NHK.

The point is not that a BBC or a NHK, or even television organizations in smaller countries such as Canada, are without necessary production facilities. Indeed, CBC has studios that would be the envy of some American producers. But only Sir Lew Grade, unencumbered by the social responsibilities governments tend to impose on their own stations and capable of mustering the necessary ingredients for U.S.-scale productions, was able to make a dent from abroad in the American commercial market. Even the rich German stations only can afford an occasional local television program with production values comparable to those routinely done in the United States.

In conclusion, commercial American television matured into a system that consumed enormous quantities of expensively produced film programming. Although these huge stocks of telefilm were intended essentially for domestic viewing, canned images and sound priced far below original production costs proved to be highly exportable, too.

AMERICAN TELEVISION ABROAD: DREAMS AND REALITIES

I am convinced . . . that the word "International" has an increasing significance for our industry.

—Leonard H. Goldenson
President, ABC
4 March 1964

It was really a self liquidating business. . . .

—Gerald Adler
Former President, NBC Enterprises
25 February 1975

American television executives once dreamed not just of selling film programs abroad, but of extending their companies, indeed their industry, around the world. The suddenness with which the domestic market had bountifully peaked meant that during the 1960s the still young pioneers of television faced the choice of either being contented with harvesting the thoroughly plowed but very fertile U.S. domestic soil or chasing new rainbows overseas. The new horizon abroad was irresistible, for a mixture of altruistic and economic reasons. No contradiction was felt when industry leaders spoke of their commercial enterprises abroad as being similarly beneficial to the work of the Peace Corps in less developed countries and of the U.S. Information Service's American image building programs abroad.

If a domestic network was good, would not an international network of affiliated foreign stations be better? If owning five VHF (the statutory limit) American stations[67] was handsomely profitable, would not more than five abroad be better? Then too, television was a complicated electronic medium, requiring a complex structure of studios, transmitters, trained personnel, and much else. Why should any new station abroad trust its fate to novices when Americans had available expertise? Why even produce expensive programs, when U.S. shows could be had for attractive prices?

Such questions had an inherent logic that made the international market appealing. But, as the Americans were to ruefully learn, their optimism was to confront differing foreign attitudes. Perhaps they could have anticipated difficulties if they had turned their perspective around for a moment and inquired of themselves: how would Americans feel if some foreigners were asking the same question about the United States?

But during the late 1950s, only Americans who then were unsurpassed leaders in television could ask such questions. And they were being asked for three reasons. First was the fact that television, as we have seen, had blanketed the American market so rapidly; networks were "right up against the ceiling," as a former industry insider put it.[68] Limited by government regulation to owning only five (VHF) stations, and fearful that the government soon would—they eventually did—limit the number of hours of network programming, networks looked for new opportunities abroad.

Second, internationalism then was an attractive American notion. The United States was *the* world power and in those heady pre-Vietnam years, network executives were no less immune to global allurement than other would-be multinational businessmen. Broadcasters had as much, sometimes more, pride in having a few of their corporate emblems in foreign countries than a hundred scattered throughout the infinitely more profitable American market. Having flags on the world map and traveling on international airlines were "in" activities.

Third, several broadcasters, notably Time-Life Broadcasting and the American Broadcasting Company, were late entrants into the American market. As Johnny-come-latelies, they dined on domestic leftovers. They were determined not to be tardy when the international dinner was served.

In sum, American broadcast executives were what stockbrokers would call "bullish" about the prospects of investing in the international television market. Because they had the know-how, Americans were optimistic. But in the end there would only be potential deals, bad deals, and short-term training/advisory contracts. With a few minor exceptions, nationalism would prompt foreign governments to deny outsiders control of the sensitive and powerful medium of television. By the end of the 1960s, America's involvement in television abroad would be restricted almost entirely to program sales, and even there the industry would have reached a plateau.

It should be said here that—altruistic statements notwithstanding—there is little evidence that American television organizations wanted to make investments abroad for any reasons other than profit motivations. True, there was a snobbish attitude of "we-know-what-is-best-for-the-world" in the United States prior to both the shattering of domestic tranquility by the American civil rights movement and to the diminution of U.S. assertiveness abroad through the Vietnam fiasco. Nonetheless, neither a hunger for political control nor a thirst for cultural domination explicitly lay behind American desires to invest in foreign television. This explains why the U.S. investors had policies of only being junior partners who provided capital and know-how to indigenous operators who were to exercise majority control.

Right at the outset there was an ominous sign: NBC's attempt to invest in Britain's newly created commercial television service was thwarted. The British government, urged by American-controlled advertising firms, among others,[69] decided in 1954 to permit a commercial system of production companies whose programs would be telecast through facilities operated by the Independent Television Authority.

One of the prospective licencees was TWW Ltd. which intended to have NBC as its junior partner if TWW succeeded in securing the rights to serve Wales. As the deadline for awarding the franchise drew near, TWW was informed that it would be the leading contender, except for its prospective partnership with the U.S. firm. NBC withdrew, TWW got the franchise and then entered into a service contract with its spurned partner. But helping set up a new television operation has its limits and thus the arrangement was financially less rewarding for NBC than part ownership would have been.

Why did Britain's television authority not want NBC? "Because," said Gerald Adler who then represented NBC in London, "of the tremendous feeling of nationalism in any country . . . the tremendous opposition to being swallowed up by the Americans."[70]

Even though NBC's attempt to make a television investment in one of the world's most democratic countries had come a cropper, network officials did not see their failure in Britain as a watershed. Rather it was a bridgehead. Already in the mid-fifties, NBC knew, Adler said, that "there were times we would have to be satisfied without ownership but at the same time we would wind up with profits," from the management services contract with TWW and other foreign stations.

In competition against CBS, NBC was to make two more abortive tries at European investments, plus a solo attempt that Adler described as a "wild scheme." Both networks failed in bids to invest in either the second West German channel or in Ireland's television service. NBC thought that if investment was impossible in Irish TV, then a management service contract would be a good second best, as it had been in Britain. But the wily Irish outmaneuvered the men from Rockefeller Plaza by hiring away NBC's key man in the proposed service deal. The "wild scheme" was an attempt to set up a station in

Italy outside the state-franchised monopoly. Although NBC thought there was a loophole in Italian law, Milan police disagreed, raided the station, and padlocked it.

Outside Europe, NBC encountered another failure in Rhodesia and "wisely," according to Adler, turned down an opportunity to be part owner of a Beirut television station. NBC was not so wise in Kenya, Mexico, Argentina, Peru, and Venezuela. Investments in television stations in those countries, all since liquidated, proved to be unprofitable.

Two decades after failing to become a partner with TWW in Wales, and despite considerable effort, NBC had minor interests in three foreign television stations: one in Hong Kong, another in Sydney, the third in Brisbane, Australia. Whether these investments ever generated enough revenues for NBC to offset losses, especially those incurred in South America, is not known. But whatever the actual balance sheet on foreign investments by NBC, there is no doubt that expectations fell so far short of realities that the psychological balance certainly was written in red.

NBC Enterprises, as the division that handled international affairs was called, did considerably better in the management services business. Setting up television systems in Saudi Arabia, South Vietnam, and Nigeria was among its biggest operations. But, said Adler, "management services . . . all had an end. It was really a self-liquidating business. I had no illusions about it . . . there are only so many countries in the world."

But still, there were program sales that generated ten times more revenues abroad than the other foreign businesses of NBC Enterprises. That too, however, went by the boards for the networks when the U.S. Federal Communications Commission placed restrictions on network syndication. Beginning in September 1970, NBC, CBS, and ABC could acquire telefilms for national broadcast, but not for resale. Within three years, NBC was to fold its Enterprises Division and the division president, Gerald Adler, was to depart network television for private law practice. The last page of a brief chapter in the short history of international television had been turned.

The record of CBS's international involvement is similar to that of NBC's, although perhaps not quite as extensive. Its major investments in South America suffered the same fate as those of NBC's, and one particular service contract, assisting Israel in setting up a national television system, has turned out to be costly since it resulted in CBS being put on the Arab economic boycott blacklist.

At ABC, where Leonard Goldenson was mindful that his network had suffered because it had organized later than its two rivals, thinking regarding the potential of the international market was on an even grander scale. Goldenson's vision was that international television would develop as it had in the United States, that is, he foresaw world television networks. ABC, he decided, would be first this time. Starting about 1960, his plan was not only to invest abroad and help set up new stations, but also to establish foreign affiliations with a network ABC called Worldvision. A veteran participant in that plan described ABC's concept this way: "What we tried to do was to establish relations with the strongest local partners we could. We would help them with know-how, finances, engineering, programming and also act as their international sales representatives. And later when satellites became feasible, we could sell the [global] network to advertisers."

By 1964, when Goldenson was awarded the television society's gold medal, ABC had brought forty-eight stations in twenty-one countries into the Worldvision network. Included was a Central American subregional television network of stations in which ABC had made investments.

The dream, while never quite a nightmare, certainly became impractical. Advertisers were insufficiently interested to reorganize themselves to make global buying commitments and this, coupled with the same realities encountered by the other networks abroad, doomed ABC's bigger idea.

By 1975, ABC had what one network official termed "tiny" investments in two Japanese television stations, plus television interests in Bermuda and Central America. One lingering aspect of the Worldvision concept has been that ABC alone among the networks has been a sales representative and program buying agent for stations in about a dozen Latin American and Pacific countries.

Finally, there is the story of Time-Life television abroad. The American magazine publishing corporation, like ABC, had gotten into domestic television late. It owned a chain of stations in what American broadcasters call the second twenty markets—financially good, but not nearly as good as stations in the twenty biggest metropolitan areas. So Time-Life too did not want to be left behind in going abroad. Additionally, it had an extra incentive: foreign editions of the company's magazines had piled up what one knowledgeable source indicated were sizeable earnings abroad. For tax reasons, these funds were better spent there than repatriated to the U.S. Like the networks, Time-Life's interest in television abroad was financial, not social, influence. Accordingly, editor-in-chief Henry Luce left such a responsibility to savvy business colleagues like Andrew Heiskell and James A. Linen.

The person however, with the most involvement was Sig Mickelson who came to the publishing firm after heading CBS News. During the early 1960s, Mickelson roamed the world for Time-Life in quest of television investments.

The first was in Beirut, where for $350,000 Time-Life bought a 20 percent interest in a local station; the same station NBC had "wisely" stayed out of. Within two years, Mickelson discovered that the French government, which had influence as a motive, had become, in effect, a secret partner in the Beirut station. That was not exactly the sort of arrangement a private commercial firm desired. So Time-Life pulled out of Beirut in 1963.

Meanwhile, Mickelson unsuccessfully tried to make television investments for his company in Holland and Germany. The strategy in the latter case was to own part of a production company, but neither it nor a similar company in which Time-Life invested later in Sweden ever were licensed to broadcast TV programs.

True to form, Time-Life entered markets in Latin America and the Pacific region. Along with CBS, the publishing firm had backed Latin television impresario, Goar Mestre. He had begun by building a television system in Cuba, which Fidel Castro seized when he came to power and turned to his own skillful use. Mestre left Castro's Cuba for Argentina and there, as well as later in Venezuela, he got into the television business. Time-Life and CBS financially backed Mestre's production companies, Proartel in Buenos Aires and Proventel in Caracas, both of which provided programming to sister companies that actually operated stations. Initially, Mickelson recalled in an interview,[71] the Argentine investment was profitable for the Americans. But all too quickly the situation turned around and both it and the Venezuelan investment were costly mistakes. Time-Life also entered Brazil with local partners, but under government pressure the U.S. company was forced to withdraw.

Elsewhere Time-Life contributed to setting up an experimental television station at a 1962 Karachi trade fair, but hopes for establishing a commercial TV system in Pakistan were never realized. Similarly, an attempt to get a pay-TV system started in Britain fizzled. Only a 15 percent investment in a station in New Castle, Australia and a 10 percent share of the Hong Kong station (HK-TVB) in which NBC also had a share, paid off for Time-Life.

By the 1970s, Mickelson was a professor of journalism at Northwestern University and Time-Life's foreign television business was a small film service. In collaboration with the BBC, the company produced and distributed, primarily in the U.S. and Latin America, educational television programs such as the much praised "The Ascent of Man."

The networks came to have miniscule foreign businesses on a par with Time-Life films because of the FCC decision forcing them to discontinue syndication of programs the networks themselves did not produce. If foreign television viewers were to forever "Love Lucy" in reruns of CBS's all-time comedy favorite starring Lucille Ball, they would have to buy "I Love Lucy" episodes from Viacom International, which had been spun off by CBS as a separate corporation in compliance with the government ruling.

At NBC, one man, William Kratch, working in the sports sales office, represented the network's commitment to international operations in 1974. A year before, NBC had a vice president for International Enterprises who, in turn, had a half dozen subordinate directors for Canadian Operations, Far East Operations, European Operations, Latin American Operations, International Sales, and International Management Services.

Kratch worked in sports sales, for the simple reason that NBC itself produced more of that kind of exportable programming than anything else. Newsfilm shot by NBC cameramen went into foreign circulation via Visnews, a London based consortium started by the BBC. Occasionally, NBC documentaries or entertainment programs were consigned by the network to independent distributors.

The foreign market for sports was, however, barely large enough to employ a single person. Kratch has occupied himself selling broadcast rights to NBC's television coverage of American major league baseball to clients in Canada, Puerto Rico, the Dominican Republic, Mexico, Central America, Venezuela, and Colombia. More limited sales of American Football League telecasts have been made in Canada, Mexico, and Puerto Rico. In addition, there have been a few special deals —the final game of baseball's world series (once televised on a delayed basis in Britain and Australia); Stanley Cup championship hockey matches in Switzerland; and what may be the most unusual sale, football in Japan.

In 1974, a Tokyo station (NET) adopted the Miami Dolphins as its favorite American football team. The station bought from NBC the rights to telecast thirteen games on a delayed basis. That American football was little more than a curiosity in Japan is revealed by the fact that the station edited each half of the game to fit one broadcast hour and then televised the edited halves a week apart.

NBC's only significant attempt to undertake a new venture in international television was an agreement in 1973 with the Soviet

Union. But, although the pact suggested possibilities of bilateral programs deals, "it never really came to be much," according to a network official.

Hollywood's TV program producers also have made futile efforts to do business in Moscow. "We feel there is a great market there. But," according to MCA vice president Ralph Franklin, "unfortunately no American company has been able to crack it, except on an exchange basis, which we are not interested in," but that has been the preferred Soviet way of doing business. Moscow's trade policy long has been to barter when possible rather than spend any of its limited "hard" monetary reserves.

Franklin, who in 1975 was running the world's largest telefilm syndication sales service, explained that MCA felt exchanging films with the USSR would be a bad precedent because, as he put it, "We don't do business that way in any other place in the world."[72]

In sum, twenty years after NBC's initial hoped-for partnership deal with TWW in Britain had fallen through, virtually every American hope for foreign ownership had been shattered; the training/advisory business had run its course, and program sales appeared to have leveled off abroad—indeed, in one area there was retrenchment.

CBS News decided in 1974 to discontinue international distribution of its newsfilm. Although it had nearly a hundred clients in over fifty countries, the semiautonomous CBS News organization felt the service was turning into the proverbial tail that wagged the dog. "Instead of being an ancillary service of reusing CBS newsfilm," a well informed source explained, "it was becoming so tailored and custom-made; hundreds of stories a year were being shot for syndication service." For example, the source said, Australian stations always wanted far more coverage of Britain than interested CBS editors for the U.S. market. While officials at Viacom, which handled the sale of CBS newsfilm, would not disclose any information concerning finances, the decision to quit international newsfilm distribution clearly implies that the service was at best marginally profitable to CBS even though it had wide usage. Foreign stations could still get CBS news material in the form of video tape highlights of the network's daily news programs, the chief means of distribution being via London into the European Broadcast Union's electronic news exchange service. But practically speaking, CBS was out of the international newsfilm business and no other American organization had a major commitment to it: ABC operated a small independent service, stressing sports coverage; NBC put its newsfilm into foreign circulation through an agreement with Visnews, a worldwide service organized by the BBC, Reuters, and the Canadian and Australian Broadcasting Corporations which had 172 subscribers in 91 countries and territories; UPI was a partner in a smaller British-based newsfilm service organized by Britain's independent television.

Filmed entertainment programs, mainly the action-adventure type, on the other hand, have continued to be steady sellers for American television organizations abroad. When in 1970 the trade publication, *Variety*, began issuing annual reports on international television, the foreign market for exported American telefilms was described as "stable."[73] This aspect of American business abroad was, in other words, neither booming nor busting—a trend that has continued in subsequent years. And, however measured, either in financial terms ($130 million in foreign sales in 1973) or in number of program hours exported (at least 100,000 hours in 1971), foreign dissemination of American telefilms held an important place in the world of television.

When the American networks bowed out of international syndication in 1970, with minor exceptions such as telecasting baseball games to a handful of neighboring countries, the business of foreign program sales belonged to three groups: producer/distributors who were direct descendants of the once great Hollywood motion picture studios; distributors who handled other organizations' productions; and independents who were small producer/distributors and did not belong to (that is, were independent of) the association of ("major") exporters. The nine "majors," a reference to members of the Motion Picture Export Association of America, Inc., were Allied Artists, Avco Embassy Pictures, Columbia Pictures, MGM, Paramount, 20th Century-Fox, United Artists, Universal Pictures (MCA), and Warner Brothers.

The leading producer/distributor has been MCA, the parent company of Universal Television. From offices located on Manhattan's fashionable Park Avenue, the foreign operations of MCA Television were being directed during the mid-1970s by Ralph Franklin, a business executive with the suave and assured manner of a veteran diplomat. Franklin spoke during an interview[74] of America being the "Mecca" of international television programming, but foreign buyers did not need to visit the U.S. in order to acquire broadcast rights for any of MCA's many popular programs. "We cover every television market in the world with our own representatives," Franklin said. Indeed, MCA had thirteen offices abroad—London, Paris, Amsterdam, Rome, Munich, Beirut, Tokyo, Sydney, Sao Paulo, Mexico City, San Juan, Toronto, and Montreal.

MCA's general operating procedure has been to produce a series for an American network. Once that sale, which could run $200,000 and up per program, was made, filmed copies of the program were sent to representatives abroad who in turn sold the same programs for anywhere from $50 up—dubbing costs extra.

Exactly how much MCA has earned from foreign syndication has not been revealed. However, based on a general rule of thumb that sales abroad add about one-fifth to U.S. generated revenues, MCA probably grossed around $25 million in foreign sales in 1973. If this estimate is near correct, an analysis of the company's annual report suggest that MCA counted on foreign sales not merely for its margin of profit, but indeed also to make up a small difference left between multimillion dollar domestic deals and exorbitant production costs. Put succinctly, an MCA film series sold *only* in the U.S. market probably would be a financial loss for the company, but a series sold *only* abroad would be a financial disaster. MCA profits when a series is well amortized by domestic sale and then also sold abroad.

The leading representative in the second category of U.S. television program sales organizations abroad is Viacom International, a company that derived its name from its commitment to the business of visual-audio communications. Essentially, Viacom's Enterprises Division took over the distribution of television programs produced for CBS when that network ended its syndication business. CBS Film Sales became Viacom Enterprises.

In a handsome, three-color, six-language (English, Spanish, Portuguese [for Brazil], French, Japanese, and German) catalogue, the company introduces its wares this way:

Viacom is a world leader in the distribution of the finest television programs in all categories: comedies; westerns; variety; drama; adventure; mysteries and detective shows; informational and cultural programs; and specials. Many of these programs were developed for network television in the United States. Others were created in a partnership with leading independent producers specifically for international markets. Viacom distributes programs in over 100 countries.

We translate, dub and subtitle these programs in a variety of languages.

Well over 100,000 film and videotape prints are shipped each year from Viacom's strategically located distribution centers on four continents. Programs or events of special timeliness are often transmitted via satellite.[75]

From offices a few blocks down Park Avenue from those of MCA, Lawrence Hilford, a shirtsleeves executive, directs a worldwide operation for Viacom similar to that commanded by Ralph Franklin. But there is a basic difference between the two companies: most of the programming sold by Franklin was produced by MCA, whereas Hilford first had to acquire the broadcast rights to telefilms and then sell them. Both companies have strayed at times from their basic operations, but not so much as to alter the fundamental character of their businesses. Partly because it distributes what others produce, Viacom's revenues from television programming are much smaller than MCA's —$35 million gross revenues in 1972 of which $10 millon was earned abroad, according to knowledgeable sources.

The third type of American telefilm exporter are independents, such as Metromedia Producers Corporation. This organization has an image of itself similar to that of MCA, but it is not part of the producer/distributor's association (hence the independent label). As a small unit of Metromedia Incorporated, which might be described as an entertainment media conglomerate, the Producers Corporation "creates movies-of-the-week, documentary specials and entertainment series for the [American] television networks and syndicates productions of its own as well as other production companies," according to a self-description.[76] But the scale of its operations has been minor in comparison to that of the members of the Export Association, which is why MCA and its brethren are referred to within the American visual industry as "majors."

Unlike much bigger MCA and Viacom, the Metromedia Producers Corporation did not establish a string of offices around the world. Rather it has relied on sixteen local representatives, usually non-Americans, trying to sell the corporation's television programming abroad. Moreover, while Metromedia has a full line of programs in its catalogue, it has specialized in educational documentaries in order to "compete with quality," according to Klaus Lehmann who directs the firm's foreign operations.[77] Lehmann referred in particular to four programs: "The Undersea World of Jacques Cousteau," "Jane Goodall and the World of Animal Behavior," "Untamed World," which is a coproduction with Canada's privately owned network, CTV, and a series of specials produced with the National Geographic Society.

The financial rewards of what amounts to nibbling in the international TV market with "quality" shows apparently have been miniscule. Metromedia's 1973 annual statement, which reported revenues of $200 million, omitted any reference to foreign syndication. Successful nibbling, however, could start a trend, because "quality" shows apparently are not so offensive to foreign nationalists as other formats. Apparently, such programs appeal to intellectuals who frequently champion, indeed lead, nationalistic movements.

While action-adventures, with their mass appeal, continued to dominate the world of telefilm commerce, there were other signs, too, that a quality program trend was developing in the mid-1970s. Time-Life Films produced "Wild, Wild World of Animals" and "Other People, Other Places" and distributed them with some success. The children's program hit on American public television, "Sesame Street," has been successfully exported. A program buyer for Central American stations who secured the rights for "Plaza Sesamo," a Spanish language version of the show, commented that even commercial stations abroad desire more educational TV programs.

More notable signs of the quality program trend came from Sir Lew Grade. Britain's knighted showman signed up England's famed Old Vic National Theatre Company, then directed by Sir Lawrence Olivier, to produce classic plays for television; Sir Lew's own ATV Studios offered a TV series entitled "The Royal Victorians," and with Italy's RAI television system ATV was coproducing four programs for international distribution—"Moses the Lawgiver," "The Roots of the Mafia," "The Life of Christ," and "The Life and Times of Shakespeare." Sir Lew's basic formula, especially for the coproductions with RAI, mixed the high production values of action-adventure programs with historical themes that acted to transcend cultural barriers and skirt many political sensitivities.

If historical programs are less likely to run afoul of nationalistic sentiments, so, too, might a futuristic show, or so Sir Lew apparently had reasoned. His concept was being tested with an outer space telefilm, which, if successful in international sales, would no doubt be a forerunner of a rash of such programs. The space telefilm series also combined high production values of action-adventure with a near universal palatable theme of people working together for a common good.

The major American producer/distributors—who first cater to the rich U.S. domestic market and then seek resales in the international market—have been cautious in either promoting or exploiting new trends for television programming. Although MCA's Ralph Franklin has said that he is "very optimistic" that "Americans are going to be in the lead in new program ideas [and] new techniques" in television production, Hollywood's record in the mid-1970s has not been impressive.

Indeed, the most innovative idea from the big West Coast studios has been seventy-four minute movies, otherwise known as movies-for-television. This is hardly a new concept, for what is offered is merely a refinement of the network strategy to secure a large share of the prime time evening viewing audience. The seventy-four-minute movie (which leaves sixteen minutes for commercial and other announcements) ensures a hold on an audience share for ninety minutes; that's half of the evening, or three of the normal thirty-minute program blocks. Beyond also functioning as occasional pilots for possible future telefilm series, usually of the standard drama, adventure, mystery, detective, or western varieties, made-for-TV movies seldom offer much originality. The point is not that they are without popularity; they are, which is the reason the networks have nightly programmed movies, sometimes even double features, in quest of 30 percent-plus audience shares. TV movies have not been innovative, however.

New ideas increasingly have been imported by the United States, especially from Britain. Bud Yorkin and Norman Lear bought the rights for the development of "All In the Family" from the British producers of "Till Death Us Do Part," a program about a middle-aged bigot who shared the same household with his liberal son-in-law. For three years the program won high ratings on the BBC and stimulated much controversy before coming to the United States where Alf Garnett was recast as Archie Bunker with the same ratings results on CBS. Similarly, Britain's "Steptoe and Son" became "Sanford and Son" in America. A third British program, "Upstairs Downstairs," a soap opera about an upper-class family and their servants set in early twentieth-century England, came to the U.S. as a presentation of the Public Broadcast Service; the idea was adapted for CBS in an American series entitled "Beacon Hill"; its venue was Boston circa 1920s.

The non-commercial, and thereby comparatively underfinanced, American Public Broadcast Service which was envisioned as a source of alternative television programming, has relied heavily on imports. So heavily, in fact, that when PBS presented a BBC profile of American opera star Beverly Sills, a *New York Times* critic praised the program, but then added, "Its very success returns full circle to the question of public television's enormous debt to imported programs. When the American public has to rely on the British Broadcasting Corporation for an outstanding portrayal of a renowned American artist, something, somewhere, is very wrong with the American system."[78]

What is "wrong" with the system, if one wishes to put it that way, is much the same situation that once existed in the motion picture field. Hollywood, once converted to the television medium, again became trapped by its very success into assembly line production of banal films for mass television consumption, while the creative artistry of the medium has resided elsewhere. That PBS has had to rely on telefilm imports only updates the earlier reliance of theatrical art houses on foreign movies.

Essentially then, the American system, insofar as prime time commercial network television is concerned, has been given over to the disciples of Thomas Ince who pioneered formula Hollywood film making, while the would-be television successors of D. W. Griffith, the creative genius of early American movie making, must work on the periphery in independent studios or in other media. This system in turn creates huge stores of expensively produced telefilms that foreign television organizations cannot afford to produce themselves but that Hollywood sells abroad at bargain prices.

The whole evolution of American involvement with television abroad can be understood within the concept of Americans offering, at an acceptable price, what would be substantially more costly to do locally. Adding to the complexities of this global business are political and cultural factors that influence and, in some cases, determine whether deals are made and under what conditions.

Looking back to the period of attempted and fruitless American investments in foreign television stations, one sees that there was great reluctance abroad to allow outsiders to become even minor part-owners of local TV stations.[79] The few deals that were made, principally in Latin America, turned out to be costly mistakes for the U.S. investors who discovered belatedly that their local partners desired American capital and know-how, nothing else. Once those ingredients had been transferred, the Americans were virtually powerless to reap any benefits from less than scrupulous indigenous partners and nationalistic governments.

There was, perhaps, a certain inevitability about that, for television in every country generally has been the offspring of the preexisting radio system. Just because television was a new medium did not necessarily signal that there would be new policies regarding control. Furthermore, even when a rare break with previous broadcast policy occurred, such as the establishment of commercial television in Britain nearly a score of years before commercial radio there, new policies, if not explicitly xenophobic, were designed to better serve local, not foreign, interests. That some Americans thought otherwise reflected misconception, if not naïveté.

Except for communist-aligned countries where, for political reasons, autarchy was, and more or less has continued to be, the watchword in television, American expertise was welcomed abroad within the concept of acquiring everything from technology to techniques at lower than local costs. The Federal Nigerian Government could have started a TV service in Lagos without the help of seventeen Americans there under contract with NBC New York. Austria's ORF could have introduced color television without eighteen months of advice from an NBC technician. But in both cases, and numerous others, the importation of American assistance was economically prudent, while seemingly of little if any political or cultural consequence.

The importation of American television programs, which also has a strong economic relationale given their low costs, rarely if ever, however, has been considered apolitical or acultural. Moreover, the social complexion of foreign viewers affects the international flow of these programs.

Typically, the flow of American programs to any foreign market came about as follows: after establishing a television system, sometimes with American help, a foreign broadcaster turned to the United States as the most readily available source for programs. Prior to the shift of televison production from New York to Hollywood, the American telefilm supply was not large; still, what was available was desired abroad. The reason was twofold. With limited budgets, foreign stations could purchase American telefilms far cheaper than creating local productions; they could thus telecast for longer periods than otherwise would be possible. And secondly, the initial audience for television in any society is usually composed of those who can most easily afford to buy TV sets. Therefore, foreign systems began with a wealthy elite audience whose tastes tended to be more cosmopolitan than those of the middle class who later greatly enlarged the viewing audience. The result was that available telefilms like "I Love Lucy," an unsophisticated comedy program with middle class appeal in the United States, was telecast during the 1960s around the world to appreciative upper class audiences.

But as foreign television systems matured, just as had the American system, their audience base broadened, they increased the number of telecasting hours, and they acquired more wherewithal to do their own productions that had greater local appeal. This development did not necessarily diminish the amount of imported programming, but rather the kind. With more air time to fill, the inexpensive import remained desirable, but the type of shows preferred changed. Whereas at first any film, almost irrespective of its political/cultural dimensions, could be exported, the new situation reduced the scope of the international telefilm market to entertainment action-adventures. Foreign stations could and would do their own musical comedies, soap operas, and political documentaries. What they still could not afford to do was what Hollywood did so well: the western with the great exterior scenes, the cops and robbers story with a big chase, and the dramatic adventure with special production effects.

91

The world no longer loved "Lucy" once every national television system was able to put local comedians before the TV camera. But even if a non-American television station wanted its own "Kojak," none could afford the quarter of a million dollars a week that MCA was spending in the mid-1970s to produce that popular police-action program. Moreover, "Kojak," which has been widely syndicated abroad, had a transnational, albeit Americanized, theme.

Writing in the *New Republic,* Roger Rosenblatt described Kojak, the surname of a fictitious New York City detective, as "at once old-world justice and new-world law. . . ."[80] With such a universality of emotional appeal and availability to foreign television stations at a fraction of the original production cost, no wonder that "Kojak" has challenged, if only temporarily, Sherlock Holmes as the best known detective in the world.

"Kojak" and a few other similar American programs have regained top ratings abroad, something the early U.S. telefilm exports lost when local productions more sensitive to indigenous cultural and political needs arrived. In Japan, for instance, where local productions surged in the late 1960s, a few years later a pair of offbeat American television detectives, "McCloud" and "Columbo," became pop-cultural favorites among the Japanese. Their acceptance in Japan was in the tradition of the Beatles and other international rock music groups.

Even though foreign buyers of American telefilms have certain preferences, they do not have much leverage in getting Hollywood to produce programs more suitable to their needs. Essentially they buy according to their tastes from what is available. Viacom's Lawrence Hilford has said that he tends "to be sensitive to shows that flaunt the American flag" and would "rather not have any U.S. telefilms be specifically nationalistic." In other words, he prefers programs that do not offend foreign sensitivities. But Hilford distributes what others produce and producers are mainly concerned about American, not foreign, tastes. So America-first production policies have prevailed. At MCA Ralph Franklin said, "Generally we don't go abroad unless we have a sale to an American network." Since the networks put up the most money, their sensitivities do count with producers. Moreover, the glut of telefilms available for sale abroad, caused by the networks' shift to filmed programming, has turned the international sale of television programs into a buyers' market. Thus telefilm export prices have remained low, an economic reality that limits the influence foreign buyers have over the content of programs in the commercial U.S. market. With the upward price adjustment campaign started in 1970, the situation will likely change, however.

Hilford pointed to the situation in Britain, one of the U.S. exporters' best markets, as having been typical. "England, with roughly about 20 million TV sets, less than a third of what we have here in the U.S.," he said, should be paying "something like a third of the production costs of a program." But the BBC and ITA, Hilford continued, pay "infinitely less, probably less than four percent, definitely less than four percent."

If prices have been too low from the U.S. exporters' standpoint, the American industry must in part blame itself. In the beginning, very little attention was paid to the international market, so little, in fact, that when foreign broadcasters made their first program buying trips to the United States the U.S. industry was astonished and unprepared. As Hilford put it, "People would come in here from Australia and to everybody's surprise would buy programs." The industry's reaction was, Hilford recalled, "Isn't that sensational!" Because such sales were random from the American perspective, foreigners bought at bargain prices. By the time American television businessmen realized the potential of the market abroad, the pattern of low prices had been established and reinforced by an oversupply of telefilms.

Looked at from the other perspective, which frequently prompts cries of cultural imperialism and dumping, one can see that importers of U.S. telefilms have a trade-off between low prices on one hand and their inability to influence program content on the other. Such trade-offs, however, have not always seemed fair to some importers. French Canadians, for instance, have complained that American programs dubbed in France are not suitable for broadcast in Quebec Province where a different French dialect is spoken. American exporters, their reactions tempered by what they consider low prices, have been unsympathetic, because dubbing again in Montreal would be, as one American executive put it, "economically unviable for the producers," unless the French Canadians would pay the added expense.

After a decade of acquiescence to what they considered unfair prices, American exporters during the 1970s have tried to raise prices. Since this is the most sensitive area of their business, the results of such efforts have been unclear. The industry did realize a jump from $93 million to $130 million in sales from 1972 to 1973, but some of this 40 percent rise was offset by inflation and included several unusually large long-term package deals of feature films. Still, through a policy of the Exporters' Association establishing minimum price agreements, prices for American telefilms were being adjusted upward.

Moreover, there has been other evidence that the almost casual attention paid to the international television market since network top

executives' dreams of foreign investments were dashed may be an attitude of the past. While the networks essentially are out of the international picture, their Hollywood program suppliers increasingly have
come to depend on foreign sales, as shown by the fact that the $130
million earned in 1973 was more than one-fifth of the industry's total
earnings that year of $600 million.[81]

After distribution costs are subtracted, what is left over from foreign
sales, according to an industry source, "isn't enormously significant in
terms of percentage of production costs. But in the last few years
[1973–74]," he said, "with production costs going up and network
[payments] not going up proportionally, it has become more important."

Furthermore, MCA's Franklin commented that, "There are certain
things that have been done abroad, more shooting [although] not
necessarily entire programs [but] within the body of the segments.
There's a bit more of going abroad, certainly not in a great rush."
However, he quickly added, "The business is essentially an American
product, uniquely American, done with American style, American
polish, American gloss which nobody around the world can match,
except in very unusual cases." He might have added: and done with
American unions. Mindful that the Hollywood motion picture industry was a "runaway" to foreign countries, unions have been determined not to allow that episode in the history of American visual
media to repeat itself with telefilm production.

So there have been contending pressures for and against the U.S.
television industry to move further away from its role of being a
national exporter of American telefilms toward that of a multinational
producer. By the mid-1970s, the prospects for an internationally controlled telefilm production industry, similar to what happened to
motion pictures in the late 1960s, seemed remote. One might speculate,
however, with some confidence, that a multinational industry is inevitable.

The reason is that the networks, already under pressure to hold their
mass audiences against the competition of a near equal number of
independent stations, will require ever more expensively produced
programs. This pressure will likely be heightened both if cable television, with its promised twenty or more channels, goes into widespread use and if advertisers are able to improve their cost effectiveness
by emphasizing the use of local stations or regional hookups at the
expense of national network distribution. An erosion of both audience
size and revenues would force the networks to demand of their Hollywood program suppliers even better (that is, more expensive) shows,

94

but not at commensurate higher prices. This in turn will make cheaper foreign productions more attractive in the U.S. market and encourage U.S. producers toward multinational production arrangements to safeguard, indeed expand, progressively more vital shares of the international telefilm market. The pace of such an evolution depends on numerous factors, of which the already mentioned American unions are important.

Foremost, however, are the questions of the reliance of the American networks upon telefilms as the principal source to retain the networks prime-time mass viewing audience, and at what costs. Conceivably the networks could turn their backs on the Hollywood film makers and instead substitute more sports, game shows, magazine programs, and sexier soap operas. But, should they stick with film, the once exlusively American character of that industry probably will become increasingly multinational in complexion.

As things stood in the mid-1970s, American television was a hybrid between what had been radio, with its information and in-studio entertainment programming, and what had been the motion picture industry, with its big Hollywood studios cranking out formula films. The former never was exportable, the latter always was. Radio remained nationalistic; movies were so transnational in character that they traveled full cycle from national film exporter, to multinational movie making, to international motion picture coparticipation deals, back to national exporter.

Whither American telefilm?

AMERICA'S PRINT MEDIA MERCHANTS

here are only two forces that can carry light to all corners of the globe—the sun in the heavens, and the Associated Press down here.

—Mark Twain

Foreign news media are relying more and more on UPI for global coverage.

—United Press International
Progress Report, 23 April 1973

SUPPLEMENTAL NEWS for foreign readers:
—*International Herald Tribune*
The New York Times News Service
The Washington Post/Los Angeles Times News Service

Again this week more people around the world will get their news from TIME than any other single source.

—*Time* advertisement, 5 May 1975

The world's first *truly* international magazine was born January 1, 1973.

—*Newsweek* promotional announcement

Reader's Digest
  A World of Difference
    Multinational Editions
      World's Best Seller
Vive la différence!

—*Reader's Digest* International
Editions promotional poster

THE GLOBAL FLOW OF AMERICAN PRINT MEDIA

American print media has been as ubiquitous around the world as visual media, indeed more so in some places. In South Africa, for instance, where television did not make even an experimental debut until 1975, *Reader's Digest* has had the highest magazine circulation, while *Time*, with a far lower circulation than general interest publications, has been the most widely read newsmagazine there. And South Africa is not a unique case; *RD* has been the most popular magazine in all Spanish-speaking countries, and *Time*'s circulation in the United Kingdom has outdistanced the *Economist* by nearly two to one.

The reach of indirect print media has been even greater, for media wholesalers whose wares can be locally filtered do not confront the same barriers as retailers. By the 1970s, every communist news service except those of Albania, North Vietnam, North Korea, and Mongolia was receiving the Associated Press's copy. Even ships at sea could avail themselves of a special service provided by United Press International, America's other general news agency.

Whether direct to readers or indirect to foreign media, American print merchants have established themselves as leading currents in the global flow of information. What the man-in-the-street in Bangkok and the man-in-the-street in Bogotá learned about crises in Berlin probably came from information disseminated by these merchants.

Americans, to be sure, have no exclusive print media rights around the world. While they frequently compete against each other, they also face formidable foreign merchants in world markets. Globally, there are three non-American news agencies: Reuters of Britain, Agence France Presse of France, and Tass of the Soviet Union. Regionally, there are not only numerous other news services but scores of publications as well. No fewer than two dozen West German newspapers and magazines spill over into adjacent countries in substantial numbers. Yet, no country has approached the United States in sheer volume or scope of print material distributed externally—the *International Herald Tribune* and *Newsweek International* have been striking examples of publications with near universal transnational perspectives. Despite the global reach of these media, they, like visual media, maintain an imbalanced, one-way flow pattern essentially within other industrialized, noncommunist countries.

The pattern can be seen in the foreign distribution of the supplemental news services, one operated by the *New York Times* and another operated jointly by the *Washington Post* and the *Los Angeles Times*. In 1973, the two services together had more than 200 foreign newspapers subscribing to their services. With the exception of a Belgrade client, there were no subscribers in communist countries; in Africa, outside the neighboring white-ruled states of Rhodesia and South Africa, there were but a few; subscribers in Australia and New

Zealand outnumbered the total in all of Asia; and the list of Canadian newspaper subscribers was nearly as long as that for all the countries of Latin America, with Brazil accounting for slightly more than half those in the hemisphere. In Britain and Japan, where national, instead of local, newspapers dominate, the number was tiny but the subscribers were prestigious.[1]

Flow pattern is but one parallel characteristic between U.S. visual and print media: print merchants, too, have experienced their greatest expansion abroad since the end of World War II through the usual process of starting with random exports; seldom have they attempted to buy into other countries, preferring instead to replicate in foreign markets the same strategies successfully employed domestically; the financial rewards of their efforts appear to have been substantial, with the aggregate annual revenue generated abroad by all these merchants estimated in 1975 to be at about several hundred million dollars;[2] noteworthy, too, have been aggravations of censorship, monetary controls, and other restrictions.

Finally, it should be said that, while print media have not experienced a technological achievement comparable to the advent of television, the role of American print merchants abroad has been, like that of the visual merchants, an evolutionary one. Phases of that ever changing process are revealed in the following sections which describe the merchants individually.

THE ASSOCIATED PRESS

"You are part of the most extensive news and photo distribution network in the history of communications."[3] So begins a hefty, 208-page looseleaf book published for internal use by the Associated Press. The stated intent of *World Service Signposts* is to give "every AP man a clear understanding of AP's global news and photo distribution." Not that all of AP's 2500 journalists must read the volume from cover to cover; they use it rather as a reference guide in order, the news agency's management hopes, to better "contribute to AP growth and success abroad by remaining alert to stories and photos with foreign news interest."

For instance, AP's more than 150 world-wide bureaus are on notice that a primary photo interest in Yugoslavia, a communist but Western-linked country, is not in pictures from Eastern or Western Europe but, says *Signposts*, in "pictures from Africa, Asia and Latin America, and particularly the non-aligned countries. . . ." Cosmopolitan political scientists would not find this surprising, but without the *Signposts* guide a novice AP staffer is apt to mistakenly bypass a picture that editors in Belgrade would gladly have.

While the pages of *Signposts* assist AP personnel in carrying out their international responsibilities in the competitive world of news agencies, the book itself stands as a testimonial to a global commitment by the Associated Press. Since AP first began regular foreign service to Cuba in 1902, the premier American news agency has expanded its world service to more than 100 countries where, a senior AP official estimates, "over one billion people a day make their value judgements on international developments on the basis of AP news."[4]

While that statement, at first reading, exaggerates the impact of AP abroad, it does reflect the pervasive distribution of AP service. Some ten thousand foreign newspapers and broadcast stations have been receiving AP's news and photo services and then have been selectively making them available to nearly one-third of the world's population; the inhabitants of North and South America, Western Europe, and Japan account for two-thirds of the total. How much AP-transmitted information filters through to mass audiences is not accurately known because broadcast measurements are virtually impossible. A few indicators of newspaper usage, on the other hand, do exist. A 1972 survey of selected newspapers around the world revealed that newspapers everywhere devote only approximately one-fourth of their available columns to international news.[5] What part of that one-fourth is AP material and what type of stories are used depends, of course, on decisions of local editors, something AP monitors by keeping daily records, called logs, of newspapers' contents.

Founded in 1848 by six New York newspaper publishers, AP claims to be the oldest news agency in the world. The claim rests on the contention that even though three European news service pioneers— Havas in France, Reuters in Britain, and Wolff in Germany—actually had launched their organizations as much as thirteen years earlier, their original businesses were concerned with gathering and disseminating market prices and other economic intelligence for private clients, not for publicly distributed newspapers.

What lay behind the formation of the Associated Press was an economic impetus. Mass circulation newspapers, known as the "penny press," were taking hold in America, the result being that newspaper content was shifting from opinion to information. This development, combined with the introduction in 1844 of the telegraph in the United States, prompted the six New York publishers to pool their out-of-town news collection resources. The concept was successful. AP's first foreign bureau was at Halifax, Nova Scotia, where in 1849 Daniel Craig gathered overseas news from Cunard Liners at their first North American port of call and then telegraphed the information to New York.

During the early 1890s, the Associated Press underwent a fundamental domestic reorganization and also became party to a foreign scheme it was to regret.

The New York Associated Press, beset with scandal and pressured by regional newspaper associations, no longer could maintain its once lucrative monopoly. The Associated Press was reorganized as a nonprofit cooperative of American newspapers wishing to participate as members, with shared costs. Shortly after the 1892 reorganization, AP agreed to a news exchange arrangement with Reuters, the British news agency, which had championed an international cartel together with Havas and Wolff. The three European news agencies had carved up the world into parts more or less paralleling their home governments' spheres of influence. Reuter had Great Britain, its colonies, Egypt, Turkey, Japan, China, and, until its agreement with AP, North America. Havas had the French Empire, Switzerland, and all Latin countries—Italy, Spain, Portugal, and those in South America. Wolff's share was Germany, Scandinavia, Russia, the Slav countries, and Austria.

The cartel controlled the international flow of news, a reality that AP passively accepted until 8 September 1914. On that day, Kent Cooper, then chief of traffic for the news service, came across a cablegram from *La Nación*. The message from the Buenos Aires newspaper requested that AP provide it with the texts of German war communiqués and other official news about World War I. Upon learning that Havas had exclusive rights in South America, Cooper, later to become AP general manager, mounted a personal crusade to bring the *Barriers Down*, as he was to entitle a book about AP's campaign to break the European news monopoly.[6]

While Cooper's altruistic motives (expressed in the words, "True and Unbiased News—the highest original moral concept ever developed in America and given the world."[7]) no doubt were genuine, it also is true that with the "barriers up" the young United Press was outdistancing its older American competitor abroad. Ironically, one of UP's first foreign clients was *La Nación*, which applied to it for the same service AP was unable to provide. (Subsequently, *La Nación* switched to AP.)

In stages, Cooper fought, both within his own organization and against Reuters, to free AP of its international restrictions. Starting with South America, a major breakthrough came with the acceptance of twenty-five South and Central American newspapers as Associated Press members on 1 January 1919. Within the next fifteen years the barriers were dismantled in Europe and the Far East as well. The culmination came on 12 February 1934, when AP signed a new contract with Reuter based on a policy of freedom of international news exchange.

Now Cooper could realize what he called his "fondest dream"[8]—the building of the Associated Press's World Service, which would both collect and disseminate news abroad. The scheme, however, would be somewhat different than in the United States, for, in accordance with New York State law, foreign newspapers no longer could be admitted as *members* of the nonprofit AP organization. They could, of course, subscribe to the service in the same way that United Press, a profit-seeking organization, sold news to *clients* abroad.

Initial planning for the World Service was only partially complete when World War II erupted and forced delay. But even before the fighting ended, Cooper pursued his cherished idea by assigning Lloyd Stratton, an assistant general manager, to visit every inhabited continent to study the feasibility of full-scale foreign operations. Stratton reported to the AP's Board of Directors in October 1944 that the organization faced a competitive situation with regard to foreign news and service. The board, urged to action by Cooper, authorized up to $1 million to initiate a World Service, which Stratton originally directed.

In the postwar period, the service mushroomed to include some sixty foreign bureaus with subscribers virtually everywhere. Mark Twain, the nineteenth-century American humorist, had been a bit premature in saying that AP, like the sun, carried light to all corners of the globe. But by the middle of the twentieth century, the saying was indisputably accurate.

The system, put together by Stratton and later refined by his successors, works in the following manner. Radio teleprinter transmitters in New York, San Francisco, London, and Tokyo reach every part of the world continuously with AP news. Where the foreign news and newsphoto flows are heaviest, more reliable means of telecommunications are used. Leased cables, operating around the clock, link the United States and Europe. Satellite circuits as well as cables provide connections with key points in Asia. Two-way service for parts of Latin America is furnished via satellite, microwave, and cable. The gathering and distributing of news pictures follows the same pattern.

AP news travels internationally in English and is translated into the languages of the various countries upon arrival. Latin America is an exception in that Spanish language transmissions originate in New York. (In Brazil, the AP's Spanish service is translated locally into Portuguese.)

While situations vary somewhat from country to country, an examination of a typical AP operation abroad, Argentina, one of the first foreign countries served by AP, provides some insight into the workings of the system. The AP bureau in Buenos Aires has been headed by an American, Mort Rosenblum, a linguist with previous AP foreign service experience in Africa and Southeast Asia. Another American plus a dozen or so Latin Americans, although not necessarily Argentinians, made up the staff in the mid-1970s. Rosenblum and his colleagues were responsible for reporting Argentine news of international interest and watching over AP's local interests. The bureau, for a few years, also prepared a national or local report—news about Argentina for Argentina—but in 1973 the Perón Government banned internal news service by outside organizations. The decision did not displease the American organization, according to AP officials, because its general policy is to avoid operating local services.

AP's basic service to Argentina is the Spanish-language radio teletype report that originates in New York. This is supplemented daily, via commercial cable or satellite transmission, by a so-called "Specials Cast" and an hour or two of the English-language main U.S. news service, known as the AAA wire. The bureau receives this material and routinely, albeit somewhat selectively, refiles it over a leased circuit to Buenos Aires subscribers and to the national post office for relay to interior subscribers. No one receives service directly from New York, although in an emergency several interior subscribers could do so.

AP's dissemination in Argentina is wide, yet not nearly inclusive. In 1972, 33 of the country's 162 newspapers were AP subscribers, including 2 of the 5 major newspapers in Buenos Aires—*La Nación* and *Clarín*. Nine of Argentina's 91 radio and 3 of the country's 26 television stations were AP clients.[9] Picture subscribers numbered 16 radiophoto, 11 mail, and 42 "casual" or nonregular clients. Unfortunately, there is insufficient data to more precisely indicate AP's penetration of the Argentine mass media market. An exception is newspaper circulation. Based on statistics published by the United Nations and the U.S. Council on Foreign Relations, countrywide newspaper circulation in Argentina totals almost 3.7 million, of which 1.6 million is in Buenos Aires. Of that number, AP newspaper subscribers account for nearly 700,000 of the daily newspapers distributed in the capital.

To best serve its Argentine subscribers, AP's *Signposts* is a handy reference for editorial deadlines (in Greenwich Mean Time, which is standard for the AP World Service), dates of Argentine holidays on which newspapers are not published, and the wordage limit on stories (major, 1500; secondary, 500).

Regarding Argentina's general and specialized interests in services offered by AP, *Signposts* for that country provides a 450-word summary with such remarks as "Argentine newspapers have cut back on space available for foreign copy. They expect well-backgrounded spot news coverage. . . . Vatican and Roman Catholic news is important. . . . We require good coverage of world financial news, especially currency stability, grain, wool, meat and petroleum. . . . Soccer and auto racing are very important. . . . *Clarin* likes photos illustrating major news stories, sports and features. . . . Magazines want photos of movie actors all over the world, features, European fashions. . . ."[10]

Since Argentine newspapers "expect well-backgrounded spot news coverage," let's trace the process of how AP would satisfy that need for a hypothetical foreign story which, incidentally, originally was constructed in an article by AP newsman George A. Krimsky and has been adapted here.[11]

The hypothetical story begins with an AP correspondent in Malaysia witnessing an assassination attempt on an important visiting head of state at the Kuala Lumpur airport arrival ceremony. The correspondent dashes to a telephone and calls a bulletin—a short one-paragraph item—to a colleague in the AP bureau, who in turn hands it to a teletype operator. From a teletype machine in Kuala Lumpur, the bulletin moves in the form of an electronic signal via land line and microwave transmission to AP's Singapore bureau, where it is automatically relayed by undersea cable to Hong Kong. Without delay of human interference, the signal is passed to Manila by bouncing it off a satellite 25,000 miles overhead, Intelsat Four. Manila processes the signal through submarine cable via Tokyo to San Francisco, where it is relayed across the United States by land line to AP headquarters in New York. The entire transmission process from Kuala Lumpur to 50 Rockefeller Plaza in Manhattan takes less than one minute.

Half the process has been completed. Now the World Desk takes over; first editing the bulletin for accuracy and style, then transmitting it to clients using a computerized system. For those in Argentina, this means sending the story to the Spanish Desk for translation to be followed by filing on the radio teletype circuit to Latin America. Within an hour of the actual assassination attempt, Argentine subscribers to the Associated Press will have been informed of the event.

But more is required than a mere one paragraph bulletin if Associated Press is to fulfill the interests of Argentine newspaper editors for "well-backgrounded" coverage.

From the Kuala Lumpur airport, AP's correspondent on the scene provides details of the event and subsequent developments. Meanwhile, the AP bureau in the home country of the intended victim and AP diplomatic correspondents in Washington begin, either on their own or in response to requests from the World Desk, to collect and transmit information pertinent to the main story. This information funnels through New York, perhaps as separate stories known as sidebars, or incorporated into the main story, or both. Possibly, too, a story for Latin American distribution only will be prepared if there is an angle of interest to that region alone. The initiative for a special story for Latin America might be a request from a subscriber there for a specific piece of information. For instance, assuming the head of state was on a world tour, an Argentine newspaper nearing its deadline would want to know urgently whether the dignitary's scheduled visit to South America would be affected. Associated Press would attempt to get an answer prior to the client's deadline. It has been the practice of AP to extend the policy of attempting to satisfactorily answer every request from domestic member newspapers to the agency's foreign clients. When the Associated Press moved into global operations after World War II, its other domestic policies were generally applied abroad, too. But for various political reasons this was not always possible or desirable.

Since June 1945, when the U.S. Supreme Court outlawed an AP by-law permitting local franchise rights, the agency's policy has been to distribute its service as widely as possible. Abroad, however, the politically sensitive issue was not whether a single newspaper should have exclusive market rights to AP, but whether AP should operate as a local news agency. Realizing that getting involved in foreign countries on the same level as indigenous media was risky political business, the agency wanted to avoid such ventures. At the other extreme was an alternative just short of no distribution, namely selling to national news agencies. That too was distasteful. The result was a vocal commitment to the principle of direct distribution, with pragmatism prevailing when indirect was the only-or-nothing course. A principle AP did not dilute, however, was that national news agencies who purchased AP had to guarantee in writing, just as other subscribers, that they would not alter the content of stories and still credit the Associated Press as the originator. This "integrity" provision does not, however, prohibit abuse of AP material with the agency's logo removed.

Wherever direct distribution to newspapers and broadcast stations has been forbidden by local law, AP has entered into contractual agreements with national news agencies when service could be provided on a mutually agreeable basis. Sometimes these agreements are a two-way street in which AP *exchanges* news with a national agency; an example being the arrangement AP negotiated with Peking's Hsinhua agency, a no-money exchange deal, made in the wake of President Nixon's 1972 trip to China. In at least one case, AP buys news from a national agency—Italy's Agenzia Nazionale Stampa Associata. Predictably, AP is limited to doing business only with national news agencies in communist countries, where there has been strict adherence to the integrity clause, and with the more nationalist-minded developing countries, where infractions have occurred at times.

Countries and geographic regions where the Associated Press has been permitted to operate without going through a national news agency are:[12]

Norway	Philippines
Sweden	Malaysia
Denmark	Hong Kong
West Germany	Thailand
Holland	Iceland
Belgium	Turkey
Switzerland	Greece
Italy	Entire Middle East
France	All of Latin America
Austria	All Caribbean
Japan	Africa

In three countries, the AP has operated as both an international and local news agency, the latter in violation of its own policy. The reason, explained World Service Chief Stanley Swinton, was that at the conclusion of the Second World War, publishers in both West Germany and France asked AP to provide such a service and a similar request came from Argentine news executives in 1969.[13] The return of General Juan Perón to power in Buenos Aires brought the Argentine operation to an end in 1973 ("We were happy," Swinton said), while the local German service has continued to function fully and the French service has lingered on providing supplemental material that was not competitive with the indigenous general news service, Agence France Presse.

Two other policies have helped to keep the American news organization out of foreign troubles: AP correspondents go abroad with instructions to stay out of local politics, and the company had neither attempted to make investments overseas nor considered accepting offers that typically come from small foreign photo agencies to buy them out.

Still, these policies have not provided foolproof insurance against politically motivated accusations aimed at AP abroad. A case in point was a charge of malice-in-reporting leveled at Arnold Zeitlin, the Associated Press bureau chief in Manila, by the Media Advisory Council established in conjunction with the imposition of martial law in the Philippines in 1973 by President Ferdinand E. Marcos.

The accusation was based on a story by Zeitlin, then the only American newsman based in Manila, filed for AP in February 1974, about fighting between government troops and Moslem rebels. Although the official complaint focused on an allegedly inaccurate battle casualty report, the heart of the matter as stated by the Advisory Council chairman, Primitivo Mijares, was that Zeitlin attempted to "alienate the Philippine government and people from the Arab world" at a time when the Marcos government was having difficulties negotiating with Kuwait and other Moslem countries for oil.[14] In reporting this incident, the *New York Times* also quoted a diplomatic note sent by the Philippine foreign ministry to Kuwait, Saudi Arabia, and Egypt as saying the AP correspondent was "suspected to be a Jewish journalist."

That the Philippines, which were once under United States guardianship and since their independence in 1946 have had extremely close relations with the U.S., should apparently contrive to blame an American journalist for any adverse reactions by Arab oilmen to the military campaign against Moslem rebels, is but one example of how tenuous relations between foreign governments and American correspondents can be.

In the two decades between the end of World War II and the United States plunge into the Vietnam quagmire, the position of American journalists in countries allied with the U.S. was near sacrosanct. But by the 1970s, the relative weakening of American power abroad, in relation to both increased military and economic strength of other countries, had the side effect of diminishing the once high stature of American foreign correspondents.

In a discussion of the Philippine and similar incidents with World Service Chief Swinton, he discounted the notion that fervent nationalism had been reborn. To the contrary, Swinton argued, at the height of U.S. power abroad foreign governments were no less sensitive about the activities of U.S. newsmen in their countries. But, he continued, "they swallowed their unhappiness in the past . . . now they cry out."[15]

Swinton, incidentally, had a distinguished career as an AP foreign correspondent, having worked in more than 100 countries including Indonesia, Vietnam, Malaya, and Burma, where he learned firsthand about nationalism by covering revolutions.

In going abroad, AP not only has consciously tried to avoid, with mixed results, getting embroiled in foreign politics, but it also has modified its American character somewhat. Only about one-tenth of its 800 employees abroad are U.S. citizens. Usually they have been prepared for foreign assignments by language training and several years' work on the World Desk in New York. Many have special qualifications, such as advanced university degrees in international affairs. Their instructions, and those of the New York editors, are to refrain, to the extent humanly possible, from injecting either an American or host-country viewpoint into AP stories. "We try to avoid bias . . . to avoid trigger words," Swinton said. Accordingly, AP copy is not supposed to be embellished with adjectives and is to be free from characterizations such as "enemy" unless the usage is within a quotation.

Because the Associated Press is not a national news agency, Swinton said, it can "try to see people as they really are." AP's non-American staff has played a major role in this perception process as exemplified by the fact that three of AP's five Pulitzer Prizes for journalistic excellence in Vietnam were awarded separately to a New Zealander, a German, and a Vietnamese. Many of the non-American journalists employed by AP got started on the road of dual loyalty (to both their native country and AP) when they came to the United States as university students. Others had their AP loyalty reinforced during company-paid training programs in the U.S. In all, AP has more than 700 non-Americans working abroad. A handful belong to the regular AP foreign service of journalists who are available for assignments, including bureau chief posts, worldwide. The remainder are employed in their native countries. The employment practices of AP abroad and the scope of the World Services operations imbue the American news organization with a multinational character. That character is reinforced by AP not being a national agency and by the nature of its product—factual news which, like water, is universally desirable. But no news service can be completely free of biases and value judgments, even one with a tradition begun in 1856 when AP's Washington correspondent said, "My business is to communicate facts. My instructions do not allow me to make any comments upon the facts." But the correspondent himself recognized that in practice his instructions required him to make decisions about legitimacy of information and in so doing he could only attempt to be accurate and fair. Accordingly, he went on to say, "I therefore confine myself to what I consider legitimate news and try to be truthful and impartial."[16] So the definition of "factual news" long has been somewhat subjective in implementation at AP, for it cannot be absolutely objective.

Although the once wholly American news service has acquired a multinational perspective, it has remained U.S. controlled. Moreover, internationalization of the Associated Press, that is, sharing of essential control with non-Americans, is not likely. AP's Board of Directors has continued to be composed of "newspaper publishers in the United States, many of whom also operate radio and television stations."[17] The agency has made a point of mentioning that some board members are broadcasters as well as publishers in deference to the importance of 3500 U.S. radio and television subscribers. They, like subscribers abroad, are not *members* of the Associated Press.

There is also another similarity between the two: broadcast and foreign subscribers each have accounted for about 20 percent of the organizations' budget, which in 1974 totaled $82 million. Furthermore, both the broadcast and World Services, according to reliable sources, have earned more money for the AP than they spent. The amount, these sources said, was not large, a few million dollars, but it provided what was described as a financial cushion.

If the American newspaper publishers who always have controlled AP ever dilute their power, the benefactors would be U.S. radio and television stations, not foreign subscribers, whose access to the board room has been blocked by New York law excluding foreign membership in nonprofit corporations. Although subscribers abroad are entitled to the same service as American member newspapers, they neither can vote at the AP general meeting nor sit on the organization's board of directors. This limitation on the ability of foreigners to influence policy-making at AP suggests that unless there is a change, the world's oldest and largest news agency, the Associated Press, will continue to be international in operation, but not in control.

UNITED PRESS INTERNATIONAL

From amidst the treasures of a Tennessee flea market, a UPI staffer plucked a May 1933 issue of *Fortune* magazine and among its pages discovered an article about the then young United Press (its name was lengthened twenty-five years later to United Press International in a merger with the International News Service of the American Hearst newspaper chain). The article, written by a noted poet and novelist, was worthy of reprinting, thought UPI management. So on 27 February 1974, Editor-in-Chief H. L. Stevenson sent copies to the staff whom he addressed as "Unipressers" in a transmittal letter that began with a quotation: " 'To a press association the world is a local assignment,' Stephen Vincent Benet wrote 40 years ago." Editor Stevenson continued, "He spoke of the unusual *esprit de corps* that binds Unipressers and he told of the struggle to get started and the men who put our logotype in newspapers on every continent." The letter concluded, "Today as we embark on revolutionary technological transitions in news and pictures, telling the world what it is doing is still predicated on accuracy and speed and what Benet described as our 'utter impartiality.' " The letter, in keeping with company tradition, bore an informal signature—"Steve."[18]

The incident tells much about United Press International. The chance finding of a valuable record of its past bespeaks of an earlier period of immaturity when apparently there was not even a company archive; the informality of "Steve," up from the ranks like every UPI executive, writing to his brethren gives a sense that "Unipressers" have been more like members of an affinity group than employees of a profit-seeking firm; the reminder of the early *esprit* and struggle for worldwide acceptance parallels a kind of Washington at Valley Forge or Mao on the Long March reference; the reaffirmation of basics (accuracy, speed, impartiality) and the pledge of commitment to the electronic age point up an ardent desire to maintain high standards. Even the use of the word "revolutionary," although applied to technology, is symbolic, for in its field UPI has been not unlike other rebel movements.

When at the turn of the century foreign news agencies either were government-operated or -supported, and most U.S. newspapers exchanged news through the nonprofit AP cooperative, the fledgling United Press was fiercely independent and in the news business for profit. Three-quarters of a century later, having grown large (nearly 7000 subscribers, including 2000 abroad[19] and displaying new signs of respectability (annual "progress" reports were inaugurated in 1973; an advisory board was created in 1974), UPI not only was transitioning to sophisticated electronic equipment, but was also experiencing the transformations of a movement entering the establishment.

With a 1975 budget of approximately $64 million (eight times greater than that of the UP about which Benet had written), a communications network stretching 1.2 million miles to every part of the world carrying 4.5 million words a day plus hundreds of pictures and special broadcast reports, and 238 bureaus in 62 countries staffed by 10,000 full- and part-time journalists and technicians,[20] the fragile news service that E. W. Scripps formed in 1907 for what he said was "not only a selfish [one-man control] but also an altruistic motive [disbelief in monopolies],"[21] had passed a test of time and was establishing itself as a computer-modern enterprise. Having embarked on this course, management apparently wanted to avoid abandoning old values, as evidenced by Stevenson's letter. UPI had reached this point after what Stevenson appropriately termed a "struggle" in which foreign operations played a significant role in giving UPI a multinational character.

E. W. Scripps founded the United Press shortly after the turn of the century on the strength of the Scripps-McRae newspaper chain and the pooled resources of three smaller associations, two of which he had formed and a third he had acquired. A reluctance to join the reorganized Associated Press provided another impetus. The ambitions of the new United Press, wrote Benet in 1933, were "to be a profit-making, non-exclusive organization, selling news to any client, anywhere, at any time." Its credo stipulated that "it must never be obligated to any financial, business, governmental, or political interest." Benet continued, "It must never be dominated by any newspaper or group of newspapers. It must be colorful and enterprising but utterly impartial. It must be *international in point of view*. . . ."[22] (emphasis added)

That UP had to have an international perspective should not be surprising for it hardly could have been otherwise and still have been competitive. The Associated Press, through its link with the European news cartel, provided its members with comprehensive foreign, if sometimes biased, reporting, and even that could be rectified somewhat by stationing a few AP correspondents abroad. United Press had no such advantage. As a result it had to build up a string of foreign bureaus. On the other hand, not being a party to the cartel covenant, UP could sell its news abroad—something it began doing in 1909 to the Japanese Telegraph News Agency (Nippon Dempo Tsushin Sha) and to the London Exchange Telegraph.

A few years later, UP flirted with the idea of joining the cartel that had indicated a willingness to dump AP in favor of UP. Roy W. Howard, who in 1912 at age twenty-nine became president of United Press, discussed the subject in London with Herbert Reuter, whose father, Julius, had started the Reuters Agency. But the idea went no further, UP having decided to pursue its old policy. The decision was to have significance not realized at the time.

With the outbreak of war in Europe in 1914, UP's foreign staff, unrestricted by an alliance with the cartel, scored a succession of beats in the early days of war for the organization's steadily growing number of almost 500 American newspaper clients. Howard quickly saw the Great War as an opportunity for UP; it also provided the occasion for a great embarrassment for the agency as a whole and for Howard personally.

With limited reporting resources, UP frequently was late with official war news, but easily compensated for that inadequacy with people-oriented stories that not only were more interesting, but more credible, too. Unipressers vividly reported on working-class Englishmen in the trenches, French taxi drivers at the Marne, and life in once-gay Munich without its young men.

In 1916, two years after *La Nación* had turned to UP for war coverage that AP originally had been requested to provide but could not under terms of its agreement with the European news cartel, Howard sailed for South America. In Buenos Aires he concluded a deal with *La Nación*'s director, Don Jorge Mitre, for a joint news service which Howard then sold to other South American newspapers. The arrangement was to net each partner around $75,000 a year.[23] But it got off to a shaky start.

South American editors were dissatisfied with the news diet sent by Havas and were unable to get Wolff's reports from Germany for balance and to satisfy the interests of South America's sizeable German community. It was into this vacuum that UP stepped and then immediately tripped. The same dramatic, colorful, and romantic war stories that delighted North American editors had the opposite effect in South America. One dispatch describing a French peasant woman placidly milking her cow while the German military machine rolled by, drew a curt cablegram from the hemisphere: "Cowmilkings unwanted." In response, UP's correspondents were instructed to provide well backgrounded political and economic stories for which the new foreign clients were willing to pay handsomely. At first the serious reporting was handled separately, but with some hesitation New York editors began distributing the copy intended primarily for South America to domestic subscribers, too.

The partnership with *La Nación* soon eroded; Mitre pursued the establishment of his own news service, and AP decided to enter the South American market. The promising start of 1916 was coming a cropper within two years. But then, on 1 June 1919, a breakthrough of long-lasting significance occurred: *La Prensa*, Buenos Aires' other influential and fiercely competitive newspaper, subscribed to the United Press service. In time, *La Prensa* reportedly paid UP more than a half-million dollars annually, for which it demanded a comprehensive and detailed, at least 5000 words a day, world news file.[24] All this news, of course, UP could sell elsewhere, too.

The deal with *La Prensa* cannot be underestimated, for it came at a critical juncture when the rising fortunes of UP suffered a severe setback. During the war, UP had increased by 200 to 700 its number of North American clients, the South American service had flourished, and the international service was expanding. Then came 7 November 1918, a day of tragedy for United Press.

Howard was in France visiting U.S. Admiral Henry Wilson at Brest. The naval officer handed him a piece of paper with permission to file it verbatim. It was from the American Embassy in Paris. The message read, "Armistice signed at 11 A.M." Howard dashed to the cable office and filed the story to UP's New York headquarters. His subordinates were amazed and a bit leery, but nevertheless went ahead and transmitted UP's biggest exclusive ever. The information was, of course, wrong. The actual end of the war would not come for another four days. But for the two hours before an official denial came, the nation, which had come to trust United Press, celebrated the end of a war that was not yet over. The U.S. embassy had been hoaxed, Howard had been hoaxed, and in turn, the world had been hoaxed. Even though Admiral Wilson explained what happened, the false armistice story blackened the reputation of United Press.

Nonetheless, the organization was to rebound, although not without difficulties, especially during the world depression of the 1930s. And despite the calamitous ending of its World War I coverage, the South American ventures had lasting importance. For, as Benet has written, "with the founding of the South American report UP, for the first time, began to be truly world-minded."[25]

That attitude has deepened considerably since, as UPI has striven to serve its foreign subscribers who primarily have been in Latin America, Western Europe, the Pacific region, and Canada. Over the years, the American news agency has offered a variety of services abroad—local, regional, and international, not unlike the mix of services available in the domestic market. The information that flows through these channels, however, is tailored to different audiences. Not only are news items different on, say, the European and American West Coast regional wires, but stories selected for transmission also vary in type according to subscribers' interests. Abroad, for instance, UPI stresses so-called hard news coverage—natural disasters, election results, and similar events that lend themselves to objective, factual coverage. It attempts abroad to be more or less a neutral observer, because to do otherwise risks offending foreign sensitivities. In the United States, however, UPI believes its role also encompasses the responsibility of being a public guardian or watchdog.

It may be argued that the roles of observer and watchdog, especially in practice, are not far different. But the difference in perceptions does indicate a willingness by UPI to adjust and adapt its services around the world. A policy of flexibility was evident in a remark by one of the company's top editors. Interviewed in 1975, Associate Editor Paul Eberhardt said that UPI as an *international* agency had to "try to see countries and people as they see themselves."[26] To accomplish this, UPI maintains a multinational staff, including two non-American senior executives—Julius B. Humi, vice-president and general manager for Europe, Africa, and the Middle East, was born an Austrian but later acquired British citizenship through World War II service with the British army; Claude Hippeau, director of South American operations, was born and educated in Paris.

Moreover, just as *La Prensa* and the other original South American clients provided the first commercial incentive for UP to broaden its perspective, a steady growth in foreign clientele, which has accounted for as much as one-fourth of UPI's annual revenue, has continued to reinforce a striving for a nonethnocentric viewpoint.

By the time AP broke with Reuters in 1934 and began planning its World Service, UP already had 340 foreign clients, or roughly one-third of its total subscribers. The ratio was nearly the same in 1975, although the number of subscribers abroad had multiplied to 1,948.[27]

The methods by which United Press International has served newspapers and broadcast stations around the world are practically the same as those of AP. In the hypothetical story about an assassination attempt, a UPI newsperson also would have been at the Kuala Lumpur airport, with the UPI story routed via New York to subscribers worldwide in English, except for a Spanish service to Latin America. The one fundamental difference between the two American general news agencies is that UPI is a profit-seeking, whereas AP is a nonprofit, cooperative. Abroad, however, this difference is virtually nil, since AP cannot legally accept foreign members.

The profit incentive, however, seems to have made UPI somewhat more venturesome than AP. This impression is gained more by examining the organization's history than financial records, since little fiscal data about UPI has been publicly available. The agency has remained part of the privately owned Scripps-Howard Company, so named after Roy Howard quit the UP presidency in 1920 in order to help reorganize the old chain of Scripps-McRae newspapers.

Abroad, for instance, UPI was not reluctant to establish local news agencies in Western Europe, Scandanavia, South America, and Canada. Toward the end of the 1960s, however, UPI began discontinuing many of these services, because they no longer could compete with national news agencies. Politics, however, not economics, forced the closure in 1973 of UPI's local service (and AP's) in Argentina after the return to presidential office of Juan Perón. Only the Canadian service, begun in 1922, has continued to function at a substantial level, although UPI's Canadian subsidiary does not attempt to compete with the indigenous Canadian Press on anything but major national and international coverage.

But even as foreign local services were being eliminated, UPI was ready with new services for sale abroad: a newsfilm business was started in 1967 jointly with Britain's Independent Television News; the surprisingly successful audio service for domestic radio stations was offered abroad about the same time; automatic teletypesetter service was introduced to newspapers in Canada and Japan in 1974; and no doubt more was to come from the U.S. news agency. UPI's international sales director, John Alius, has said, "We don't try to sell America to anybody,"[28] and could have added, but United Press International does try to sell services to *everybody*.

AMERICAN NEWSPAPERS ABROAD

The story of American newspapers abroad is neither long nor complicated, for the simple reason that there's not much to it. The only American-owned daily outside the United States of any real significance is the *International Herald Tribune*, a joint venture of the *Washington Post*, the *New York Times*, and the corporate remnant of the old *New York Herald-Tribune*, which once was sole owner. Additionally, both the *Post* and the *Times* commercially distribute their news copy abroad through foreign extension of their domestic supplementary news services.

There have continued to be several other American newspapers with regular circulation in foreign countries, but with the exception of the

Stars & Stripes, published for U.S. military personnel overseas, none has approached the *International Tribune* in size.

The *Christian Science Monitor* has sought foreign readership since its church sponsor inaugurated the highly respected newspaper in 1908. Until April of 1975, the *Monitor* printed a daily edition in London from material prepared at the home office in Boston. But rising costs necessitated a decision to eliminate the daily in favor of an international weekly, still printed in London. From there, some 12,000 copies a week have been distributed by mail, with the largest readership (an estimated 60 percent) in Britain.[29]

In Rome, the *Daily American* was established to serve readers primarily in the Mediterranean region. The paper, with a circulation below 10,000, has traveled a rocky financial road and its survivability has been in doubt. A third U.S. newspaper with regular service abroad has been the *Miami Herald,* which has reached Latin America daily with two air express editions of a dozen or so pages. One edition has been designed for Panama, where about 4,000 copies have circulated both in the country and the Canal Zone. The other has a circulation of about 10,000 in the rest of Central and South America and the Caribbean.[30]

By comparison, the *International Herald Tribune* has a circulation of about 120,000 a day and readers in over seventy countries[31]—and more during the summer tourist season.

Throughout most of its long history, the *IHT* had the image of being "an American in Paris," but that was changed after World War II and the image has further softened since the *Trib,* as the paper frequently is called, broadened both its ownership and readership during the 1960s. It has evolved into perhaps the world's only newspaper that can truly claim to be international, although its American character and perspective have remained nearly intact.

In a variety of ways, the newspaper emits a sense of prestige—its headquarters at 21 rue de Berri is off the Champs Élysées. Two of its owners are leaders in U.S. publishing, its readers are elites in international society, its contents are culled from the best of American journalism. No wonder then that the small (usually fourteen to sixteen pages) and expensive (between forty and sixty cents) *International Herald Tribune* has continued to be so highly regarded. Some of the accolades the paper has received were summarized in the *Columbia Journalism Review:* "The 'most readable and informative daily published anywhere' (*Time*), 'the only truly European paper despite being American' (a Common Market official), in many ways a 'superior production to our own national dailies' (Britain's *New*

Statesman), and 'superbly edited' (columnist William F. Buckley, Jr.)."[32]

Since the mid-1960s, the paper has been a joint venture that ended more than three-quarters of a century of ownership by a parent New York City newspaper. The founder was James Gordon Bennett, whose father had started the *New York Herald* in 1835. The younger Bennett, who had a reputation for never doing anything commonplace, arrived in Paris from New York in the late nineteenth century apparently having been ostracized for incidents of alleged offensive social conduct. Whatever the reason, Bennett decided that the prosperous paper his father had bequeathed him in New York should have a Paris offspring. So in 1887, he began the Paris *Herald*.

His personality and that of the paper were said to be intertwined. One account put it this way: "Immensely wealthy, self-willed, authoritarian, suspicious, capricious, socially charming and vain in almost everything, Bennett created the American-in-Paris image and sustained it with his newspaper. He was the most colorful American expatriate the French ever laid eyes on. For forty years he enchanted Europe as publisher and playboy."[33] He pioneered foreign news by cable and introduced automatic typesetting machines (linotypes) to Europe before his death in 1918. Afterwards the paper passed through another set of hands prior to the amalgamation of the *New York Herald* and its Paris edition with the *New York Tribune* in 1924.

Between the two World Wars, the Paris *Herald Tribune* successfully outlasted several competitors, including a Paris edition of the Chicago *Tribune*, by catering to American expatriots and tourists. With the Nazis about to enter the French capital in the summer of 1940, the paper ceased publication until 22 December 1944. Postwar readership widened with the inclusion of U.S. servicemen. The circulation went up to around 50,000 with seasonal fluctuations.

In 1949, the *New York Times*, which for a number of years had an overseas air edition, decided for reasons of stature and prestige to enter the European market directly. At first the *Times* merely printed a slim edition in Amsterdam that had been editorially produced in New York. But in 1960, with its printing moved to Paris where it used teletypesetter circuits that enabled it to publish complete U.S. stock market tables, and with an editorial staff on the continent, the *Times* offered formidable, if costly, competition. For the next half-dozen years, the *Trib* is said to have lost at least $200,000 a year and the *Times* more than thrice that amount.

In 1966, the Paris *Trib*, its New York parent in serious financial trouble and soon to fold, searched for a partner. In August, a deal selling 45 percent of the paper to the *Washington Post* was announced. A year later, the *New York Times* having failed in an attempt to overtake the better established *Trib* overseas, gave up on its European edition and formed a merger with its continental competitor. In the new arrangement, the *Times* and the *Post* each had approximately a one-third interest, with the other third held by the senior partner, the Whitney Communications Corporation, the last owner of the defunct *New York Herald Tribune*. In the years since, the circulation has soared past 100,000; the value of the paper has quintupled to $20 million; deficits have turned to profits; a satellite printing plant has opened in Britain and another is planned for Frankfurt; ambitious talk of an Asian edition has flourished, and serious questions of identity have begun to arise.

The last had been triggered by the realization that the readership of the *International Herald Tribune* no longer was restricted to Americans abroad, in fact nearly half were non-Americans, mainly Europeans, according to surveys in the early 1970s.[34] Given its high price, averaging fifty cents a copy, the *IHT* draws a foreign readership of that breed of elite internationalists—businessmen, diplomats, and journalists—who are fluent in English. One survey, for example, revealed that among the regular readers of the *IHT* have been 12 percent of the senior executives in European companies that have more than 500 employees.[35] The bulk of all readers live in Europe, more than half in the nine Common Market countries alone.

The question of how to best serve these new readers is what has confronted the *IHT* with an identity crisis. In the mid-1970s a so-called "mid-Atlantic" viewpoint prevailed at the newspaper, a label that connoted a much more serious purpose and altered perspective than the days when humorist Art Buchwald, through his column, which he began at the Paris *Trib* in 1949, typified the "bumbling American boy in Paris, an innocent abroad with a sure touch for the irritations and surprises of the average foreign traveler in France."[36] The policy that has been practiced in serving all its non-American readers has been to publish a newspaper which, in effect, is a digest of stories from the *Washington Post*, the *New York Times*, and the commercial news agencies, with a limited amount of original copy. The strategy, however, of publisher Robert T. MacDonald has reportedly been to move the *IHT* further out from under the wings of its parents in order to get coverage more suitable to the paper's non-American readers. The concept has run afoul of three obstacles: the kind of coverage envisioned is expensive; the *Post* and the *Times* naturally want the *Trib* to showcase their stories; and the other half of the *IHT* readership, Americans abroad, have continued to want back-home news. Since any newspaper has a finite amount of resources and space, questions of how much to pay for printing and what to print have become central to adjusting the character of the *International Herald Tribune*.

The unanswered question has been the extent to which the *IHT* will remain American or become more multinational in perspective. A notable tension in this regard has been on the sports page where American baseball box scores compete against European cycling results for space. The editorial page, on the other hand, features some European-originated material but mostly American commentary, tempered somewhat by the contributions of a New York based writer, Harry W. Baehr Jr., who weekly prepares four "mid-Atlantic" commentaries exclusively for the *IHT*.

If publisher MacDonald and his staff have desired to be more relevant to the readership while the owners think the readership should be getting mainly a diet of American-made news, one wonders what the readers themselves want from this international newspaper. Several incidents in which the French government complained about coverage of local events by the *IHT* suggest that trying to be on a par with indigenous newspapers can be tricky, and indeed, in the long run, may be a risky business. If that is accepted, then the issue becomes balancing coverage of America and the rest of the world, with the complicating question of who does the actual coverage. Both matters, one suspects, will be resolved in the nitty-gritty process of deciding over time how much economic resources will be allocated to the newspaper.

One thing that did not seem likely, however, in the mid-1970s, was for the *IHT* to pass out of American hands. It is not inconceivable, of course, that the world's only international newspaper should someday come under international control, too. Still, the two American newspapers who are part-owners of the *Trib* were more or less getting their wares displayed abroad and turning a tidy profit at the same time— one report said $1.3 million in accumulated profits were repatriated to the United States in 1973 by the owners.[37]

Besides the shared ownership of the *IHT*, another foreign activity of both the *Times* and the *Post*, first offered domestically in the early 1960s, is the export of their copy to newspapers around the world wishing to buy supplemental coverage. The *Post*'s service is operated jointly with the *Los Angeles Times*. The *New York Times* has been the bigger of the two, both in number of foreign subscribers (136 versus about 100 in 1973) and amount of wordage supplied (40–50,000 versus 20,000). Some of the material has been available in Spanish, French, and German.

What does a foreign newspaper get from these sources? They get pretty much what American newspaper subscribers get: international and national coverage, articles on science and culture, and commentary. Local politics and American sports are of little interest abroad so they are excluded. But the latest from the White House as reported by the *Post*, or an economic story from Japan by a *Los Angeles Times* man, or the U.S. national mood as assessed by *New York Times* columnist James Reston have been deemed by an increasing number of foreign newspapers to be welcome additional material.

In practice, what takes place is something like this. A Hong Kong correspondent of the *New York Times* writes and then cables to New York a story about, say, the Chinese communist leadership. His dispatch is edited for the next edition of the *Times* but it is also picked up by the *Times* news service, which sends it across the United States and around the world, a near instantaneous process in this electronic era. One result is that the story appears not only in the newspaper of origin but in the *South China Morning Post*, one of Hong Kong's own English language dailies, too. For the reading public of that British colony the window on China has been, in this instance, via New York and through American eyes.

With only about 200 foreign outlets combined, these services do not rival in size the general news agencies that have thousands of subscribers abroad plus distribution to numerous national news agencies. But among the ranks of the 200 are many of the world's most influential newspapers. And even though these papers, at times, print little of what they get (*Le Figaro*, for instance, has published none of the supplemental copy it has bought), the material is useful for background and as sources for stories that eventually do get printed. Put another way, there now is an international extension of the domestic journalistic game of follow the leaders.

Both the *New York Times* and the *Washington Post-Los Angeles Times* news services have been spin-offs of their normal news operations. Neither does much to tailor its service beyond minor editing and a limited amount of translating. The financial rewards apparently have been so meager that no mention of the news services has been made in annual corporate reports. While the exporting of the supplementary news services has gone beyond the random stage to the point of being done systematically, neither the *Times* nor the *Post* has considered the foreign sale of their news copy to be anything more than a means to earn a bit more revenue. Essentially, then, these have been exporting, not multinational, enterprises.

TIME

On 5 May 1975, for 5 Philippine pesos, or 35 Belgium francs, or 7 Indian rupees, or 2000 Uruguayan dollars, or 75 Canadian or U.S. cents, inquisitive readers around the world—their attention perhaps grasped by a colorful cover photo on Hanoi's triumph—routinely paid for the shared experience of reading a weekly digest of news published by *Time*, America's, and the world's leading newsmagazine.

Had the military situation in Vietnam stabilized, however, chances are that Portugal's first elections since the military coup a year earlier would have been that week's cover story, except perhaps for *Time's* Asian editions whose readership interests hardly would have rated Vietnam's bloody final contest below that of a small European country's peaceful political struggle.

The question of "whither Portugal?" had risen so high on *Time's* news agenda, that Managing Editor Henry Anatole Grunwald had traveled to Lisbon to personally interview the key political figures in advance of the long-promised balloting. But with the agonizing second Indochina war nearing its climax, Grunwald, his exclusive interviews notwithstanding, directed a new course. *Time's* European Bureau was advised by cablegram that "Portugal" was being downgraded to a major (180-line) inside story (nonetheless, the staff in New York who would prepare the finished story still wanted to know "what Moscow thinks about the Portugal situation"). Meanwhile, a special editorial team was assembled just to handle the Vietnam story.

The cover switch from Portugal to Vietnam was but one, albeit the most important one, of countless decisions taken at *Time* in preparation of its 5 May 1975 issue.[38] So many decisions are made, so rapidly, in publishing a weekly newsmagazine, that the system bears some resemblance to that of a Wall Street brokerage house handling a mutual fund. The investors, in this analogy, are readers who trust the editors of *Time* to make a weekly purchase of information for them. There always is much to choose from, with an infinite variety of ways to implement any choice. Mutual fund managers who decide to buy big into manufacturing stocks must first evaluate and then select from among numerous corporate offerings. Similarly the staff of *Time* implemented the Vietnam cover decision with a subset of decisions ranging from an evaluation of first-hand reports (known as "files") from field correspondents to selecting from among hundreds of photographs, collected by a photo researcher, a dozen or so to illustrate the cover story.

What lay behind the multidecision-making process, which has been institutionalized on the twenty-fifth floor of Time Inc.'s glass and steel Manhattan skyscraper complete with a "hot line" communications system and a simply furnished editorial "board room," is the weekly business of publishing a newsmagazine. From an inauspicious beginning in February 1923, when two young Yale graduates turned out 9,000 copies of a twenty-eight-page publication called *TIME: The Weekly NewsMagazine*, that business has grown large, prosperous, and influential.

The 5 May 1975 issue had at least fifty-two pages, some editions had many more depending on the amount of advertising. The issue circulated approximately 5,821,440 copies[39] to an upper class readership interested in news in-depth and what *Time* calls "back-of-the-book" coverage of subjects ranging from cinema to science.

None of this may seem surprising. After all, Henry Luce, who co-founded the magazine with Briton Hadden, was a legend in his lifetime because of his original contribution to American journalism. Moreover, the innovative practice of centralized editing and writing as a team, so-called "group journalism," has brought both public praise and criticism to *Time*, and the impact of the magazine's authoritative presentation on its influential American readers has been controversial at times.

But while all this has been more or less widely known, what is less generally appreciated is the fact that of the nearly six million copies of the 5 May issue, *Time Canada*'s share of the total amounted to approximately 549,785 copies, *Time Europe*'s share was 458,620, while editions for the Pacific region and Latin America accounted for 369,261 and 136,136 copies, respectively. In sum, *Time*, with a quarter of its readership abroad, has become *The WORLDWIDE Weekly Newsmagazine*.

The story of how this came to be begins in 1940, seventeen years after the magazine first appeared in the U.S. That year, Luce, who shared with his associates a special concern about Latin American affairs, approved a recommendation to translate an 8,000 word excerpt from the American magazine for syndication to South American newspapers. The experiment proved successful and gave inspiration to an air express edition printed on lightweight paper in the United States for distribution by mail throughout the hemisphere. The edition was quickly both popular (circulation soon reached 20,000)[40] and controversial. The acting president of Argentina, Ramon Castillo, complained that his portrait on the first cover made him look like an outlaw. The remark prompted *Time*'s Buenos Aires correspondent to recommend special handling of Latin American news; a plea U.S. officials were soon to repeat regarding American news in hopes of curbing dissemination abroad of unfavorable U.S. news. But a survey of subscribers revealed that they opposed any tampering.

What began as an experiment in 1940 mushroomed during American participation in the Second World War. Truncated versions of the magazine, known as pony editions, followed American servicemen overseas. By war's end, no fewer than twenty ponies were being printed in places as far separated as Calcutta and Paris, Tokyo and Buenos Aires, Rome and Manila, Stockholm and Sao Paulo, and Cairo and Sydney. Total military and civilian circulation exceeded one million. *Time*'s pictorial companion publication, *Life*, also had an overseas war-time edition which had a fortnightly circulation of 625,000. Together they had been a patriotic, if expensive, undertaking. By 1945, their annual deficit was exceeding half a million dollars, but the cost was small in terms of goodwill and, significantly, in opening management's eyes to the potential of the international marketplace.

In September 1945, Luce appointed C. D. Jackson to the newly-created post of managing director of Time-Life International, which was to have overall control of foreign operations including a corps of postwar foreign correspondents whose reporting had replaced the magazine's reliance on the Associated Press. Jackson consolidated the wartime editions into four principal editions—Atlantic, Pacific, Latin American, and Canadian.

Time Canada actually had appeared already in 1943, when a separate edition had been created for the purpose of conserving the company's war-diminished paper supply by eliminating from it all advertising except that directed at the Canadian market. The thinness of the publication drew complaints from Canadian readers to which *Time*'s management responded by establishing a two-page section in the new edition entitled "Canada at War." Half of the section appeared for a time in the U.S. edition, too. Within a year, *Time Canada* became a profitable subsidiary and eventually did so well that its very success embroiled the magazine in a bitter, and for *Time* a losing, controversy, which will be discussed in Chapter four.

The three other postwar editions of *Time* and a bi-weekly edition of *Life International* did not fare so well initially. Jackson's TLI division reported losses of more than $2 million in its first three years,[41] as it encountered unanticipated problems with distribution, censorship, and currency restrictions. And with the troops back home, the high war-time circulation abroad of over one million had plummeted by 75 percent.

Nevertheless, Jackson—whose talents Luce then used in revitalizing *Fortune*, a magazine for businessmen—had laid a foundation upon which both *Time* and *Life* could plan strategies to build up their foreign circulations. For both magazines, a financial incentive to do just that came a few years later, in 1951.

The postwar economic recovery in the United States, bolstered by the Korean War, had increased the profit margins of Time Inc. to the point where Luce declared that half of an estimated $10 million in accumulated capital "was available for suitable investment in our business."[42] Among the ideas suggested were investing $1 million to start up a British edition of *Time* and publishing a Spanish-language edition of *Life*. The former, which proposed a different format than the American edition of the newsmagazine and envisioned incorporating original material for British readers, was rejected after some initial enthusiasm. Luce reportedly commented that the project had merit as "a great experiment."[43] His principal business associate, Roy E. Larsen, then corporate president, thought otherwise. *Life en Español*, on the other hand, was capitalized at an undisclosed amount and began publication in January 1953.

Two decades later, the concept of *Time-in-Britain* was resuscitated, if neither consciously nor in detail. A new set of political/economic realities across the Atlantic and the established popularity of the American format abroad suggested that the old, perhaps even forgotten, concept was out of focus and too radical. Nonetheless, a vintage idea took form with the appearance of *Time Europe* on 12 March 1973, or, as the corporate newsletter put it, "in the first week of *Time*'s 51st year."[44] Incidentally, *Life en Español*, after attaining a circulation of 400,000, but showing profits in only three of its years, folded in 1969. Its sister publication in English, *Life International*, with an even higher circulation of 600,000, succumbed to the same financial illness a year later.[45]

The fiscal problems that beset the two foreign editions of *Life* stemmed not from total circulation, but from insufficient penetration of international advertising markets. These markets, formed on a geographic basis, for the most part eluded *Life*, which in turn was unable to attract enough advertising to support the special foreign editions. Then, too, the parent magazine had similar fatal problems at home.

123

Time, on the other hand, had no costly commitments to publish special international editions—except in Canada, where circulation became proportionately higher than in the United States and *Time Canada* was a great success with Canadian advertisers. *Time* management, while keenly interested in international affairs which were monitored intensely by a network of able foreign correspondents, had adopted a laissez-faire attitude toward the international marketplace. Exporting the magazine was almost a random part of its business, except for creating special advertising editions. That skill, perfected in the rich U.S. market, was applied to accommodate advertisers' geographic requirements abroad and, of course, to generate additional revenue. But virtually nothing was done to tailor the editorial content of the magazine to better serve the interests of readers abroad, perhaps because the corporate assumption was that most were expatriate Americans anyway.

This attitude prevailed into the 1960s, even though the overwhelming majority of readers abroad were discovered, through surveys, to be non-Americans. In the meantime, the magazine was reaping substantial revenues overseas as indicated by the company's futile and/or frustrating attempts, described previously, to use unrepatriated foreign earnings to finance investments in television stations abroad. While Luce must have considered the growing international circulation of his newsmagazine to be valuable in terms of prestige, the economic policy seemed to be a benign acceptance of whatever revenues might accrue.

But with the approach of a new decade came a reappraisal, motivated, if not initiated, by business concerns. *Time* abroad no longer could be considered a random export activity, for foreign earnings were estimated to account for something on the order of 20 percent, or about 30 million, of *Time*'s 1970 revenues.[46] Moreover, *Time Canada,* the only foreign edition with a section of additional pertinent news for its readers, was, by far, more successful than *Time*'s other international editions whose growth rate had slowed.

Meanwhile, a pilot study, conducted in Italy in the spring of 1970 and subsequently expanded to cover the rest of Western Europe, provided useful new insights into *Time*'s overseas readership. The research, repeated later with similar results in Latin America and Asia, revealed that the typical *Time* reader abroad was an affluent, multilingual, cosmopolitan, and comparatively young, business executive, who was "likely to be internationally oriented in his economic and political opinions."[47]

Statistically, 91 percent of *Time*'s readers abroad were non-Americans and of those, 63 percent were businessmen, most of whom, like another 19 percent of professionals and 10 percent of government officials and military personnel, were members of a new class, or breed, of multinational elites who traveled about in Boeing 707 jetliners and stayed in Hilton Hotels. The remaining 8 percent—students, housewives, and others—neither were statistically important nor very influential transnationalists.[48]

These "multinational" readers had to be kept in mind if something was to be done to put new vitality into the magazine's international editions in terms of greater circulation, advertising, and impact. The obvious place to begin was Europe. The Atlantic edition, with two-thirds of its 400,000 plus circulation in Europe, ranked second to *Time Canada* in foreign circulation, but the European reader, unlike his Canadian counterpart, got the same editorial diet as an American.

In June 1971, three Time Inc. executives—Robert Ball, *Fortune*'s European editor, David Borie, assistant to the *Time* publisher, and R. Edward Jackson, deputy chief of correspondents—conducted a feasibility study that concluded that *Time* could provide valuable additional editorial material for a Europe that "is uniting . . . [and] increasingly speaks English."[49] Publisher Ralph Davidson agreed. "The need for a European edition has been there for probably three years and more likely for five," he said.[50]

By adding a few extra pages at the beginning of the magazine, the new edition, patterned after *Time Canada*, was not intended to alter the image of *Time* as an American magazine for the world. Rather, it was to enlarge that perspective in order to tell Europeans about themselves and to inform them how others, especially Americans, view European issues. To accomplish this, a five-person writer-researcher staff was assembled in Paris under the editorship of Jesse L. Birnbaum, who previously was the magazine's European cultural correspondent. Coordination of the specialized work of the Paris office with the rest of the magazine became the responsibility of Ed Jackson, whose role on the feasibility study led to his promotion to international editor. From *Time*'s New York headquarters, he not only handled editing and layout chores for *Time Europe* but for the Asian and Latin American editions as well, both of which had the same editorial, although not advertising, contents as the U.S. edition, except for occasional changes, mainly in the Asian editions.

In early 1976, *Time* realigned the resources it had devoted to its international editions in order, according to Jackson, to do more in Asia. To accomplish this, the Paris staff was returned to New York to work on both the Europe and Asia editions. One journalist, however, remained on the continent to supplement for the European section the work of *Time*'s regular correspondents.

Until the realignment, the way in which the international editions were edited (and in a general sense still are) may be illustrated by reviewing a typical work day for Jackson. On Thursday, 24 April 1975, as pressure to meet Saturday night's editorial deadline for the 5 May issue mounted with each passing hour, his day went something like this.

10:40 A.M.—A transatlantic telephone call was made to Birnbaum in Paris, one of a dozen during the week, to discuss, among other things, kudos from managing editor Henry Grunwald for a special European cover story on Princess Caroline of Monaco.

10:57 A.M.—Jackson snapped on a mini electronic calculator as he began figuring out how many lines could be "fitted" into the space allotted to the Europe section of the magazine.

11:10 A.M.—Bonn correspondent Bruce Nelan advised *Time* headquarters by cable that terrorists had raided the West Germany embassy in Stockholm. At some point that developing story too may have to be fitted into the magazine.

11:15 A.M.—Jackson read some of the backlog of a never ending stream of cables, memos, and story lists which a highly efficient message center carries through the headquarters building, but, as was soon observed, the paperwork always was playing catch up. Jackson has appropriately labeled files handy in order to save relevant dispatches, but, like a world wall map, they are more decorative than useful. In twenty-five years of covering foreign affairs, Jackson had learned that Lesotho is surrounded by South Africa and that his memory, not his files, is essential. (A box marked "action," he admitted, held "three-year-old stuff.")

Noon—Jackson attended his first of many makeup meetings, where preliminary decisions were to be taken on the content and layout of the "World" section. Jackson needed to know what the "World" section would publish in order to coordinate it with the international editions. Jason McManus, a confident, fortyish, senior editor, who was *Time*'s Oxford stringer while a Rhodes scholar, presided with good humor. During the next forty-three minutes McManus rhetorically asked, "Who cares about Honduras?" as he rejected a story about an American payoff scandal there; Managing Editor Grunwald used his hot line to inform "World" that the section had lost another page so that the Indochina story could be further expanded; makeup specialist Charlie Jackson moaned, "Oh, this makes me so nervous—all these changes"; and, finally, with much undecided, McManus chirped, "So many multiple choices [for] Henry [Grunwald] to decide."

12:45 P.M.—The makeup meeting shifted locations to what, in effect, is an editorial board room, where the managing editor presided. Grunwald remarked he felt "contrite about dropping Honduras, [the story was later reinstated] but it's been an unusual week," he added with reference to the Vietnam climax. For the same reason, he abandoned a desire for more pictures to accompany his interviews with Portugal's leaders. "I want to see the picture of me asleep," he quipped to the mild amusement of his lesser colleagues. In ten minutes the session was over, but it and others like it for every section of the 5 May edition of *Time*, including the international editions, were to be repeated nearly endlessly before the printing presses started.

Lunch—In response to questions about *Time*'s international operations, Grunwald, with Jackson and McManus in agreement, commented that the newsmagazine should apply the same journalistic standards worldwide, although he said that little investigative reporting is done due to limited resources. On *Time*'s foreign impact he remarked that it is partly the result of the magazine being American and that's part of the service. On the United Nations' principle of free flow of information he said that it never lived and admitted that perhaps *Time* has been too passive in not protesting more when copies of the magazine are censored abroad, something that occurs somewhere every week in *Time*'s world.

3:05 P.M.—Jackson got a message from Paris saying the *Time Europe* staff did not plan to write a story on the German embassy attack and suggested the "World" staff handle it.

3:35 P.M.—Jackson telephoned Birnbaum at his Paris home to discuss what stories should be eliminated from *Time Europe*, necessitated by Grunwald's decision to devote more space to Vietnam.

While Jackson was on the phone, a messenger delivered a cablegram from the European Correspondent Bureau in which the correspondents suggested that for the edition of 12 May (eighteen days hence) they report on five stories—Portugal's election aftermath, Britain's labor crisis, Britain's waivering on the issue of Common Market membership, Northern Ireland's going back to the polls, and the Cyprus talks in Vienna.

By midafternoon, Jackson's work day was but half-finished (he was to sleep in a Manhattan hotel the next two nights), and already he was involved in deciding what to cover in the issue after next. But for the next forty-eight hours at a minimum, he and other *Time* staffers

127

would spend nearly every waking hour preparing the 5 May editions of *Time*.

For Jackson, however, it was an unusually easy period, unlike a week earlier when three different cover stories appeared among the seven foreign editions for which he had responsibility. The U.S. cover about tennis champion Jimmy Connors was published in the South Pacific editions which were printed in Melbourne and Auckland; a Vietnam cover ran on the Asian editions printed in Tokyo and Hong Kong, as well as the Latin American edition printed in the U.S.; but the Atlantic edition split—Connors was on the cover of the issue printed in Johannesburg, but Princess Caroline, dubbed by *Time* "The Superkid from Monaco," was the cover story that came off the presses in Holland.

But this week, with the same cover running worldwide, and no other special adjustments required, Jackson's work was routine, if time consuming. Among his regular duties was preparation of a two-page contents guide for readers which appears in English in the Hong Kong edition and is translated into Japanese in the Tokyo edition—*Time*'s only non-English material. By Saturday night, all assignments were completed and then an incredibly fast printing and distribution schedule began.

The process started after texts had been fed through a computer with final editing done on print-outs to ensure that the copy fit the allotted columns. Then the material was electronically transmitted to a printing plant in Chicago where films were made of the international editions for air shipment to other plants around the world where *Time* actually came off the presses in magazine form. With luck, nearly 1.5 million copies reached the initial subscription or newsstand-buyer readership four or five days *before* 5 May. Since initial readers tend to pass along the magazine to others, the total foreign readership of the 5 May issue probably exceeded seven million persons.[51]

Readers everywhere got fifteen pages of Indochina coverage, four columns about assorted presidential activities of Gerald Ford, another four on the U.S. economy pulling out of a deep recession, an article on "Aiding Ailing Hearts," another on "Moynihan to the U.N.," and so forth. For Canadian readers there were additional stories, like "Air Canada's Turbulence at the Top," while only in *Time Europe*, in its section of added news, was there an item on the retirement of Jean Monnet, an elder statesman affectionately known as "the father of Europe."

Time's ability to tailor the contents of the magazine is a function of its printing and distribution system. For advertisers abroad, the magazine has offered more than sixty different editions based on geography (ergo, Time Toronto Metro, Time Common Market Six, Time East Asia, etc.)

In theory, *Time* could vary the editorial content of each of its foreign advertising editions. But the restrictive time deadlines under which newsmagazines operate suggest that may be impractical. More importantly, the costs would be prohibitive given the economic realities of magazine publishing, circa 1975. Nonetheless, with the appearance of *Time Europe* and the realignment of the international staff a few years later, the concept of tailoring editorial material for foreign readers already has gained a significant degree of acceptance.

In January 1974 *Time* inaugurated an annual forecast of the coming year for its readers in the Asia/Pacific region. How long it would be before the *Time Europe* pattern would be repeated weekly in that part of the world has been a much discussed question at Time Inc. And while there has been no formal talk about a *Time Latin America*, the possibility of such an edition someday has not been foreclosed.

Time has been feeling its way with the regional concept, mindful that the national edition so long successful in Canada finally came a cropper. Moreover, management has fretted over diluting the American character of the magazine, for it—some have felt more strongly than others—has continued to be the essence of the magazine's strength abroad. On the other hand, *Time*'s publisher admitted the magazine had been slow off the mark to recognize and adjust to the new reality of an evolving Europe.

As its second half century of being "The Weekly Newsmagazine" unfolded, the international marketplace presented both new opportunities and uncertainties to *Time*. By the mid-1970s, *Time* had gone beyond the stage of merely exporting magazines and was evolving into a multinational medium for a multinational audience. How far that evolution might go depended, in the final analysis, on how successful that concept was financially. For the days when journalist Luce characteristically commented that a *Time-in-Britain* might be a worthwhile "great experiment" died with him in 1967. Since then more businesslike pronouncements such as, serving audiences according to their size, to paraphrase a remark by a *Time* executive,[52] have been more typical at Time Inc.

NEWSWEEK

Newsweek International, which announced a major expansion program in late 1972, enjoyed its first full year as "the world's first truly international news magazine." With the formation of its own editorial and commercial staffs, the edition reached its goal to be fully responsive to the needs of overseas readers. During the year, for example, *Newsweek International* ran hundreds of exclusive stories and featured 22 covers different from the domestic edition.

—The Washington Post Company, 1973 Annual Report[53]

If the corporate parent of *Newsweek* has continued to keep count of covers abroad that were different than those in the United States, the 5 May 1975 issue may have given the tabulators some difficulty. The overseas cover pictured a young Vietnamese lad, an improvised name tag with identification number hung conspicuously from his neck, waiting forlornly somewhere in the refugee-evacuation pipeline during "The Last Days" of the Vietnam war. *Newsweek's* domestic edition featured the same youth but substituted a background stressing a more American theme: "End of an Era." In the United States, the photograph's original background of refugees amid their luggage was replaced by grim pictorial reminders of the American involvement in Vietnam—memorable pictures of wounded GIs, the execution of a suspected Viet Cong, self-immolation by a Buddhist monk, and a young girl, screaming in pain, fleeing a bombing strike.

"The Last Days" and "End of An Era"—the two phrases, in large print on the 5 May covers of the foreign and domestic editions of *Newsweek,* respectively, may seem to create an identical impression, with different words. Perhaps. But while each came as the result of the same process (group journalism), the phrases that set the tone and image for *Newsweek's* coverage of the Vietnam climax were arrived at from separate perspectives.

By midday Friday, 25 April Editor Robert C. Christopher had decided to pick up for use in *Newsweek International* the verbatim domestic version of the Vietnam story. He had committed himself, and *Newsweek,* to publishing the same twenty-one pages of information about "The War in Indochina" worldwide. But then Christopher elected to begin work on the cover independently. For seven minutes, starting at 12:02 P.M., the editor's midtown Manhattan office became a think tank awash with "slash" suggestions from Christopher and his principal assistants, Managing Editor Maynard Parker, and Assistant Managing Editor Richard Z. Chesnoff. Parker began. A good slash word, he thought, would be "exodus." But Christopher ruled that the emphasis was wrong and then offered and rejected in the same breath "bugging out" because "it's not universally understood." More suggestions followed, were considered, and rejected. At 12:09 P.M., the editor, having heard "How about, 'The Last Days'?" a moment earlier and having sensed an instant consensus, agreed—"Yeah, let's do that."

An independent "slash" line decision not many years earlier would have been impossible, if not unthinkable, at *Newsweek*. But starting in 1969, the newsmagazine began infrequently to use substitute covers on its international editions, a practice built upon experiments of occasionally substituting stories of foreign interest for those of purely American concern in overseas advertising editions. Then in 1972, Christopher, a newsmagazine veteran whose career had been chiefly in foreign affairs, conceived and launched the International Edition of *Newsweek* in collaboration with Peter A. Derow, a rising young vice-president whose fascination with the newsmagazine business began when he interrupted his Harvard education for a year's work in London for the *Economist*.

Newsweek always had been number two behind *Time*, more so in the international field where *Time* had a two-to-one circulation lead— over three-to-one, if *Time Canada*, with a special tax advantage not enjoyed by its American competitor, was included. During the years when foreign circulation consisted of random exports, being in second place abroad caused little concern at *Newsweek*. But following a surge in foreign circulation during the late 1960s,[54] Christopher, the journalist, and Derow, the businessman, shared the opinion that the international marketplace was becoming increasingly important. Therefore, it should neither be neglected, nor, worse, left to *Time* by default.

The concept was for a newsmagazine explicitly designed for non-American readership, but one that drew on *Newsweek*'s American resources, both tangible (capital and talent) and intangible (publishing experience and the U.S. position in world affairs).

Christopher argued that elite citizens of an interdependent world had an unsatisfied information need that he envisioned could be filled by a medium through which, for instance, Japanese and Common Market businessmen might communicate about topics of mutual interests in addition to receiving an American perspective on external, not purely internal, affairs. Derow calculated that this made good business sense, for the readership to which the magazine already appealed was very affluent[55] and therefore could afford a premium price. The significance of this is that *Newsweek* domestically generated 70 percent of its revenues from advertising and 30 percent from circulation; while abroad, where the price per copy has been 25 percent higher than in the U.S., the statistics were advertising 45 percent, circulation 55 percent. For the domestic and foreign percentages to be the same, Derow explained in an interview,[56] *Newsweek* would have to greatly expand its international advertising sales staff at a cost that probably would be counterproductive.

Essentially where *Newsweek* differed from *Time* in evaluation of the international market was in thinking globally as opposed to regionally. Indigenous regional publications, reasoned *Newsweek*, were bound to be competitive, so why not "leapfrog ahead of regionals," as Derow put it.[57] This then was the thinking behind a *Newsweek* announcement that read, "The world's first *truly* international newsmagazine was born January 1, 1973."[58]

Actually, *Newsweek*'s foreign history goes back to the Second World War when a miniature version of the magazine known as "Battle Baby" was published. It, and six other wartime editions for service personnel, had a combined overseas military and civilian audience of more than a million. At war's end, these editions were consolidated into two, one printed in Tokyo, the other in Paris. Latin America, then and since, has been served by copies of the U.S. edition via airmail. This pattern has continued, with some alterations. What was called the "Atlantic book" was subdivided into twelve advertising editions and printing was shifted from Paris to Slough, England; its counterpart, the "Pacific book" was equally subdivided in order to serve geographic areas of specific interest to advertisers, and two additional printing locations—Hong Kong and Sydney—were added to Tokyo to facilitate distribution.

The editorial content of the first postwar international editions, the pinup girls of the "Battle Baby" having been eliminated, was the same as in the United States. Then, in the decade following acquisition of the magazine by the Washington Post Company in 1961, minor revisions appeared on an ad hoc basis and two regular features were added: a column about "New Products and Processes," and signed opinions, prepared individually by three leading American foreign affairs specialists—George Ball, Zbigniew Brzezinski, and William P. Bundy. Subsequently, their commentaries appeared at tri-weekly intervals in the U.S. edition, too.[59]

The situation, then, when *Newsweek* announced its new international concept in 1973, was unsystematic and limited editorial modifications of the overseas advertising editions, which had been rapidly growing in circulation. The new intent was to create a *Newsweek International* that would be more relevant to the information needs of its elite foreign readership and would thereby enhance its business prospects.

Because of a paucity of available data, it is difficult to estimate the economic condition of the international editions at the time of the change. But whatever the situation was at the start, *Newsweek International*, despite an enlarged payroll, was financially viable by its second year. Overseas advertising pages had increased to 1,771, up 60 pages from the first year, while circulation grew during the same year from 398,000 to 415,000. The overall result: "an outstanding year and . . . an operating profit," according to the Washington Post Company 1974 annual report.[60] From a corporate viewpoint, the commendable performance of the new enterprise apparently came at an opportune time. After two consecutive years of substantial growth in income from its magazine and book division, the company's 1974 income of $10.2 million in that line of business reflected a comparatively unimpressive 10 percent increase.[61]

The editorial concept that led to the business success of *Newsweek International* was implemented by assembling a staff separate from the domestic magazine for the purpose of publishing an edition on an average of 50 percent different from its U.S. parent. Besides the key American editors in New York who, in addition to deciding what to put in the magazine, supervised writer-researcher teams and did makeup, two regional editorships were created and commentaries by distinguished non-American journalists and analysts were added.

The regional editors have on-the-scene responsibility for news coverage in the "Europe" and "Asia" sections of the magazine. Some stories they themselves cover, others are handled by regular staff correspondents abroad, still others by part-time reporters known as "stringers." Edward S. Behr, a Cambridge-educated British national who was born in Paris, has been regional editor for Europe since the start. He has been based in Paris, where he previously was *Newsweek*'s bureau chief following a similar assignment in Hong Kong. In January 1975, Richard M. Smith, an American who for three of the previous four years had written about international affairs for *Newsweek*, was posted to Hong Kong as regional editor for Asia.

In order to further refine its U.S. accent, the international editions rarely have published any of *Newsweek*'s American columnists, preferring instead the signed opinions of non-American contributing editors. Their roster in 1975 numbered eight; their specialties were politics and economics; their instructions were to observe and comment on an interdependent world. They were: Donald Horne (Australia), Arrigo Levi (Italy), Bernard Levin (Britain), Mochtar Lubis (Indonesia), Theo Sommer (West Germany), Olivier Todd (France), Jiro Tokuyama (Japan), and Varindra Tarzie Vittachi (Sri Lanka).

The only Americans whose opinions have appeared in the *Newsweek International* are political cartoonist Ranan Lurie and domestic columnist Bill Moyers, a former White House aide turned journalist, who frequently wrote on foreign affairs before discontinuation of his column.

The extent to which *Newsweek* differs around the world is illustrated by comparing the 5 May 1975 issues of the American edition and the two international editorial editions—Atlantic and Pacific— which essentially have the same contents. The only regular difference between the two has been placement of the Asia section before Europe in the Pacific edition and vice versa in the Atlantic.

Back-of-the-book content abroad has not been, however, always uniform. The reason is twofold. First the amount of space for editorial text is determined in relation to the amount of advertising in each edition and, second, stories once written to a prescribed length, cannot be easily expanded or contracted. The result is that when adjustments are necessary, they are made in the soft-news sections dealing with books, movies, science, and the like.

In the 5 May issue, for instance, each of the various advertising editions in the Atlantic "book" totaled fifty-six pages, four more than in Asia. The space allotted to editorial copy on those four pages allowed Editor Christopher to add a story to the "Business and Finance" section ("Superlong cigarettes," a pick-up from an earlier issue of the U.S. magazine) and also to publish short sections on "Medicine" and "Music," neither of which appeared in the Pacific edition.

These intramural differences are minor, however, in comparison to the radical content changes from the U.S. edition. Superficially, the U.S. and international editions of *Newsweek* have appeared similar, for indeed the style and formats have been identical. But upon closer examination of thirty-four items listed in the Pacific's table of contents for 5 May only twelve also appeared in the United States (half in the Indochina section) and four others were hybrids, that is, for instance, the "Newsmakers" and "Transition" sections both contained some original notes about people in the news plus material picked up from the U.S. edition. The additional articles that appeared in the four-page larger Atlantic edition all were done by the staff of the American magazine, so the content breakdown for its thirty-eight total items included only sixteen pickups from the U.S. edition and four hybrids.

The rest was *exclusive* for *Newsweek*'s foreign readers, including an Australian view on the meaning of the Indochina collapse by a contributing editor, Donald Horne. In the opinion of International Editor Christopher and his staff, overseas readers were more interested in the Philippines' reconsideration of its special ties with the United States than, say, a U.S. bicentennial report on art at the time of the American Revolution; or a profile of Denmark's little known, but giant, multinational trading firm, the East Asiatic Company, than, say, a page of copy devoted to America's trendy Black fashion models.

Perhaps the best illustration of *Newsweek International*'s perspective was contained in an exclusive interview with David Rockefeller, chairman of one of New York's biggest international banks, Chase Manhattan. Two questions in the interview dealt with the U.S. economic recession, another with the pending British referendum on membership in the Common Market, two with multinational corporations, two more with petrodollar investments in the U.S., and finally a pair of questions about international political developments.

What all this amounted to was what *Newsweek* has called the *other* issue, an issue U.S. readers do not see, and one intended to be more relevant to the elite readership of American newsmagazines abroad. That perspective has not been universally welcomed, for *Newsweek*, like *Time*, almost invariably has offended foreign sensitivities somewhere each week. The Singapore High Court, for example, charged *Newsweek* with disrespect after the magazine published a story on 11 November 1974 in which Singapore's jurists were alleged to have applied "selective justice" to political dissidents. The High Court held the magazine's local representatives—a distributor and a part-time reporter—in contempt. Fines and legal fees of more than $30,000 were paid by the magazine. Whether the unusual penalty served to limit the magazine's perceived journalistic license cannot be easily determined, but that seemed doubtful. The experience probably was little more than an annoyance, the expense written off as an added cost of doing business abroad.

Before and since the incident, guidance to the staff has been to "think international" in order to implement a concept that has proved financially rewarding to American-owned and -operated *Newsweek International*.

READER'S DIGEST

The Dutch call the little magazine *Het Beste*, the Finns prefer *Valitut Palat*, while to Latin Americans it's *Selecciones*. In whatever language, however, the full name ends with the words, *Reader's Digest*—the most widely read magazine in the world. Curiously, one explanation for the *Digest*'s phenomenal success abroad has been the very fact that it has not given the appearance of being an international publication, indeed just the opposite. A *Digest* editor, in testimony to a U.S. congressional subcommittee that was examining America's international image, illustrated the point with a story.

"Not long ago," the editor began, "on a train chugging through the English countryside, I picked up acquaintance with a middle-aged school mistress. On her lap as we chatted lay her *Reader's Digest.* 'Oh, do you have the *Reader's Digest* in your country, too?' she asked." The editor then went on to quote the Englishwoman as saying, "I'm so glad. So many of our English things and ways come from the States these days. I'm proud that we are sending you something for a change."[62]

The incident, which occurred a quarter century after the American *Reader's Digest* had established itself in Britain, in 1938—its first foreign edition—revealed the depth to which the monthly magazine had embedded itself into the fabric of another society. Moreover, its breadth too was unique: twenty-five national editions, printed in thirteen languages, in twenty-two foreign countries, with a circulation by 1974 of more than 11.5 million abroad, reaching something like 50 million readers in every noncommunist part of the world. Indeed, in some countries, including nearly all Spanish-speaking countries, the *Reader's Digest* was the most popular magazine.[63]

Because it applied the same skills and techniques with which it achieved unprecedented penetration of the American market (18 million circulation in 1974)[64] in combination with the good business sense to editorially mold its product to foreign environments, the *Reader's Digest* has become the world's best seller by offering a world of difference. All editions of the *Digest* from Stockholm to Sydney attempt to inform, entertain, and inspire their readers with articles written with a clarity of expression and with the ingenious titles that have been the magazine's hallmark. But a crusade for racial integration waged by the American edition, for instance, did not appear in South Africa, where *Reader's Digest* has been the largest selling magazine in that white minority-ruled country.

The example, to be fair, is an extreme, but it should be said that the magazine has not attracted an immense worldwide audience by championing unpopular causes and offending local sensitivities. While it has enjoyed a reputation for being incisive and provocative, balanced against criticisms of superficiality and over-simplification, that reputation has been rooted in a conservative philosophy of being neither outmoded nor too far advanced. Since the boundaries of such a philosophy vary from one society to the next, the *Digest* has delegated considerable autonomy to the editors of its foreign editions, each of whom is native to the area in which the edition circulates. Their subjective judgments guide them in selecting and editing the contents of twenty-five national editions, none of which, since 1964, are supposed to be a carbon copy of another.

The editors can choose from a pool of material made available by a network of editorial offices; they also can adapt or originate copy in order to serve the needs and interests of their local readers. The result is a mixture of international and local contents, commonly 70 percent of the former and 30 percent of the latter. The formula has been central to the magazine's extraordinary success abroad and explains why the little magazine, as *Reader's Digest* long has modestly called itself, has pointed to its national editions and exclaimed, *"Vive la différence!"*

From a financial standpoint, the business of being *different* had grown by the mid-1970s to an estimated $500 million annually, according to a knowledgeable source.[65] Whether the amount included revenues from the sale of books and records abroad, another major line of *Reader's Digest* business, was not revealed, nor has much other fiscal data been available about the privately owned company started by DeWitt and Lila Acheson Wallace a few years after the Great War ended in Europe.

DeWitt Wallace, son of an academician at the then struggling Macalester College in St. Paul, Minnesota, had published, with minor success, a booklet on farming prior to military service with the American Expeditionary Force in France where he was wounded. While convalescing in the A.E.F. hospital at Aix-les-Bains, Sergeant Wallace worked on condensing what he considered articles of lasting interest from current magazines, with the intention of applying this self-training to publication of a small monthly digest. After a discouraging false start, Wallace and his bride, the former Lila Bell Acheson, an energetic social-welfare worker, had sold enough trial subscriptions by mail to inaugurate, in February 1922, volume I, number I of the *Reader's Digest*. The husband and wife team, who described themselves as co-founders, co-editors, and co-owners, promised on the cover "thirty-one articles each month from leading magazines. Each article of enduring value and interest, in condensed and compact form."

From an apartment shared with another couple in New York City's Greenwich Village to a garage apartment in the rural setting of Pleasantville in nearby Westchester county, the Wallaces and their *Digest* moved in the Fall of 1922 and in that small village the magazine grew by leaps and bounds. By 1925, circulation totaled 16,500 copies and the first full-time employee was hired, a business manager. His duties at first were mundane: the *Digest* then was four years away from being sold on newsstands, five away from publishing original material, nine from its first condensed book, eleven from purchase of a wooded site in neighboring Chappaqua for construction of its handsome Georgian-style headquarters, thirteen from publication of the first international edition, and thirty from carrying any advertising in the American edition, which by 1955, when ads first appeared, had a certified U.S. circulation of 10,098,849.[66]

The precedent-shattering decision to accept advertising in the U.S. edition, taken with some reluctance, had been influenced by the experience of the *Digest*'s foreign editions. While DeWitt Wallace had not been opposed to the principle of advertising, indeed he felt it had a proper function, the magazine had been launched on the association concept. In other words, subscribers actually were members of an association, which meant, as Wallace explained in the August 1923 edition, that "*The Reader's Digest* is not a magazine in the usual sense, but rather a co-operative means of rendering a timesaving service." "Our Association is serving you," he wrote.[67] Although competition forced the *Digest* into newsstand sales in 1929, thus nullifying the association concept, the Wallaces long remained faithful to a perceived aspect of that service, no advertising.

The same spirit of altruism, however, led to the first breach of the policy ban on ads. The story began with the successful creation of a British edition of the magazine in 1938, which prompted consideration of starting another edition for Central and South America. But a study showed the costs to be prohibitive. Then in 1940, the Wallaces, with a sense of anxiety about Nazi and Fascist influence in the hemisphere, resurrected the idea of a Latin American edition, which, when it appeared, set two precedents. First, the standard price of 25 cents, thought too high for Latin Americans, was halved and the edition was opened for advertising. Second, it was published in Spanish, a forerunner of numerous subsequent non-English editions. *Selecciones del Reader's Digest* became a profitable success immediately; the initial press run of 125,000 copies was sold out.[68] Not only did an anticipated deficit not result, but *Selecciones* suggested to the Wallaces that their little magazine had previously undreamed of possibilities abroad.

Two years later a Portuguese edition appeared, then a Swedish one, and about the same time an Arabic version, the latter two started at the urging of the U.S. Office of War Information. In 1943, a special edition for Canada made its debut. After World War II, the parent magazine provided an even stronger base for foreign expansion, because during the war the American edition had doubled its circulation to 8 million. New editions appeared across the face of Europe—French, German, Austrian, Belgian, and Swiss—"in many cases," according to one account, "at the urging of readers . . . and in some instances—including Egypt and Italy—at the direct request of governmental officials in those countries."[69]

By 1954, there were twenty international editions which reprinted material taken from the current or recent American editions. All the foreign editions carried advertising, up to 30 percent of their pages, and their earnings from ads that year totaled about $13.5 million.[70] Of at least equal significance was the fact that the British and Canadian editions increased their circulations at a more rapid rate *after* they had begun to publish advertising than before. It was against this background that the *Digest* announced, in November 1954, that instead of increasing the U.S. purchase price which was still 25 cents—the same throughout its thirty-three years—a limited amount of advertising would be accepted in the parent magazine, too.

Originally, American multinational business corporations were the major advertisers in the international editions, but over the years the pendulum has swung the other way. The ratio in 1974, according to an *RD* official, was 80 percent local and 20 percent international.[71] This high volume of local ads combined with a decision in 1964 to tailor the editorial content of the non-American editions have fostered the image of *Reader's Digest* as a collection of national magazines as opposed to a single international publication.

Advertising policy abroad, like editorial policy, has been flexible. For instance, the American magazine has pledged never to accept liquor ads, but that prohibition has not been applied outside the United States. And ads have appeared from time to time which censors, who almost never interfere with the magazine's editorial content, have found objectionable.

The editorial contents of the international editions vary widely, even the amount of copy has been far from uniform; the range in the number of articles has been from a low average of twenty in the French edition for Belgium to a high average of thirty-seven in Canada.[72] The criteria for selection of material in every issue, however, has been the same: "Each issue is composed of articles on a wide variety of subjects of specific and general interest, appealing equally to men and women, carefully chosen to produce a balanced table of contents covering local and international topics in concise form."[73] If that statement, which appeared in a "fact sheet" for each national edition of the *Reader's Digest,* sounds somewhat fuzzy, it is. The key word, obviously, is "balance," but since there are neither objective standards nor significant competitors by which to judge, balance in practice meant what got published.

For British Edition Editor Michael Randolph, "balance" in January 1974 meant pairing locally originated articles (a profile of Britain's Ambassador to the Common Market, a consumer report asking, "Should You Invest in Unit Trusts?", an in-depth study of Britain's famous painter L. S. Lowry) with international features (how millions of Indians are to be educated by a communications satellite, a study of American presidential inaugurations, and a report on the "other" China—Taiwan). All of these same and similar articles were available for adaptation in any of the *Digest's* twelve other languages. But, of course, the content "balance" achieved by Editor Randolph in Britain was not the same as that of, say, Editor Ana Kviat for the Latin American editions, whose readership might share an interest in India's experience with teaching by satellite but hardly in whether British consumers should invest in unit trusts.

So from an editorial standpoint, the *Reader's Digest's* trick of bridging cultures has more to do with selectivity than sameness, although, whatever the final content selections for the separate editions, all material has been uniformly presented everywhere in the unique *Reader's Digest* style. That style is akin to that of American newsmagazines, but group journalism as practiced at *RD* has been essentially different because the *Digest* has neither a limited focus nor intense deadline pressures. The editors, wordsmiths, and researchers at the *Digest,* therefore, have enjoyed an unusual amount of freedom to apply their techniques to every article, whether original or acquired.

Over the years, original articles have become more numerous than those condensed from other publications. Originals first began to appear in the early 1930s, when DeWitt Wallace, who began by securing republishing rights free, began paying substantial fees to leading magazines for exclusive reprint privileges. Obviously costly acquisition rights were an incentive to originate part of the editorial content.

Similarly there were financial incentives for much of the *Digest's* international expansion, motivations like those that have enticed most multinational corporations. Each of the twenty-five national editions has been organizationally comparable to, for example, Ford Motor assembly plants abroad. Both have shared resources and rights of a parent firm in the United States, participated in globally efficient systems, benefited from economies of scale, and had considerable local autonomy to make adjustments in order to enhance probabilities for success.

Success is, of course, a relative term, but by all apparent indications *Reader's Digest* has created a highly successful business strategy abroad which evolved from the unselfish motive back in 1940 of countering Axis influence in South America. Among the indicators were favorable —to advertisers—demographic characteristics of its non-American readership.

The *Digest* has reported, for the benefit of advertisers, that its readers everywhere belong to a "quality audience" of affluent, well-educated, well-informed individuals.[74] Judging by research commissioned by the magazine, that seems true—in a *national* context. In other words, among their countrymen, *Digest* readers as a group stand well above average on the social ladder. The various national audiences of the magazine have not, however, composed a single international readership as nearly alike, for instance, as that of the American newsmagazines. The "decisionmakers," as *Time* and *Newsweek* refer to their readers from Tokyo to Toronto and Melbourne to Milan, are a fairly homogeneous group with similar information needs that the newsmagazines attempt to satisfy—one with a regional, the other with a global, strategy. By comparison, *Reader's Digest*, in catering to national interests, has acquired a worldwide audience, with more heterogeneous characteristics.

Two *Reader's Digest* audience studies illustrate this point. Because these surveys—one in Latin America and the other in Western Europe —were conducted three years apart (1971 and 1974, respectively), the data cannot be considered fully comparable, but the information does convey a general impression of regional readership differences.

To begin with, there was a striking age difference between Europeans and Latin Americans who responded to survey questionnaires. The median European age was 45.7 years; the median for Latin America was 33.9 years. Regarding the criteria of the *Digest*'s self-described "quality audience," the surveys revealed that affluence for Latin American families who got the magazine in 1971, meant an annual median family income of $4,613, while the figure for similar European families in 1974 was $10,185. The second criterion, education, revealed other disparities, although both readerships had approximately the same percentages of persons who had attended only elementary school (Europe 14.2, Latin America 14.7), high school (Europe 25.2, Latin America 29.3), or had some higher education (Europe 60.6, Latin America 56). It was within the last category that there were significant differences. In Latin America twice as many readers (30.7 percent versus 15.6 percent) had some university schooling, whereas the situation was nearly reversed for special or professional training (Europe 45 percent, Latin America 25.3 percent).

The third ingredient of the *Digest*'s "quality audience," well-informed individuals, could not be compared, as the European study provided no data on that. The Latin American survey showed, however, that the *Digest* audience there seldom read non-Spanish publications (only 21.9 percent) and of those who did, only 5 percent read *Time*. (No percentage was reported for *Newsweek*.)[75]

In sum, a typical Latin American reader of the *Digest* was half a generation younger, and living in a family with half as much income as a counterpart in Europe. Furthermore, while some Latin Americans may have been better educated, the evidence of low English-language magazine readership there suggests a tenuous lingual bond between, say, Caracas and Cologne readers of the *Digest*. Still, since both were purchasers of the *Reader's Digest*, they shared a transnational link, or put another way, they were somewhat less than nations apart. How much less is difficult to assess without suitable additional data for analysis.

What can be concluded, however, about the *Reader's Digest* is that it alone has embodied all the structural characteristics that have been variously attributed to other media discussed in this book. It has been both an indirect and a direct medium. For, like the news agencies and the telefilm industry, the *Digest*'s global network of editorial offices has wholesaled material, albeit to an exclusive clientele of twenty-six (counting the American) editions of the *Reader's Digest* magazine. Each edition, published by a local subsidiary has selected a portion of material from the global warehouse for adaptation and mixed it with indigenously produced material to be packaged in magazine form and retailed in preselected areas, just like the *International Herald Tribune* and the newsmagazines.

Moreover, the *Digest*'s activities in the world marketplace have followed the typical pattern of first being a national exporter of its domestic magazine, then acquiring a multinational complexion, and then an international sharing of editorial control between the home office and local editors. Unlike the eventual terminal experience of Hollywood movies that followed the same cycle, the *Digest*'s operations abroad have remained dynamic because many of the foreign editions have themselves become national exporters, thus originating the cycle again. Prominent examples are: the West German national edition of *Reader's Digest*, which in 1972 was exporting 151,553 copies a month to Austria and another 31,613 to other countries; the British edition, which at the same time was being purchased by 143,502 persons a month outside the United Kingdom; the French edition, whose exports in 1973 totaled 33,406 per month; the Japanese edition, exporting 17,004 copies, including 2,992 to the U.S.; the Swedish edition, sending 17,989 copies per month to neighboring Finland; while the Finnish edition, with an indigenous circulation of 284,396 in 1973, exported, 1,449 copies to Sweden.[76]

In conclusion it could be said that the global system of the *Reader's Digest* itself is "of [longer] lasting interest" than any of the magazine articles published in conformity with that standard.

INFLUENCE
AND IRE

ust three decades after Henry Luce's memorable comments about this being the *American Century*, a period in which Americans should exercize "upon the world the full impact of our influence," the United States suffered a humiliating defeat at the United Nations. Ironically, it was the very sway that Luce and his fellow mass media merchants had achieved in the world that lay behind a procedural vote on direct broadcasting by satellite in which the United States was completely isolated 102 to 1.

During the Cold War when the American perspective was that of a world divided neatly east and west and when the allegiances of newly independent nations were up for grabs, a widely held assumption in the United States was that foreigners could be persuaded to side with the United States if only they were sufficiently exposed to the American way of life. This was the intellectual foundation upon which the U.S. Information Agency was created in 1953 for the purpose of telling "America's story to the world," combating godless communism, and conducting, in the words of President Truman, a "Campaign of Truth"[1] in which private communicators were to be soldiers as well. This phase of American external mass communications began with a heavy dose of putative political orientation.

The idea was consistent with the popular American notion of a socially responsible press, its freedom guaranteed by the First Amendment, and with a self-righteous, moralistic attitude about foreign affairs. Freedom of information was a tenet of the post-WWII pax Americana dogma of making the world safe for democracy. Since the United Nations originally was envisioned by the United States as an instrument of that concept, an early action of the U.S.-led General Assembly was, not surprisingly, to proclaim, on 10 December 1948, a Universal Declaration of Human Rights with an article declaring the "right to freedom of opinion and expression."

There was, in sum, a sort of religious conviction that if enough missionaries (read communicators) carried the true message (read American values) to foreign lands, the world would be saved. This was neither an unchallenged nor troublefree notion. The Soviet Union championed a countervailing message and there was the usual number of internal squabbles about the communicators and their effectiveness. While Moscow was both jamming foreign broadcasts and expanding its own shortwave radio facilities, Hollywood, as already mentioned, was defending itself against charges that American films were selling the country short overseas.

As the years passed and détente succeeded the Cold War, television programs followed movie exports abroad, and the hoped-for, pervasive, foreign exposure to American culture had occurred, the challenges and troubles related to American transnational communications did not diminish but multiplied. Examples abound:

—A once holy faith by Americans in the supposed value of personal communications among peoples of the world has given way to a recognition by U.S. diplomats "that increasing international contacts have (a potential) for confusion as well as for cooperation."[2]

—The days when Henry Luce used to consider the editorial policies of his publishing empire identical with U.S. foreign policies dwindled as the foreign circulation of *Time* rose.

—Détente notwithstanding, the Soviet Union still has an Iron Curtain mentality insofar as information and cultural exchange are concerned as shown by Russian recalcitrance during discussion of human rights at the European security talks.

—The newly independent, now called developing, countries were exposed, as had been hoped, to the American way and one of their reactions was to scream "cultural [sometimes informational] imperialism."

—Perhaps the unkindest cut of all is being inflicted by America's long-time best friend, Canada, where nationalists and intellectuals are successfully campaigning to limit the heavy cross-border mass media flow from the South.

A few years after World War II, what was conceived within the United States to be a well-intentioned, politically desirable means of spreading American influence around the world grew into an extensive, profit-seeking mass communications system that continues to be increasingly controversial. These media have become embroiled in the intensifying, international public policy debate over equity and control—tough issues for the United States at a time when its political power in world affairs is fading. As the abilities of the U.S. to maintain an open international system erode, the critics of freedom of operation for multinationals have come forth ready to do battle. Yet the shape of the mass communications dimension of this conflict has been rather amorphous for neither the influence of American media abroad nor the controversy is well-understood.

INFLUENCE ON
FOREIGN MASS MEDIA

The clearest impact of American mass media abroad is on foreign mass media. Evidence of this is plentiful:

—A leading figure in the Japanese communications industry, Nobutaka Shikanai, president of the Fuji-Sankei broadcasting and newspaper empire, has explained that Fuji TV's daily children's program was created "with the stimulus of the 'Sesame Street' program."[3]

—A Chinese correspondent once said that Peking's official news agency had decided to shorten the length of its stories to the size favored by American news agencies.[4]

—A press clipping survey of newspapers in a dozen European countries during nine months of 1973 revealed that *Newsweek* and *Time* were quoted or mentioned in European newspapers no less than 3385 and 2649 times respectively. By comparison, the survey found that Britain's *The Economist* was referred to in the same newspapers only 555 times.[5]

These are but a few examples of a phenomenon of international affairs that are obvious: the imprints of American media, like the footprints of Alexander the Great's soldiers, are everywhere. The impact of American mass media elsewhere has been so powerful that one observer, Professor Jeremy Tunstall of London's City University, has concluded that, "There is no country or territory in the world whose newspapers, magazines, films, records, radio and television have not been influenced by those of the United States. . . ."[6] He is no doubt correct. Because development of contemporary mass media is virtually *sui generis* to the United States, American influence on subsequent foreign varieties has been great.

The history of each mass medium—print, audio, and visual—is one in which there are either American parents or foster parents who molded the medium, giving it enduring characteristics. But this should not be an unexpected result. Mass media have developed in the United States in conformity with the product cycle model Harvard economist Raymond Vernon has described for other U.S. multinational enterprises.[7] Media merchants, like other U.S. businessmen, have responded to unique characteristics of the affluent and innovative-oriented U.S. domestic market which motivated them to offer products and processes that were to have real promise in foreign markets. The introduction of their wares abroad—and thereby the onset of their influence—began with the export of finished products, usually of high (detractors say, slick) quality that set standards. Movies were the first mass medium exported by the United States, and while today Hollywood no longer claims to be the film capital of the world, who would doubt that the bygone Hollywood era has left an indelible imprint on contemporary movie making.

A second stream of influence is the importation by the United States of foreign media, which must conform to American formats and style if they are to successfully crack the financially rewarding American market. One of the more bizarre indicators that conformity to American standards by foreign producers has taken root has come indirectly from the National Conference of (U.S.) Motion Picture and Television Unions which, in the early 1970s, became concerned about overseas production of movies, advertising commercials, and television programs by American companies seeking cheaper labor abroad. The unions got particularly upset when the American Broadcasting Company announced that it planned to have ATV, a British telefilm company, produce a program series as part of the U.S. bicentennial celebration. To the labor leaders of American cameramen, soundmen, scenic designers, actors, and others involved in television production, that was "almost blasphemous" and they threatened to mount a public campaign against the television network unless the decision was rescinded. For its part, an ABC spokesman said the American network "had had a long and satisfying relationship with the British company and knew we could expect high quality production from them."[8] Put another way, the network was saying ATV, though non-American, produced American quality programs, which the network was all too happy to import (because they are cheaper, said the unions).

The preceding examples of influence through exporting and importing imply that processes of imitation and adaptation occur within foreign mass media organizations as a result of intimate involvement with American mass media companies. But these processes can also take place without any direct contact with U.S. media. The most obvious examples are newsmagazines, obvious because the foreign mimics often are sold abroad on newsstands side-by-side with their American inspirators. The symmetry between, say, *Time* and *Newsweek* on one hand and *L'Express* and *Der Spiegel* on the other is there for all to note in the sidewalk kiosks of Paris and Frankfurt.

Less obvious, because comparisons are not so glaring, but equally valid examples of borrowing from the United States have been: the so-called "pirate" radio stations in Europe that challenged more staid government stations with American-style "top 40" pop music formats; the American-developed pyramid style of writing newspaper stories with the main facts summarized at the beginning; and the local adaptation of banal American TV program formats like quiz shows. Reinforcing the influence of American mass media on their younger, foreign relations are a host of affiliated activities—notably book publishers and phonograph record vendors.

It is argued, then, that American mass media have exerted a profound influence on mass media in other countries. For the reasons that were set forth, that may well have been inevitable. Consider, in conclusion, the case of Agencia Latino-americana de Informacion, or LATIN as the Third World's first regional news agency is better known. Formed by thirteen Latin American newspapers in 1970 with the intent of rectifying a prevailing imbalance of the flow of news, LATIN sought to report regional affairs from an internal perspective. Although it needed outside organizational assistance, which it got from Reuters, LATIN's goal necessarily involved staying as free as possible from co-opting outside influences. But a content analysis published in 1974[9] "indicated that LATIN is becoming quite similar in news coverage to the large foreign news agencies." The author of the study, John Spicer Nichols of the University of Minnesota, explained the shift in context as a likely result of LATIN's successful competition against the Associated Press, United Press International, and the French news agency, Agence France Presse. The problem then, as Nichols notes, is that "if through its success in economic competition LATIN becomes too similar to the established news agencies, it will have failed to give Latin America an independent regional voice."

INFLUENCE ON GLOBAL SOCIETY

There is a shared awareness among students and observers of international affairs that profound changes are taking place worldwide and these changes are somehow linked with mass communications. Hence a phrase coined by Marshall McLuhan, "global village," which connotes a sense that communications have figuratively shrunken the planet on which we live, has come into popular usage. The reality of a global village is manifest in the daily lives of Americans who are able from home telephones to direct dial Hong Kong as well as Hoboken. On television screens, astronauts have been seen walking the moon and Olympic skiers racing down slopes in far distant lands—within milliseconds of the actual events.

The phenomenon of instant global communications is all too real. But what does it portend? Slowly there is an emerging recognition of how societies are being affected by the transnational flow of mass communications. Among two recent academic studies are the following findings:

—The culture of student activists spread easily around the world during the mid- and late 1960s. Harvard sociologist Seymour Martin Lipset concluded that "student culture is a highly communicable one, the mood and mode of it translate from one center to another, one country to another."[10]

—Diplomats rely on the news media for their primary sources of information. The relationship between journalists and statesmen long has been considered close, how close was described by Professor W. Phillips Davison of Columbia University who found that European and American diplomats obtain much of their information from a standard set of news media, among them the *International Herald Tribune, Time,* and *Newsweek.* Because they depend on common sources, Davison found that diplomatic negotiations are often predicated on the participants beginning with the same set of facts.[11]

The findings of these scholars—Lipset and Davison—are parts of a small but mounting body of evidence that mass communications is facilitating movement toward a new social condition. That academic research, a system of data collection and analysis, points toward that conclusion should be no surprise to politicians and other less empirically oriented observers of the international landscape who innately sense, as they are fond of saying, that "we live in changing times." Exactly how the times are changing is often hotly debated, but mass communications plays an unmistakably crucial role. Before Henry Kissinger traveled secretly to Peking, a few selected, albeit influential American journalists, already had made the same trip—publicly. They were forerunners testing the international political winds. In the same vein, Arab guerrilla leader Yasir Arafat came to the United Nations in 1974 not to quietly plead the case of the Palestinians in the diplomats' lounge but to speak to the gallery of international journalists and through them to the world. It is examples such as these that illustrate that mass communications no longer are peripheral to international relationships, but have become, in some instances, the essence of the relationships themselves.

The dramatic increase in mankind's ability to communicate quickly over long distances has greatly diminished time and space dimensions that once were formidable barriers to creating larger communities and provided people with a never-recoverable degree of immunity from contagions. In the latter half of the twentieth century the expression "safe distance" has become without meaning for Western man insofar as mass communications is concerned. For the absence of the news and entertainment media in the developed world is so rare as to be freakish. And in the less developed world, the struggle for progress is accompanied by an acute appreciation of the necessity of mass communications as evidenced by the universal priority given by rebellious forces to seizing control of national broadcast systems.

In the final quarter of the twentieth century, in the wake of an explosion in communications technology and a worldwide proliferation of mass media products, both chiefly of American origin, a new set of concerns and questions arise about the impact of mass communications. Whereas earlier inquiries focused on effects of communications on particular institutions and within particular countries, the perspective here is global.

The basis for this outlook is the increasing level of mutual sensitivity among the peoples of the world—cultural, economic, and political sensitivities—which are shared through what we might call a loosely arranged central nervous system comprised of American-operated, American-affiliated, or American-inspired mass media. The question then, should one dare to ask, is what is the impact of America's transnational mass media on the social structure of the world?

At the outset a few caveats are in order. First, and most importantly, the world social structure is far from a monolith of equal or even near equal societies. Second, the lives of most people in the world are not directly affected by mass media because, according to UNESCO, about two-thirds of the world's population falls below the minimal standards for mass media availability.[12] And third, the patterns of distribution and influence of American mass media around the globe are very uneven. Nevertheless, it still seems possible to proceed, for American mass media are analogous to American airliners. They have reached every part of the world, most often traveling on the heavily trafficked routes to Europe, but also going to communist and Third World countries, either through less frequent flights of U.S. carriers or through sales of U.S. aircraft to national airlines of countries as dissimilar as Canada and China. The point is that to the extent that airliners have an impact in any country that impact has an American dimension.

Jumbo jets, 707s and the rest, obviously have had their greatest impact in the rich countries of the world, but even the poorest countries have airports and some even operate their own international airlines. So, while the development of international air travel, like mass media, has been uneven, directly affecting the lives of relatively few people while being disproportionately influenced by the U.S. airplane industry, one can still speak of a global impact of American airliners, for their presence and influence is more or less felt everywhere.

So, too, with American mass media. No society is totally immune from their effects. Therefore, these media are instrumental in shaping the social structure of the world. This thesis is based, first, on the previously stated proposition that mass media not only directly reach worldwide audiences but also influence foreign mass media, and, second, on the next-to-be-examined hypothesis that "the emerging social structure of the world," as Professor Alex Inkeles of Stanford University has put it, is discernible.[13]

If it can be shown that humankind is moving toward a new social condition, albeit with some people having different starting points and progressing at different rates, and that American mass media are in step with that movement, it then follows from what we know about communications theory and influence that American mass media are indeed a shaping force in world social order. What then is the emerging social condition and are the mass media consistent with it?

In his study of social structure, Professor Inkeles examined several possibilities—autarchy, interdependence, dependence, integration, and convergence. One must be a bit arbitrary in evaluating any social system within the confines of these very general characteristics. Nonetheless, they are useful measuring sticks in attempting to say, whither the human community?

Of the five possibilities, autarchy seems to be the least likely emerging social condition in the world. Even the most primitive societies of Indians living in the Brazilian jungles and nomads wandering the sub-Sahara are losing their isolation and, indeed, their abilities to remain completely within self-contained and self-sustaining socio-cultural systems. At the other end of the scale, the two communist giants, the Soviet Union and the People's Republic of China, no longer practice autarchy with zeal. So the primitives and the holdouts both are becoming part of an interconnected global society.

As Inkeles points out, "a very large number of indicators may be drawn on to prove the case that the national units and populations which comprise world society have been very rapidly increasing the degree of their interconnectedness over the last half century." He cites

151

a familiar, and even to a layman, unsurprising, range of growth statistics on foreign students, international mail and electronic communications, tourism, trade, overseas investment, and the staggering proliferation of international (government and private) organizations. He could have added transnational mass media to his list.

It is, of course, precisely these indicators that give credence to notions like global village, cries for world government, and expressions such as "this small planet." Furthermore, we may expect more of these expressions for the likelihood is that global interconnectivity will continue to grow. This forecast is based on the fact that most of the indicators are linked to wealth and, as Inkeles states, "wealth, however unevenly distributed, is increasing in most *countries* and in some *segments* of all countries." It is this second point that explains one reason why even in the poorest countries of the world, American mass media have a direct impact. For although the masses may be unable to avail themselves of these media, the wealthy elite can and, more often than not, do.

Assuming, then, that rising levels of connectivity will characterize the world in the foreseeable future, what are the implications of this expectation for the concepts of interdependence, dependence, and integration? Basing speculation on past performance, we may confidently anticipate that insofar as mass media are concerned they will continue to be consistent with existing general patterns of social relationships.

Briefly let's examine the prospects. The term *interdependence*, while not new, came into widespread usage following the full economic recovery of postwar Europe and Japan. It connoted the idea, especially with regard to trade, that nation-states engage in mutually beneficial international commerce for reasons of self-insufficiency and efficiency. In other words, nations are prompted to exchange goods and services because of domestic resource limitations and in quest of wider markets more suitable for efficient scales of production.

These principles characterize America's mass media business with developed countries. For instance, the sales of U.S.-produced television programs to West European countries have been predicated on the unwillingness or inability of Europeans to muster sufficient resources (talent, production facilities, capital) to locally produce enough programming of comparable quality to that turned out in Hollywood studios. For their part, the Americans have sought to offset their high production costs partially through foreign sales. U.S. producers were so successful in doing this that foreign sales quickly evolved from a random, to a vital, business.

152

Dependence, as contrasted with interdependence, implies a relationship in which equality is not the hallmark; rather, it is a relationship in which one party has a greater stake than the other. The word dependence is most often associated with the poorer countries of the world who must depend on the richer ones for all manner of things, including mass media products. It is fair to say that dependence has characterized the relationship between American mass media organizations and the Third World countries and that this relationship will persist unless the developing countries close themselves off or until the volume of foreign mass media business rises beyond what the exporters consider the random level. The first option, isolation, so far has been politically unacceptable to noncommunist developing countries with Burma a possible and unattractive exception. The second alternative is economically difficult to achieve.

Overall the amount of business most of the U.S. mass communications companies do in the Third World has remained at the random, unessential level and thus its relatively casual importance for them defines situations of dependency for the handful of mass media consumers in the Third World. These are situations in which the producers have a more or less take-it-or-leave-it attitude and the buyers have minimal bargaining power.

While increasing interconnections via mass media give rise to notions of interdependence and dependence, there has been little real *integration* involving U.S. mass media abroad. One can go further and say there has been very little international integration of *any* mass media, which is another way of also acknowledging that political integration has taken few steps forward since the end of World War II. Countries are not disposed to surrender control over their media, for to do so would be, in effect, to give up an element of their sovereignty.

Virtually the only place where there has been movement toward media integration is Europe, which also is the only region in the world where political integration is even a talked-about possibility. Thus it is not surprising that Europeans are engaged in television program exchanges and have formed an alliance of European news agencies, and that the four-country (Britain, France, Germany, and Italy) newspaper supplement, *Europa,* has gotten off the ground.

But if Europeans have an incipient taste for political solidarity and this gets reflected in a few integrated mass media arrangements on the continent, the phenomenon is exceptional and local. The rest of the world, meanwhile, remains nationalistic in politics and press, or, as is especially the case of some American media, transnationalistic. The present general condition, then, of mass media around the world parallels that of politics—neither is approaching or even heading toward integration.

Finally we come to the concept of *convergence* and now ask whether American mass media abroad are homogenizing agents, that is, are they influencing the variety of world social systems to converge on a common norm? The answer is yes, although one can hardly be confident that a single, pervasive world culture is inevitable—certainly not in the foreseeable future. Obviously, so long as the human community is racked with dualisms like developed and less developed countries, Christians and pagans, haves and have-nots, there will be much diversity on this planet. The we/they syndrome of classification seems to be a strongly fixed notion, one not likely to have a sudden or early demise.[14] Nevertheless, it is equally obvious that a great deal of uniformity now characterizes the international landscape, with the modern industrial society serving as a model. A standard feature of that model is mass media, which themselves are much alike everywhere having more or less adopted American standards. Thus we might add *Time* to the frequently cited Coca Cola sign as a symbol of the so-called Americanization process underway in a bilevel world of both modern cultural similarities and traditional cultural differences.

In sum, we may expect American mass media to be links in a world of ever more interpendence, considerable dependence, and very little integration.

INFLUENCE ON
INTERNATIONAL POLITICS

The word transnational is a recent addition to the lexicon of political scientists who, a quarter century after the end of World War II, began to focus greater attention on a set of activities distinct from the more usual course of international affairs. Of course, a problem of definition arises immediately when a new term is introduced. In popular usage the words international, multinational, and transnational are used so freely that a statement like, multinational business corporations are engaged in transnational operations that affect international relations, is, to say the least, confusing. Yet, clearly the notorious case in which ITT proposed collaboration with the CIA to "destabilize" the Chilean government of the late Marxist president, Salvadore Allende, publicized an unusual dimension in world politics. And the behavior of the big oil companies during the energy crisis in the winter of 1973–74 was another disquieting sign that the chessboard of international politics had some new players, or, indeed, as has been suggested, another chessboard had been added.[15]

A world accustomed to power politics in which inter-state relations are directed by central governments has suddenly, it seems, been beset by private foreign policies, terrorized by nationless hijackers, economically shaken by unknown monetary speculators, and so forth. There are, in brief, actors on the international stage who, although neither diplomats nor soldiers, are nonetheless, playing major roles. They are so-called transnational actors and American mass media merchants are among them.

Their activities have confronted and perplexed people abroad. The distinguished French journalist and sometimes politician, J. J. Servan-Schreiber, reacted by writing, "The American Challenge is not basically industrial or financial. It is, above all, a challenge to our intellectual creativity and our ability to turn ideas into practice. We should have the courage to recognize that our political and mental constructs —our very culture—are being pushed back by this irresistible force."[16] While Servan-Schreiber emphasizes the challenge, the more noteworthy point here is his assertion that European political constructs "are being pushed back" by American transnational forces that we have seen include mass media. In what ways, it may be asked, do these media have an impact on international politics?

In the case of Europe, the focus of Servan-Schreiber's concern, it is astonishing that the first mass medium to embody the concept of continental unity was *Time*. The newsmagazine's European edition, begun in 1973, has as a goal to reflect a European perspective in a special section and in so doing *Time Europe* has become a force for European integration. For an American to see Europe as a whole is not unusual, however, for one of the characteristics of American transnational organizations is that they look past national boundaries at larger, homogeneous markets, and, in so doing, they involve themselves in international politics.

As a result of transnational activities getting more deeply involved in international political relations, the normal chief participants, statesmen, begin to feel a "loss of control."[17] Their abilities to formulate and implement policies get infringed upon by transnational forces, among them the mass media which sometimes play crucial roles. A classic example has been the informal alliance between dissidents in the Soviet Union and the Western press, especially the *New York Times*. Moscow's cherished policy of détente has been made more costly by this alliance which was a powerful force behind getting the

Soviet Union to make at least temporary concessions on the issue of the immigration of Soviet Jews. Of course, the Kremlin could have prevailed over the *Times* by expelling its correspondents from Moscow, but such action, Soviet officials no doubt realized, would have been even more costly. Not only would the United States have been obliged to retaliate by kicking *Pravda* correspondents out of Washington, but an atmosphere of the chilly cold war days might have reappeared, as well. Thus, the process of relaxing bilateral tensions between the two superpowers would have been slowed, perhaps halted, even possibly thrown into reverse gear. Meanwhile, the dissidents reaped the benefits of international publicity.

The United States government, too, finds itself at loggerheads with American mass media at times. The Vietnam War alone offered numerous examples ranging from the unexpected and politically damaging reporting of Harrison Salisbury from North Vietnam in the *New York Times* to an infamous quote by an anonymous American military officer—"We had to destroy the village to save it"—carried worldwide by the Associated Press. Such reporting severely undercut public support for the U.S. government's Indochina policies. Although the government had means to curtail reporters' activities in Vietnam (withdrawing accreditation or limiting travel within the country), neither the Johnson nor Nixon administrations dared act for surely restricting the press would have resulted in even greater diminution of public support for White House war policies. Here, too, the cost of winning was too high.

Vietnam did not provide only negative examples of relations between the U.S. government and the media. Indeed, during the early American military involvement in Vietnam the press generally championed U.S. policies as illustrated by the heroic image *Time*, among others, conveyed of brave Americans fighting communism.

Whether American mass media praise or criticize détente, or were pro- or anti-Vietnam war policies is beside the point here; what is significant is that, in these and other cases, the mass media as never before have an impact on the abilities of governments to formulate and conduct their foreign policies. This impact is indirect, through public opinion that is formed partly in response to the inputs of mass media. Care should be taken to avoid the easy conclusion that public opinion is determined solely by mass media, for their role is but to contribute some of the information and images used in the opinion-making process. But one shoud not underrate the influence of media-stimulated public opinion on statesmen who feel a sense of "loss of control" over foreign policy.

American mass media have other effects on world politics, too. They engender governmental regulations made in response to the transnational flow of mass communications—film import quotas, for instance. A less obvious, but not unimportant, effect is the contribution of these media to the widening gap between elites and masses in developing countries. It is the thin, upper crust of society in poor countries that has the wherewithal to read *Time* and watch U.S.-produced TV shows, not the indigent, uneducated millions. Thus, whatever the benefits of American mass media, these benefits go to the already privileged of the Third World. Finally, at the international level, mass communications can present troublesome issues that produce political fissures and defy consensus. The direct broadcast satellite controversy, at the United Nations, is a prime example of such an issue.

That American mass media have an impact on international politics is clear; that they generally exercise their influence unintentionally is ironic but true, since the inclination of these organizations is to avoid foreign politics. Seldom do they buy up mass media outlets abroad or consider themselves as having an adversary relationship with foreign governments. Contrary to numerous complaints that the American press meddles in the internal affairs of other countries, the conduct of American journalists abroad belies such accusations. While proud of their fourth estate status at home, the American press abroad have not sought such a role in foreign countries. Investigative reporting and television documentaries mainly belong to the American domestic genre of media organizations, not their foreign extensions.

The most politicized American media abroad are, in fact, not private but government-operated (by the U.S. Information Agency) or government-funded broadcast stations in Munich, Germany (Radio Free Europe and Radio Liberty which beam signals to Eastern Europe and the Soviet Union respectively). Moreover, there is evidence that the lower the political content of a mass medium the higher its foreign dissemination. Of the media considered in this book, the *International Herald Tribune* reaches the smallest audience and proportionately has the highest amount of overt political content, whereas visual media, the bulk of which is apolitical entertainment, attracts the greatest number of non-Americans. This concept is demonstrated also by the BBC's external service which is more popular than the Voice of America. Although both are government radio stations, the former has an established reputation of political independence while the latter is the official radio station of the U.S. government. Another comparison is that between Tass, the Soviet news agency, and the two American agencies, AP and UPI. Because Tass dispatches conform to political guidance from the Kremlin, the Soviet agency does not have the degree of worldwide acceptance and credibility of AP and UPI, which are independent and thus freer from governmental manipulation.

To summarize, one of the new transnational forces in world politics is American mass media. This is not to suggest, or even hint, that governments are doomed by transnational organizations—big businesses were not when their workers organized unions. But just as once we had to expand our concept of how business operates to include labor, so now must we view world politics as having significant forces besides governments. These so-called transnational actors, among them American mass media, are complementary new players on the world stage. To be sure, they make the plot more complex, but, like unions, their impact is not to supplant, rather it is to be part of, in this case, world political drama. Mere presence on the world stage, however, does not imply full acceptance by, or cooperation from, the other actors.

SOVIET IRE

The view through Russian eyes, or at least those of Georgi Arbatov, an academician who heads the USA Institute in Moscow, is that an American communications colossus exists, albeit loosely structured, that has an anticommunist, ideological warfare raison d'être. In his book *The War of Ideas in Contemporary International Relations*,[18] Arbatov acknowledges that private, nongovernmental American media operate abroad for profit motives, but he argues that although they "derive large profits from the export of their products . . . this is not simply a matter of the commercial activities of the various firms and companies or of normal cultural exchanges between countries." Rather, he states that the *International Herald Tribune, Time, Reader's Digest,* AP, and UPI (these he specifically names), et al. are engaged in "organized foreign propaganda." The organizational system, he sees, is a compendium of every facet of the United States that extends abroad. "Imperialism's Foreign Political Propaganda Machine," he says, includes not only private media, but also foundations, business firms, and, of course, governmental activity.

To be sure, Arbatov views parts of the machine as more offensive than others. Understandably the U.S. Information Agency, the Central Intelligence Agency, the Pentagon, and especially the anticommunist radio stations, Radio Free Europe and Radio Liberty, both of which receive U.S. government subsidies to broadcast to eastern Europe and the Soviet Union, respectively, are deemed more hostile than commercial media.

Nonetheless, private mass communications are seen as part of America's "foreign political propaganda machine," which he vaguely describes as being "fairly complex and mobile." Although Arbatov carefully chooses his words and most of his information is factual, he manages to create the impression of a centrally directed, monolithic apparatus massively engaged in a global propaganda campaign. He comes closer to the truth when he asserts that a common ideology (freedom of information) is shared by all the communicators, but misses the mark in stating that all have an essential goal or even commitment in fighting communism.

Two things are misleading with his analysis. The first is that though every foreign extension of American values may in fact be countervailing to communism, the extension itself did not necessarily come about with direct reference to ideology. While during the early years of the Cold War there was domestic discussion of the propaganda value of American film exports, their successors, TV shows, are exported for money alone without so much as lip service paid to propaganda. Perhaps a socialist might have reason to complain about the imperialistic impact of "I Love Lucy," but the program's producers judge its worth abroad solely by the sale price.

The other misleading part of the Russian's analysis is the time factor. Arbatov, writing in 1970 and using recent data on the international circulation of American mass media, combined this information with a two-decade old concept, which, rightly, held that American private media abroad had a propaganda aspect, but wrongly inferred —as seen with hindsight—that the intended effect would always be positive for U.S. foreign policies. That inference only sometimes was true as, for instance, in 1966 when *Time* kept faith with U.S. foreign policy in Southeast Asia by naming General William Westmoreland, the U.S. field commander in Vietnam, "Man of the Year." But the long, tacit pact between the newsmagazine and national foreign policy had even then become tenuous, partly because of *Time*'s commitment to a growing international readership. It was breached completely over Vietnam in the wake of the Viet Cong's 1968 Tet offensive which shattered the administration's line on the war in Southeast Asia. So, active opposition to government foreign policy has gone well beyond the occasional "undesired result" that the Soviet writer notes can occur when, to cite two of his examples, film exports are excessively violent or would-be goodwill ambassadors are labeled "ugly Americans."

What the Soviet Union fails to appreciate, assuming Arbatov ac-

curately reflects the prevailing assessment there, is that harmony between U.S. government foreign policy and private American media is
supplanted by pragmatism as the foreign dissemination of these media
expands to vital commercial dimensions. When overseas distribution
was small and inconsequential for most American mass media organizations, they were most likely to see eye to eye on foreign affairs with
Washington. Arbatov himself acknowledges this indirectly when he
notes "that the highest point in the craze for psychological warfare as a
'total' weapon that can almost by itself ensure victory, was evidently
passed in the 1950s and early 1960s," a period during which the economic potential of foreign markets was appreciated only by very few
American private communications companies. Bona fide American
propagandists tend to agree, with the most frequently mentioned high
point being President Kennedy's administration during which Edward
R. Murrow, a distinguished American broadcast journalist, headed the
U.S. Information Agency.

While Kennedy and Murrow may have been very good at enlisting
private ideological cold warriors, it also is true that at the time both
government and private media generally considered the benefits of
disseminating made-in-America information abroad to be political and
that therefore it ought to be complementary with the country's foreign
policies. But private media began to opt out of "the craze for psychological warfare," as Arbatov puts it, when one after another reappraised the demands of the international marketplace in light of
significant revenues that could be earned abroad.

Contrast with that attitude the parting words of Henry Luce in
1940, when *Time* was purely a domestic publication, to the first correspondent the magazine posted to Berlin. "When you get there," said
Editor-in-Chief Luce, "remember you're second only to the American
ambassador." No longer, however, does *Time*, whose readership three
decades later is one-fourth non-American, think of itself as an extension of the State Department. Nor do other private U.S. media abroad.
As James Keogh, the former executive editor of *Time*, later wrote as
director of the U.S. Information Agency, "Their purpose is different"
(than the U.S. Information Agency's) because they "are essentially
and properly commercial enterprises."[19]

This distinction between private and government media that Keogh
has emphatically pointed out appears inconsequential to the Soviet
Union, except that there is an indication that Moscow may have
greater respect for the prowess of commercial media merchants than
governmental information programs. In the satellite TV controversy,
the Russians want states, not private companies, to be fully responsible

for these broadcast systems, the implication being that the Soviet Union thinks it could exert more pressure on the U.S. government to control satellite broadcasts than on private organizations.

While the foregoing argues that in reality there is no such thing as an American "foreign political propaganda machine" into which all informational activities emanating from the United States are integrated, the fact that the Soviet Union thinks one exists is not unimportant. For although Moscow's analysis is faulty, its perception of a monolithic U.S. communications system is operative because it conforms to the Soviet Union's unbroken commitment to ideological warfare against a unified enemy. An acknowledgment that imperialism's would-be cold war, monolithic, communications structure has fragmented for economic reasons into often contending segments would weaken Soviet Communist Party leader Leonid Brezhnev's policy that the successes of détente "do not signify in any way the possibility of relaxing the ideological struggle."[20] A cynic might conclude that the Soviet Union has a vested interest in preserving the notion of an imperialistic propaganda machine in order to justify its own propaganda apparatus and policies designed, it asserts, to counter foreign information aggression and to disseminate the correct line. But the truth could also be that Moscow actually does believe that private American enterprise and the U.S. government are still wedded in an anticommunist campaign. Moscow's analysis of the relationship between *Time* and the U.S. Information Agency has been conditioned in much the same way as was Washington's long time analysis of the relationship between the Soviet Union and China. Established patterns are hard to break.

But just as events, most dramatically the 1969 border fighting between Chinese and Russian soldiers, forced Washington to rethink its concept of monolithic communism, cautious attitudes displayed by the Western press to détente have prompted Moscow to begin revising its concept of private American media. Evidence of this reevaluation appeared in October 1974 when the Moscow monthly *Znamya* published a twenty-page "Letter from the Ideological Battlefront" in which a prominent Soviet commentator strongly chastised American, British, French, and West German newspapers for allegedly waging a "violent campaign" against détente.[21] The Soviet writer, Yuri Zhukov, reportedly vented much of his criticism on the *New York Times* for trying "to prove that the United States and other Western powers were making a serious mistake in normalizing relations with the Soviet Union and other socialist countries." Where once American media had been portrayed by Moscow as cohorts in implementing anticommunist policies of the U.S. government, now some of the same media are branded by Zhukov as "poisoners" of attempts to improve relations between the Soviet Union and the West.

Although Moscow's line regarding American mass media may be undergoing the first stage of metamorphosis, and while consistency rarely has been a Kremlin hallmark, there is a single theme—supposed hostility toward the Soviet Union—in both the "machine" and "poisoners" labels given at not widely separate times (the former in 1970, the latter in 1974) to private U.S. media by authoritative Russian writers. While Arbatov and Zhukov provide intellectual underpinning for current Soviet positions, their writings do not mask an innate Soviet characteristic of lashing out at Western media when these communications organs offend serious Soviet political interests. When Russian troops invaded Czechoslovakia in 1968, for instance, the Soviet Union resumed jamming the news broadcasts of the Voice of America. A more poignant example came during President Nixon's last visit to the Soviet Union. Then, Soviet technicians fully cooperated with American television networks in covering events related to the Nixon-Brezhnev summit, but the same technicians pulled the plug on—actually cut off—transmissions going back to the United States of reports on the activities of Soviet dissidents. One minute cooperation, the next censorship. While American network officials in New York were deploring the Soviet actions, one can imagine their Russian counterparts murmuring about two-faced American television journalists who asked to visit the Soviet Union in order to cover a summit meeting and once there sneaked off to film interviews with dissidents. Surely this was the height of irresponsibility according to Soviet journalistic standards.

And therein is a clue to understanding the real Soviet attitude toward private U.S. media. The Soviet view is conditioned by its perception of what ought to be the role of mass media. The Soviets believe the chief purpose of the mass media is to contribute to the success and continuance of the Soviet socialist system,[22] which, of course, includes the foreign policies of that system. It follows that Moscow has an ambivalent attitude toward U.S. commercial mass media that in some circumstances are beneficial for Soviet policy (coverage of the Brezhnev-Nixon summit) and at other times are contrary to it (coverage of Soviet dissidents).

Second, it may be puzzling to Soviet analysts to observe the adversary political relationship of private media to the U.S. government, to comprehend the significance of the American media's independence from government and also their profit motivations. Briefly put, the

Soviet view of mass media is that of a bridge from government to people, whereas commercial media in the United States have the reverse notion of being a bridge from people to the government. Therefore, to understand American mass media one must realize that their audiences influence their content; minimally on a story by story basis, but cumulatively by choosing to be members of a particular medium's audience. That the *New York Times* pays close attention to the plight of Soviet Jews and Israeli affairs is not unrelated to the fact that the newspaper is published in a city with a large, influential, Jewish community. The private media are more concerned with fulfilling audience information desires than in purveying government policies because the financial well-being of these organizations depends on their amounts of circulation, ratings, and similar audience indicators.

For America's media merchants it is the relationship with their audience that counts, not, as in the Soviet Union, the relationship with the government. It is the latter relationship, however, that significantly conditions the Soviet Union's attitude toward U.S. commercial mass media. The Soviet Union expects political harmony between government and mass media. Aberrations from that concept apparently perturb Soviet analysts who try to understand the role of American commercial mass media abroad.

THIRD WORLD IRE

Turning next to the Third World view of American mass media, one increasingly sees the phrase "cultural (sometimes informational) imperialism" being used. This phrase sums up a nascent feeling in less developed countries that they are being culturally exploited in much the same way as they once were politically and, to a degree, still are economically. Although the challenge inherent in the charge of cultural imperialism has not yet been well articulated or orchestrated, it seems to be this: the Third World first became intolerant of colonialism and gained its political independence; next it decried economic subservience and demanded equity; now a new danger of cultural dependence is perceived. So far few remedies have been proposed for this latest challenge from the West.

Specifically, what upsets nationalists and intellectuals, especially, in the Third World is the tight grip the developed nations have on the instrumentalities for cultural dissemination. Citizens of the less developed countries must depend on foreigners to a significant extent for the books they read, the television programs and films they watch, and the news stories they read. They rely on foreign foundations for scholarly research grants, depend on universities abroad for better-quality higher education, and, indeed, must even learn a foreign language, most often English, in order to avail themselves of desired information. All this is regarded as cultural dependency. This is a one-way street with the values, mores, and behavior of the advanced, Western countries flowing to the backward, below-the-equator nations of Asia, Africa, and Latin America.

Striving to rectify this situation has so far not been very high on the agenda of the Third World, which remains concerned with the vital task of economic development. Nonetheless, it is emerging as an issue linked negatively to development. Imported mass media are blamed for nourishing expectations that cannot be fulfilled, of carrying seeds of dissent, and, in effect, of presenting a Western model of political order and social welfare as the best one. The result is a clash between the spirit of nationalism and what is perceived within the Third World as a patronizing, condescending, Western influence.

There is a parallel here between the histories of the Third World and the American black peoples. Both, after gaining their freedom, struggled for economic equity and as these efforts slowly began to be fruitful they began to realize that still another battle had to be waged, this one to preserve their cultural identities. The first step for the American black was to assert pride in his race by flaunting its symbols —wearing Afro hair styles, learning Swahili, and most of all proclaiming to be black. Equally, if not more important, black tokenism in the mass media soon led to a rapid growth in the number of black communicators. Symbolically, this was very significant. For black reporters on television were visual proof across the country that the voices of America's largest minority group at last were being heard with equality. An interracial dialogue had begun in the United States, not only because both sides talked but both sides also *listened* with interest and respect. No such policy-influencing dialogue has been achieved between the West and the Third World that chafes at being only on the receiving end.

The plea from the Third World that says, "We listen to you, why don't you listen to us?" has been dramatically expressed in the arena of international political communications. For a year the Egyptian president, Anwar el-Sadat, kept saying another Middle East war was brewing, but his remarks were merely noted in the West and quickly discounted. In effect, when Sadat sent his troops across the Suez Canal in October 1973 he was saying, particularly to the United States, "I told you so, but you refused to take my words seriously." Another example came a year later when Prime Minister Indira Ghandi decided to test a nuclear device and by so doing attempt to reshape India's backward image in order to enhance her country's international voice.

In the purely cultural sphere, however, the Third World is less capable of dramatic action. Occasionally someone from a less developed country is acclaimed internationally, an Olympic gold medal winner for instance, but such fame is transitory and seldom do fellow countrymen come along to expand a unique honor into a national tradition. The fact is that little meaningful cultural or informational *exchange* has taken root between the developed and developing countries. And the free flow of ideas and information remains a North-South current with barely a trickle in the opposite direction. Some of those on the receiving end believe this pattern to be a new form of imperialism and their strong sentiment of discontent is plain.

A manifestation of the developing countries' feelings is that their complaint itself is rarely heard in the United States, because even their outcry is muted or ignored, due to the grossly imbalanced system of international mass communications. Among the few Americans who have heard the cry and sympathize with the Third World attitude is Professor Herbert I. Schiller of the University of California who believes "that the communications-cultural component in national life cannot be viewed as a marginal element in national policy formulation."[23] The great danger, as he sees it, is that developing nations will lose their cultural autonomy; their cultures will be homogenized with the West partly through the influence of foreign (mainly American) mass media. Schiller's antidote is twofold: "freedom from the 'free flow,'" (of information) as he puts it, coupled with formulation of national cultural policies.

Another warning has been sounded by Uhro Kekkonen, president of Finland, in an address to a symposium on the international flow of television programs at the University of Tampere, Finland, where a detailed study on that subject was done. He said that the present global movement of information "in no way possesses the depth and range which the principles of freedom require."[24] Responding to this sentiment, the Tampere symposium issued an inexplicit plea for corrective action.

Efforts should be made to redress the imbalance of resources which presently characterize the international flow and direction of information among nations, especially in areas unable to determine their own cultural destiny, whether as nations or within nations. Those [countries] who have few opportunities presently may require special assistance, subsidies or protection to permit them an enlarged role in the communications process. All nations should have the possibility to produce their own cultural-communications material.

Each nation has the right and duty to determine its own cultural destiny within this more balanced flow of information within and among nations. It is the responsibility of the world community and the obligation of media institutions to ensure that this right is respected.[25]

What was urged was nothing less than a redefinition of the international principle of freedom of information as espoused in the United Nations Declaration on Human Rights. Lest anyone complain about the loss of what had been considered a sacred basic right of mankind, advocates of redressing international communications imbalance assert that private enterprise has mistakenly associated its property rights with an individual human right. In other words, as Professor Schiller argues, the profit-seeking mass communicators have been "falsely put on an individualized basis and associated with maximizing human personal benefits by increased contacts."[26] His point is debatable since Article 19 of the U.N. Declaration says that there should be freedom of information "through any media" and it makes no exception for commercial organizations.

Similar arguments have been made in the United States with regard to the First Amendment of the Constitution. Were the Founding Fathers trying to protect only a citizen's personal right to publish freely or does the freedom of press amendment apply to modern corporate mass communications activities, too?—again, a disputable question.

In attacking the legitimacy of money-making mass media enterprises, what the challengers want to do is reorder the system, not necessarily to abandon the principle of information freedom. They see gross imbalance in a system that uses an international principle to its advantage, so the principle itself is questioned. The risk, of course, is that should the challengers succeed in altering the system, a side effect could be destruction of the freedom of information concept, too. And the opposite of freedom is oppression, and while the former is an unobtainable ideal, without a commitment to it the latter may easily prevail.

There also appears to be a bit of unrealistic utopianism in suggestions to redress the imbalance in international communications for unless a developing country decides to follow the communist path of information control and isolation from the outside there is little possibility of a quick fix. To become an information exporter not just an importer requires not only considerable capital, but talented communicators also—and both are often in short supply in the Third World. To nurture Western interest in a developing country so that more information might begin to flow in the opposite direction requires a capability to act dramatically (what communications theorists call "attention-getting"). The Shah of Iran boldly captured the West's attention by successfully championing higher oil prices in 1973. Not coincidentally, the *New York Times* opened a news bureau in Teheran the same year.

But the poorer countries of the world, because they are poor, remain somewhat anonymous, unable to stimulate Western interest, and thus thoughts of a meaningful dialogue are stillborn. If these countries are being victimized by American media merchants, they are victims of neglect, not exploitation. The less developed countries are of marginal interest to American mass communications firms whose most profitable foreign business is with other industrialized countries. That elites of developing countries absorb great quantities of Western media, which is treated by the media themselves as random distribution, is not unimportant. But the notion of making a developing country information-dependent for profit is a myth. This is clearly shown when a newsmagazine, for example, is confiscated or censored by a Third World government without a murmur of protest by its publisher. Similar action, say, by the Australian government would trigger a crisis. The position of the developing countries vis-à-vis the American media can be summed up in the expression "money talks," which for the poorer countries means nobody in the United States is listening to their complaint about cultural imperialism.

CANADIAN IRE

Another complaint against American mass media is heard in neighboring Canada where nationalism, which seems to appear in cycles there, again became prominent in the late 1960s. Although the central concern is American domination of the Canadian economy, the heavy usage by Canadians on U.S. mass media is particularly galling especially to anglophobe intellectuals who believe that there is a necessity to strengthen a sense of Canadian identity.

A starting point in any discussion of this issue must be an appreciation of the deep American penetration of the Canadian mass media market. The facts are these:

—The English language press and broadcast stations in Canada depend on U.S. sources for the bulk of their international news. This is not the case, however, in Quebec province, where the French news agency (AFP) is preferred for the obvious reason that translation is not required.[27]

—*Time* and *Reader's Digest* became giants in the Canadian publishing industry. Together they were earning, by the mid-1970s, more than half the money spent on magazine advertising in Canada based on circulations of a half million for *Time* and 1.5 million for the *Digest*.

—Canada has been, over the years, the most profitable market for American TV exports and, while there are few statistics on the volume of programs crossing the border, even a cursory glance at a Canadian television program schedule reveals a striking similarity with a U.S. counterpart. Moreover, an estimated 60 percent of the Canadian population can receive American TV directly, either by overspill from border stations or through cable.[28]

Some Canadians have long been concerned with cultural intrusion from the south. As early as 1922 Canadian magazine publishers complained about unfair U.S. competition and in 1940 a Royal Commission on National Development in the Arts, Letters, and Sciences investigated the impact of the United States on Canadian cultural development. Over the years various recommendations have been made and steps taken to curb U.S. influence and/or bolster indigenous cultural institutions. The mass communications industry is one of only four key sectors of the Canadian economy that have been legally protected against foreign takeover. Nonetheless, U.S. mass media have washed over Canada like a tidal wave which, considering that two-thirds of the Canadian population of 22 million speak English and 90 percent live proximate to the U.S. border, probably was inevitable.

While Canada-U.S. bilateral relations have generally been characterized by harmony, there have been ups and downs. No one can say for sure when Canada's latest reappraisal of its relationship with the U.S. began, but 1967, Canada's centennial year, frequently is mentioned as the starting point. What came together about that time were two sets of views that interacted. First, the once glittering image of the United States began to pale in the eyes of some Canadians who with dismay witnessed the United States being torn by racial strife, infected with assassins, and mired in a seemingly senseless war in Vietnam. Simultaneously, Canadian spectators to this American traumatic upheaval, which continued unabated through Watergate, became introspective, perhaps reacting to what they saw next-door, certainly in response to their centennial which, after all, is an appropriate time for any country to engage in self-examination. Suddenly it seemed clear, if only to a vocal minority of Canadians, that Canada needed to "de-americanize" itself and assert its own identity.

This notion gained widespread public endorsement on the economic front, but less so with regard to culture. Those who saw the latter as more important than the former were fond of quoting Harvard economist John Kenneth Galbraith, himself an ex-Canadian, who said, "Canadians . . . talk about economic autonomy . . . I would be much more concerned about maintaining the cultural integrity of the broadcasting system and with making sure that Canada has an active, independent theatre, book publishing industry, newspapers, magazines and schools of poets and painters. . . . These are the things that count."[29]

Concern and corrective action are, of course, two different things. So the key question was what if anything could or ought to be done to curb a well-established pattern of one-way, United States to Canada, cultural communications. The pattern was not a recent development, in fact, as new methods of mass communications developed in the United States there followed a quick extension into Canada. Looking back to the 1920s when mass media was taking hold in North America, Canadian historian Kenneth McNaught found that "American movies, magazines, and radio programmes penetrated Canada ever more widely. Tastes and attitudes were certainly affected."[30]

But a majority of Canadians did not decide until the mid-1960s that their way of life might be too greatly influenced by the United States. As late as 1961 a public opinion poll that specifically asked Canadians, "Do you think the Canadian way of life is, or is not being too much influenced by the United States?" was answered affirmatively by a sizable, but nonetheless minority, 39 percent of those polled. But the same question only five years later drew a 53 percent "too much" response.[31]

Although a majority of Canadians were saying by 1966 that they felt too much American presence internally, there was little unity of opinion on what to do about the situation. This parallels a popular attitude toward U.S. economic penetration of Canada, which most Canadians feel has been beneficial overall but should be better regulated. However, the means of regulation, especially if controls should adversely effect the country's living standard, are a divisive issue.[32] So, too, with imported American mass media. Canadians generally recognize the situation for what it is, but there has not emerged a consensus

169

about what should be done. Nationalists, to be sure, have advocated specific action but the public seems more inclined to accept the status quo or only slight modifications.

Two examples illustrate what is happening. In Canada, as in most other countries, the government is directly involved in broadcasting and therefore is more easily able to act in that sphere than, say, in the print media, which is entirely privately owned and insulated from governmental interference by a free press heritage. So-called "content goals" were established for television stations requiring them initially to reserve 55 percent of their broadcast hours for Canadian productions. A twofold effect was desired—one to diminish the amount of American programming and the other to build up the local industry. An unexpected result was that cable television, which could provide even more U.S. programming, began expanding dramatically. Canada soon became the most wired-up country in the world in terms of the number of cable subscribers relative to the population.

Although cable originally was intended as a means of providing TV signals to fringe areas and to improve television reception where through-the-air transmissions were not reliable, the "wire" found widespread acceptance in Canada because it also offered more programming—American shows. For a small fee, usually in the $5 to $10 per month range, a Canadian household could get cable service that included several channels from U.S. border stations. In sum, while content goals cut back on over-the-air telecasts of U.S. programs the goals also provided an incentive for through-the-wire dissemination of even more American TV into Canada. In 1959, when about one million or 17 percent of Canadian households were hooked up, cable TV was estimated to be growing at a rate of 25 percent a year.[33]

The "cable conundrum," as it has been called, is a particularly difficult challenge. Cable not only circumvents the intent of content goals but as an extensive wire system it also poses the perplexing question of how to fit cable into Canada's existing communications distribution network, because cable opens up communications possibilities beyond relaying TV programs. Mail by wire and electronic home delivery of newspapers are but two examples of how cable might revolutionize established methods of communications. Whether cable should be considered a desirable new technology or inconsistent with national communications policy will be an issue for every developed country sooner or later. For Canada alone it was a pressing issue by the decade of the 1970s.[34] It confronted the Ottawa government, it may be argued, prematurely as an unanticipated outgrowth of popular desires in Canada to watch American TV, by cable if need be.

The original decision to impose content goals on Canadian TV stations has not been regretted, as shown by the fact that even higher goals were subsequently set,[35] but it must be noted that they were not a successful quick remedy, alleviating the problem of an overwhelming flow of American TV shows into the country. More Canadian programming became available to viewers, but an increasing number of the audience had more U.S. programs, too. And that was not exactly what outspoken advocates of nationalism had sought. Moreover, the government was forced to grapple with the perplexing additional problem of trying "to pick the correct path from the interweaving possibilities presented by cable television," as a Special Senate Committee on Mass Media put it.[36]

A recurring issue of longer standing facing the Ottawa government is the case of *Time* magazine. Time Inc., the U.S. magazine publishing empire built by the late Henry Luce, established a subsidiary in Canada to publish *Time Canada*. It was a twin of its American parent except that a separate section of Canadian news, four to six pages, was added and, importantly, the magazine was filled with numerous ads paid for by Canadian firms. Because it sank deep roots in Canada, *Time*, along with *Reader's Digest* was considered, by an act of Parliament, to be Canadian for tax purposes.

This was a considerable advantage, for the law allowed local businesses to deduct the cost of advertising in these two American magazines from their taxable income. This special tax advantage was not enjoyed by other consumer-oriented American publications,[37] because the Income Tax Act Amendment of 1964 excluded from the definition of "non-Canadian" those magazines that "throughout the period of 12 months ending April 26, 1965 . . . were being edited in whole or in part in Canada and printed and published in Canada." *Time* and the *Digest* fulfilled the requirements of this grandfather clause, which obviously was contrived for their benefit.

A controversy over the status of *Time* and *Reader's Digest* in Canada first surfaced in the mid-1950s when, according to one report, "the ratio of Canadian to non-Canadian magazine circulation had fallen so that only one-fifth of all consumer magazines in Canada were Canadian."[38] Foremost among the leading foreign (read American) periodicals were *Time Canada* and *Reader's Digest* which by 1955 had garnered more than one-third of all magazine advertising revenue in Canada.[39]

The liberal government, disturbed by this situation, decided to intervene in 1956 when it introduced legislation imposing a 20 percent tax on advertising placed by Canadian companies in Canadian editions of foreign periodicals. Between then and passage of the 1964 Income Tax Act Amendment, favorable to the two American magazines, the issue became what Professors Isaiah A. Litvak and Christopher J. Maule of Carleton University have called a classic case of "Interest-Group Tactics and the Politics of Foreign Investment."[40] In the intervening years, three different Canadian governments—two liberal and one conservative—grappled with the problem. A Royal Commission examined the question. The Canadian courts were involved. Public opinion was courted. And the subject became highly contentious in Canada–U.S. bilateral relations; twice it was discussed directly between Canadian prime ministers and American presidents.

Since the matter was resolved in 1964 the image of the two U.S. publications within the industry has changed, influenced, one suspects, as a result of the work of the Magazine Association of Canada, which *Time* and the *Digest* were instrumental in creating. The Association does research and promotion for the benefit of *all* its members. By the time the issue arose anew, when a Special Canadian Senate Committee on the Mass Media took a fresh look at the situation in 1970, the major indigenous publishers were saying not only that they had learned to live with the presence of the two American magazines, but also that the Canadian editions of *Time* and *Reader's Digest* contributed to the overall well-being of Canada's shaky magazine industry.

But as the former challenger was neutralized, or at least began to equivocate on the subject, a new protagonist appeared—the Canadian nationalist. His feelings were typified by Richard Rohmer, a prominent Toronto lawyer turned novelist whose books, *Ultimatum* and *Exxoneration*, which foretell war between an energy-starved United States and a resources-rich Canada, have been best sellers. Mr. Rohmer, piqued by the fact that *Time Canada*'s list of best-selling books (in the United States) failed to include *Ultimatum* when it was number one in Canada, threatened to sue the newsmagazine for damages. The author stated his views this way:

. . . *Time*'s refusal to prepare and publish a Canadian best-sellers list of both fiction and non-fiction books is clear evidence that *Time* is not prepared to carry out even a minimal action in recognition of Canada's literary achievements. It is also evidence of the increasing arrogance of *Time* and the mounting disregard which this enormous American publishing octopus has for Canada, its people and their culture.

Time has a special tax exemption in Canada and with it goes a special responsibility. That responsibility is to editorially reflect Canada and the Canadian viewpoint. This it fails and refuses to do. Instead as it grows richer and more arrogant in Canada it insists on shoving the American point of view at all its readers in Canada.[41]

The anti-*Time* campaign gained momentum in the winter of 1974–75 and led to the introduction of legislation on 24 April 1975 by Prime Minister Pierre Trudeau's election-strengthened liberal government to remove the tax exemption for *both* the American magazines. Parliament, however, had little taste for quick action and the proposed legislation got mired in the second reading stage. Among the reasons was a distinction many lawmakers made between *Time* and *Reader's Digest*.

In the first place the *Digest* had made a far larger financial commitment in Canada than had *Time*: in 1961 it opened a new multimillion-dollar building in Montreal where an all-Canadian staff then numbering about 500 ran the *Digest*'s $10 million annual business which included publication of both English and French editions of the monthly magazine. Equally important, however, was the fact that although the *Digest* and *Time* were legally linked, the former never engendered harsh criticisms as did the latter. This can be explained by the very nature of the two periodicals. One, a weekly, pins its success on a specialized presentation of a controversial commodity (news), a close identification with the United States, and a high profile. The other, a monthly, has a comparatively bland editorial content, a non-ethnocentric viewpoint, and an image which is deceptively low key. While both have a U.S. heritage, indeed American parents, the *Digest*'s Canadian editions have emigrated to Canada, while *Time Canada* still represents an American abroad. Hence, the latter was more offensive than the former to Canadians who champion the cause of national self-identity.

Then, too, the nationalists themselves ran into criticisms over a sticky issue—content. Under the 1964 tax law, with its exemption for *Time* and *Reader's Digest*, Canadian companies are given a tax incentive to advertise in magazines that are 75 percent Canadian-owned, published in Canada (but not under a foreign license), and *not substantially the same as foreign publications*. The last provision has been the subject of much debate and ambiguous statements. Percentages of "Canadian content" have been mentioned, with amounts ranging between half and three-quarters. Talk of content goals in publishing have prompted counter-criticisms. The Canadian author, Mordecai Richler, for example, attacked "the nationalists [for having] made it clear that they are determined to win through legislation, for the second-rate but homegrown writer, what talent alone has hitherto denied him."[42] Privately, government officials said this was not so. The issue, they contended, was not Canadian content, but Canadian control over editorial content.

Meanwhile, *Reader's Digest*, no doubt concerned lest a precedent be set in Canada that might be applied to its other subsidiaries around the world, tried to stop the legislation. Ironically, *Time*, the chief target of Canadian nationalists, decided to qualify as a bona fide Canadian publication if Parliament repealed the 1964 tax amendment. *Time* felt it could accept a situation in which the newsmagazine would a) retain its advertisers by safeguarding a substantial tax advantage for them, b) become 75 percent Canadian-owned and thereby less profitable to Time Inc., and c) be substantially different from the U.S. edition of *Time*—whatever that was determined to be.

Time's decision to comply was based on an intention to begin publishing a Canadian edition about half different in editorial content than its U.S. edition. But the National Revenue Minister, J. S. G. Cullen, was even more demanding. In October 1975 he ruled that the tax law required that 80 percent of a magazine's content must be different from any foreign publication in order to qualify as Canadian. A subsequent interpretation of the "Cullen Rule" held that *Reader's Digest* was within bounds because it draws material from its own international editorial pool.

In its 26 January 1976 edition, *Time Canada* published a two-page appeal for rejection of the rule in the name of "freedom and fairness." It was in vain. A month later the House of Commons in Ottawa approved the government's tax bill. The next day the president of *Time Canada*, Stephen S. LaRue, announced that the 33-year-old Canadian edition of the U.S. newsmagazine had "no choice but to cease publication."

As shown by the examples of American television programming in Canada and the case of *Time Canada*, the controversy over American mass media in Canada has been intense. Public policy-makers were confronted on one side by an aroused, outraged, outspoken intelligentsia who asserted that U.S. media merchants had woven too many American threads into the social fabric of Canada, while on the other side was a complacent public who has not seemed eager to forego the entertainment of American TV or information of *Time*.

The question of the proper role of foreign (read American) mass media within Canadian society moved high on Canada's national agenda. The process of seeking an answer through debate, persuasion, and legislation got underway. The results may well have implications beyond North America for what was judged were the merits of one aspect of the Americanization process that has touched every country in some way.

WHY SATELLITE TV
SCARES THE WORLD[43]

Up to this point what has been examined are three attitudes about the transnational flow of commercial American mass media seen in isolation from each other. There is a forum, however, where the Soviet, Third World, and Canadian views mesh. That forum is the United Nations, where, since 1966, the subject of direct television broadcasting from satellites has been considered. Here is a topic that facilitates full venting of latent and known attitudes toward the worldwide dissemination of made-in-America mass media products. Direct Broadcast Satellites (DBS) is a perfect micro issue for appreciating how foreigners feel about American media merchants for the U.S. was expected to acquire the means for satellite TV before anyone else[44] and, since the technology was still on the horizon, candor characterized the discussion. A résumé of what has occurred at the U.N. on this subject is therefore insightful.[45]

The crux of the satellite issue at the U.N. boils down to whether a nation desiring to transmit television programs via satellite directly into homes in another country must first have permission to do so from the government of the receiver country. International shortwave radio broadcasters are not required by international law to seek permission, but foreign missionaries do need visas. Should DBS, like shortwave radio, be a beneficiary of the principle of free flow of information, or should it, like traveling clergy, be subject to prior consent? The United States has supported the former, while the latter has been favored by very nearly every other country in the world.

The isolated position of the United States was remarkably revealed on 9 November 1972, when the General Assembly voted 102 to 1 to refer a draft convention on satellite broadcasting to its Committee on the Peaceful Uses of Outer Space. The lone dissenting vote was cast by the United States. It is misleading to imply that 102 countries have abandoned the principle of freedom of information and favor a form of censorship. The issue is far more complex than that, but it is fair to say that the international community of nations is apprehensive about how the technology of satellite broadcasting, when developed, might be used and for what purposes.

It can be credibly argued that the DBS issue at the U.N. was more symbolic than real because on solid technological grounds DBS does not have the potential many envision. The basic fear is that unwanted telecasts will someday be bombarding helpless nations. In reality, to achieve an international DBS system would require at the outset cooperation between transmitting and receiving countries in order to have essential technical compatibility. Without such cooperation the system would not work. Technical feasibility, however, is assumed by many in the debate on the grounds that a country that can land men on the moon surely can transmit a TV show a few thousand miles into any foreigners' homes at will.

Whether real or symbolic makes little difference here, except that if the U.N. ever concludes its deliberations on DBS and finally passes a substantive resolution, a precedent might be set that would affect other means of international mass communications.

The Soviet Union, joined by Egypt, first introduced the satellite broadcasting issue into the U.N. during discussion of the Treaty on the Peaceful Uses of Outer Space in 1966. Two years later, Canada, in collaboration with Sweden, successfully sponsored a resolution to establish a special working group on Direct Broadcast Satellites. By the end of the 1960s, DBS was on the agenda of the United Nations, put there by a new majority of states (communist, Third World, and small powers) who felt they might be further disadvantaged in the arena of transnational communications if the United States acquired an unrestricted, space-age, delivery system.

The majority coalesced, however, for related, but not identical reasons. While all were apprehensive about the potential of DBS in the hands of the United States, the Soviet Union took the hardest stance in seeking a *convention* that mandated prior consent in the name of sovereignty; Canada's position was more moderate in advancing a set of nonbinding principles, which included prior consent, while at the same time advancing the notion of international cooperative broadcast arrangements that would allow the smaller powers to play a bigger role; the Third World was somewhat divided on exactly how to deal with the subject, but they united under the banner of "cultural imperialism," which they saw as a new form of domination.

Faced by this formidable coalition, the United States gave ground at the fifth session of the working group which met in Geneva in 1974 by proposing adoption of a set of general principles of good behavior that would neither be binding nor include a prior consent provision (Moscow had wanted both, Ottawa sought only the latter). The U.S. proposal generated some favorable reaction, notably by Britain and Japan. But still the U.S. was not out of the woods on this issue, mainly because apprehension about an unrestricted American TV satellite system actually is a surrogate for discontent over America's outsized share of transnational mass media commerce. To listen to much of the debate about Direct Broadcast Satellites is also to hear the pent-up complaints about pervasive American print and visual exports.

ASSESSING THE CONTROVERSY

If for Americans there is a familiar ring to much of the foreign criticism and complaints about their mass media abroad, there is good reason—similar commentary already has been registered in the United States. American parents who agonize about possible detrimental effects of television on their children no longer do so alone now that youngsters of many nationalities have been offered a diet of U.S.-produced TV shows. The charge that mass media in America is dominated by a handful of worn-out members of the Eastern establishment now has a global echo. Former Vice-President Agnew's one-time favorite sport of attacking media monopolies has become an international game.

Since at least the start of the 1960s, the United States has had an informal national debate going on about the proper role of mass media in American society. With hindsight one can see that what stirred up this questioning process were changes in both the mass media and the nation itself.

Suddenly it seemed Americans no longer were a nation of farmers who prized the land above all else. Now most of them lived in or near cities. The balance of political power had shifted from local governments to the federal level. And leading U.S. media, traditionally local, had become national. Scores of local newspapers failed just when their communities were most troubled. And the national medium of television not only reported disturbing events, with little sense of local sensitivity said the critics, but the very coverage itself also inspired more disruption. The civil rights movement was the pacesetter. It grew into a national movement as TV grew to be a national medium. The distance between TV coverage of civil rights demonstrations and demonstrations staged for TV was short. Television made Dr. Martin Luther King, Jr. a national figure and *Time* anointed the civil rights leader by naming him "Man of the Year." A tormented America naturally reappraised its institutions, including the mass media which were

177

associated, indeed deeply involved, with, first, the civil rights movement and then, the Vietnam misadventure.

The controversy about American mass media abroad is, in a way, an international extension of America's own recent internal debate about what role the press and broadcast organizations should play in domestic affairs. Today nations on all continents feel that their sovereignty is threatened, that their destinies are ever more influenced by outsiders, and that within their own borders they are losing control. A world accustomed to a military security game now finds new players on the chessboard, indeed a different sort of board. Governments are confronted by revolutionary groups based in foreign lands, imported unemployment, domestic repercussions to someone else's monetary crisis, multinational corporations that shift assets among countries and plan global strategies, domestic dissidents who are encouraged from abroad, and a host of other little understood and seemingly uncontrollable transnational activities.

Furthermore, there is a worldwide sense that international order is fundamentally changing—former President Nixon meeting Chairman Mao, astronomical oil prices, and fresh leadership everywhere are among the signs that a new, but as yet ill-defined, world order is emerging.

Finally, coupled with the phenomenon of transnationalism and grave uncertainty is a global sense of immediacy. Modern modes of transportation and communications have ushered in a "now" world in which problems are presented and solutions demanded in the same breath.

These recent changes in the international landscape have been accompanied by the worldwide expansion of commercial mass media. In fact, much of what is known about change in world order comes from information disseminated by giant U.S. mass media organizations. It follows then that for better or worse, American communications resources are related, as they had been at home, to a sense of global change. Consequently, when change itself is disturbing, so too are the media that appear to both reflect and be part of what is taking place. The phenomenon is not new.

In their distinguished paper on "Communications . . . Taste and . . . Action,"[46] Professors Paul F. Lazarsfeld and Robert K. Merton suggest that many critics are hostile to the mass media "because they feel themselves duped by the turn of events." Writing in 1948, the pair of Columbia University sociologists noted that "reform movements" in the United States had achieved great successes, resulting in more leisure time for individuals. The freedom and opportunity acquired from newly won forty-hour work weeks, child labor laws, and universal public education, among others, carried the promise of mass involvement with high culture. Instead, the great body of the liberated population got hooked on the low culture of the mass media, occupying their newly acquired free time with soap and horse—not classic—operas. "These mass media seem somehow," Lazarsfeld and Merton wrote, "to have cheated *reformers* of the fruits of their victories," (emphasis added) and created in them a sense of betrayal. Without the powerful mass media, so went this argument, people would neither have been corrupted by marginal values nor misdirected to indulge in low-taste culture.

So, besides being associated with undesired changes, American media abroad, like the proverbial messenger who bore bad news, also may spark the ire of foreign critics who either feel cheated or need a scapegoat when desired ends have not been obtained. For dissatisfied reformers, whoever and wherever they may be—American New Dealers, Soviet ideologists, Third World xenophobists, Canadian nationalists—U.S. mass media wares are perhaps an irresistible target to attack. This is understandable, for the normal role of the mass media is to support the status quo and cater to popular tastes. Thus criticisms of these media imply discontent with established values and preferences as well.

Overall then and stated succinctly, America's mass media merchants have become controversial both for what they say and for having their ability to say it.

A
CRITIQUE

his book was written at a time when a catchy phrase, "media event," was in vogue. Acts of terrorism were media events. Typically, a bomber telephoned pertinent, self-serving bits of information about his antisocial deed to a news bureau which then obligingly functioned as a publicist for the terrorist. President Nixon, in his foremost diplomatic achievement, showed a remarkable appreciation for media events, too. Preparations for his historic trip to China included sending ahead a ground station for satellite television transmissions. Mr. Nixon's downfall featured two other media events: the televised Senate Watergate hearings and later, the televised House impeachment hearings. Media event, like the more traditional power-of-the-press, is a vague but nonetheless disturbing cliché, for it is another phrase that triggers debate on the role of mass media in our societies. My own view regarding the role of America's mass media merchants occupies the final pages.

THE CENTRAL QUESTION:
GOOD OR BAD?

From perspectives as personal as one's own emotions or as grand as high politics, come judgments about the mass media discussed in the preceding chapters. And these judgments become inescapably intertwined with the environments the media have penetrated. It could hardly be otherwise, for some notable changes in societies, both foreign and domestic, have been accompanied by new modes of communications that, in some instances, have included introduction of American mass media. Can it be denied that there were links between television and the U.S. civil rights movement or between the American-sponsored Radio Free Europe and the bloody Hungarian uprising in 1956? Yet, can it be proven that either medium played a causal role in either situation? Here are both puzzling and troublesome questions that are taken from but a pair of examples between the complex and multitudinous ties between media and events.

Regarding the relationship between American commercial mass media and foreign societies, my own conclusions are that in the absence of convincing cause-and-effect evidence, transnational media can only be considered as contributing factors in the decision-making processes affecting societies, and, secondly, that through the marketplace system by which America's mass media merchants communicate with their foreign consumers both parties enjoy different but still useful benefits.

Admittedly, my conclusions fall far short of asserting that greedy media hucksters are people manipulators. It seems to me that such accusations are derived from a word used at the outset of this book—ubiquitous. The mass media by definition are virtually everywhere. Statistics about the number of hours the average person, whether American, British, Japanese, Malaysian, Nigerian, Guatemalan, or whoever, watches TV reinforces what is already assumed—television has invaded lives everywhere. That the *New York Times* has begun to export its copy hardly can be surprising in a world, as social scientists tell us, that suffers from information overload.

But it does not logically follow—given the ability of American mass media merchants to make their wares near-universally available—that they possess inherent powers of persuasion to bring about the adoption of values contrary to their audiences' true beliefs in a system that benefits the communicator only. One is reminded here of the old saying, you can lead a horse to water but you can't make him drink.

Indeed, there is evidence that what mass media most successfully accomplish is reinforcement of established values. According to a study done at Columbia University, propagandists have a much better chance of accomplishing their goals when they attempt "canalization rather than change of basic values."[1] This is particularly so if the only instruments available to propagandists are mass media. These media can suggest alternative behaviors, but they cannot effectively turn around attitudes for they are unable to impose either the necessary conditions of monopolization or supplementary personal contact. Commercial mass media never have complete communications control.

Put differently, the context in which American mass media function includes the information demands of their audiences who, in an open marketplace, strike bargains with the merchants over media contents. My contention is neither to imply that these media merchants are always on the side of the angels or to suggest that the roles for their wares are nothing more than casual (as opposed to causal). Indeed, the adage of buyer beware seems good advice for foreign consumers of American mass media because their impact, even when marginal, can be potentially decisive.

But the point is that while American media surely played significant roles in both the domestic civil rights movement and the Hungarian uprising, it cannot be overlooked that the central motivations of those struggles were the quests of American blacks for equal rights and of Hungarians for freedom. Neither group had to be convinced by outside media that racial segregation laws and secret police tactics were contrary to basic human values.

But there is no doubt that individual and collective decisions made in Birmingham and Budapest to actively oppose, instead of continuing to passively accept, repression were made in light of information provided by outside media. The contribution of the media in both instances, then, was to change the "information environment" in which decisions were made. So, as seen in these cases, the media can have important roles, but their influence is to mediate the environment, not to impel persons to act against their wills.

When American mass media enter foreign countries, they function as new institutions in those societies, one of their roles being "surveillance of the environment, disclosing threats and opportunities affecting the value positions of the community and of the component parts within it," as Professor Harold Lasswell has written.[2] Since the role of watchman can be of considerable importance, how, it may be asked, do external media perform this task?

Here we may return to two sets of characterizations made earlier. The first was whether a medium was merely a national export with the consequent status of being foreign, multinationally composed, or one under international control, by which is meant that its activities are governed by representatives of two or more countries. The second set of characterizations divide media into categories of direct and indirect. The former is a retailer, that is, a merchant who sells a finished product directly to an end-user, while the latter is a wholesaler who supplies raw or semi-finished materials.

The significance of these distinctions can be appreciated by briefly reviewing the experiences of *Time* and *Reader's Digest* in Canada. *Time Canada*, a direct medium, operated as something between a true national exporter and a multinational one because it had a small local staff in Montreal to tailor a four- to six-page section of Canadian national news in an otherwise purely U.S. magazine. The *Digest*, on the other hand, while not quite an information wholesaler like a news agency, has functioned as an indirect medium in the sense that its editions for Canada (English and French), both entirely edited by Canadians, contain some material selected from a worldwide pool for local adaptation and publication along with original articles. The process was multinational in character, but not quite international until *Reader's Digest*, in order to qualify its subsidiary as Canadian under the 1976 tax bill, was forced to surrender a greater degree of U.S. parent control. Prior to the tax bill, both magazines, however, shared the same legal status in Canada as bona fide Canadian publications.

When Canadian nationalists began to take note of these two institutions of mass communications in their society, their fiery criticisms were more directed at *Time* than *RD*, and not just because newsmagazines are usually more controversial than general interest publications. *Time*, in the eyes of Canadian nationalists, had essentially remained foreign, whereas the *Digest* had acquired a more or less indigenous image.

Lest the impression be left that *Time Canada*'s Yankee image had been a liability to the giant U.S. publishing company and offensive to all Canadians, *Time* officials have said that readership surveys in Canada revealed just the opposite.[3] Given the newsmagazine's high circulation there, the claim seems valid.

So the character of an outside medium affects internal attitudes about it. But one cannot predict a priori what those attitudes will be, based solely on whether the medium is an export, a product of a multinational process, or under the control of representatives of several different nationalities. Internal circumstances, as in the Canadian case of a resurgence of nationalism, are crucial factors.

Moreover, whatever the characterization of an American medium abroad at a given time, the history of these media's foreign operations reveals that none have stayed the same after the threshold level of random exporting was exceeded. Accompanying their evolutionary performance cycle has been an equally discernible impact pattern, too. The clearest demonstration of this was seen in the economic realm. Because mass media are essentially labor-intensive intellectual services, initial advantages of practitioners can easily erode. Hence, the monopolies American mass media merchants might enjoy at the outset cannot be maintained over time.

Hollywood movies were the first case in point. Originally, the movie industry developed in the United States with American audiences in mind. But because the pictures had universal human appeal, they quickly were imported by local entrepreneurs for showing abroad.

Before long, however, in Mexico and Japan, in Italy and India, local producers discovered they too could make movies. While their indigenous products did not match the slickness of Hollywood, the local films were better attuned to local tastes. Faced with these new competitors, American producers, who also were pressed at home by television's challenge, did not abandon the world market; instead they increasingly catered to it with multinational productions. This forced the genie of movie-making further out of the bottle and finally nothing but the financing and distribution of foreign productions (control shared internationally) was left to the Americans. Eventually that too eroded.

For a while the profitable screen world belonged exclusively to Hollywood. But the longer-lasting impact was to stimulate the growth of national movie industries around the world founded on the base of those foreign entrepreneurs who got into the local movie business by handling Hollywood exports.

The political impact of American mass media abroad has been, if anything, less understood, although not for a lack of attention. The political arena, after all, is where the controversy occurs. Much of the argumentation is a mixture of local prejudices and preferences about media in general coupled with the clashing ideas of the free flow of information and cultural imperialism.

What the issue usually boils down to is a question of sovereignty—information sovereignty. In a world in which statesmen feel a "loss of control," as a study of transnational affairs put it,[4] external media are another of those activities, like multinational business corporations, toward which governments hold ambivalent attitudes. This is so because officials like to control the environment within their own turfs while American media desire to practice their craft according to their own independent policies. The situation can produce anything from harmony to antagonism between indigenous politicians and American mass media merchants.

Take the case of Singapore and *Newsweek International*, for example. In 1973, the newsmagazine published a cover story favorably depicting the island republic as a great economic success. The story could hardly have pleased the Singapore government more, for it was then trying to entice even more industry to the small Southeast Asia country. A year later *Newsweek* printed a story that began, "One of the less admirable aspects of the thriving city-state of Singapore is the treatment accorded political dissenters there." The story, critical of Singapore's judicial system, resulted in the levy of stiff fines against the magazine's local representatives.

Direct media, like *Newsweek*, pose the hardest dilemma for foreign officials because their distribution is direct to the audience. Thus their impact, too, is greater. Indirect media, on the other hand, can be filtered. The difference was reflected in the Kremlin's policies regarding American news services during the Cold War. AP and UPI had arrangements then to enter the Soviet Union via TASS, the Soviet state news agency. But newscasts by Western radio stations, mainly compiled from the same U.S. agencies and broadcast directly into the Soviet Union, were jammed. In other words, Kremlin officials found the AP and UPI's services useful under one set of conditions and intolerable under another, illustrating the fact that whether the American media are viewed as good or bad depends on the situation.

The usefulness of AP and UPI to the Soviet Union, beyond normal intelligence gathering, was in performing the same functions, albeit in a highly selective manner, that news media do elsewhere: informing the public what to think about and conferring status, either positively or negatively, by publicizing subjects. Assume for a moment that a Kremlin goal was to get the United States to abandon plans to build a new strategic bomber. And assume further an American congressman had spoken out against the proposed warplane. Radio Moscow could enhance an antibomber publicity campaign by quoting an American news dispatch about the congressman's remarks. In effect, listeners would be told that being opposed to the bomber was a legitimate item on the world's agenda and information from a credible source would help them think about it.

All information, of course, is not presented in such a blatantly self serving manner, but all of it is selected for distribution. It's the choosing and the disseminating processes that can be politically very sensitive. As we've seen, American mass media are aware of sensitivities abroad, but for commercial reasons audience interests tend to come before politicians' concerns. And the two views do not always coincide.

When provided with an economic incentive to serve audience interests, these media oblige and will gladly surrender a piece of their once totally American character, ergo the section of national news in *Time Canada*. Without that section, Canadian nationalists would probably have been even more outraged. But one wonders why *Time*'s compromise position—agreeing to majority Canadian ownership of its subsidiary and publication of an editorially half-different newsmagazine—proved unsatisfactory.

The question probes the central issue of how much information sovereignty is enough, which in turn raises a more fundamental question: who should have overall sovereignty over what turf? That, of course, has been an all too frequently pressing, if not violent, political problem rooted in what Professor Harold R. Isaacs of MIT has called "the great and bewildering paradox of our time: we are fragmenting and globalizing at the same time."[5] Because nearly every country in the world is inhabited by a heterogeneous society, there are pressures to preserve what Professor Isaacs calls "tribal separatenesses" and yet there are also obvious needs for ever greater togetherness to ensure a semblance of world order. The situation is fraught with tension, and at times, conflict results.

It is in this politically charged milieu that American transnational media and national leaders sometimes cooperate, sometimes clash, sometimes just coexist, but seldom ignore each other. Their relationships are dynamic, not static. The relationships get caught up in the quest to maintain national identities and the necessity to defuze the we-they syndrome, ever more dangerous as humankind begins to appreciate that the earth's resources are finite. The imperatives of a world culture are balanced against preferences for separate nationalities, which in turn present their own problems. The nation-state arrangement, after all, is far from perfect as evidenced by separatist movements around the world and similar causes in virtually every society.

The adjustments that people make in these situations are called dualisms and they abound today to the point that we live in a truly hyphenated world—Irish-Catholics, Chinese-Communists, Mexican-Americans. The list goes on endlessly for it includes everyone who has transnational loyalties, from local employees of foreign multinational business corporations to non-American readers of *Time*.

Dual loyalties are nothing new, but their numbers, as reflected by the mushrooming post-World War II growth of international non-governmental organizations, have soared. In a wide spectrum of fields, people have banded together across borders. Among some of the better known groups are: the International Air Transport Association, the International Olympic Committee, the World Council of Churches, and the World Federation of Trade Unions. According to Norwegian scholar Kjell Skelsbaek, the number of such organizations, which stood at a mere 300 or so at war's end, leaped to nearly 2,000 by 1968.[6]

Does this mean that diverse cultures are being homogenized? Not necessarily. For anyone who has witnessed an Olympiad knows that under the quadrennial banner of transnational sports competition, nationalism flourishes; even subnationalism lives as shown by the conduct of some black-American athletes at the 1968 Olympic games in Mexico City.

Dualism, then, is an accommodation that people can and do make when confronted by the societal paradox of simultaneously fragmenting and globalizing. In so-called closed societies, such accommodations with foreign mass media are deemed antistate activities, while in open societies there is a much greater tolerance of those media. Whether closed or open, each society weighs the advantages and disadvantages of having American or any foreign information or entertainment media in their midst. And since, with a few possible exceptions such as Japan, societies are heterogeneously composed, various members easily reach differing conclusions at different times. For instance, the gateway for American media abroad has been through elite groups, but when the imported media penetrate deeper into the foreign society some of the same elites cry cultural imperialism in reaction to their middle-class countrymen enjoying the same American wares.

But are indigenous cultures really endangered? In the first instance what may occur is a greater practice of dualism, while in the second, the American medium, with the incentive of a larger local market, either will begin adjusting itself to local tastes or be supplanted by an indigenous mimic. For those who see dualisms as unnecessary infringements upon cultural integrity and are distressed during the periods of change, the phenomenon of transnational American commercial media is painful. The offended are like factory owners who oppose unions. But then, what of the workers' rights?

Management versus labor is analogous to that of the principle of freedom of information versus information sovereignty, for in both cases the issue gets very much embroiled in who decides what is best for whom and when. Economics, politics, and culture all may be central factors when this question is posed about transnational commercial mass media. Answers may not come easily.

With regard to economic considerations, for instance, the protection argument should not stand up for it has been shown that over time the initial advantages of the American mass media merchants erode to the benefit of local citizens. But this does not prevent indigenous merchants, who say they cannot wait, from demanding immediate relief from the perceived unfair competition of imports.

Similarly, national leaders who want to maintain control over the political environments of their home turfs have difficulties sometimes seeing transnational media as offering new opportunities as well as challenges. For example, the role American media have played abroad in presenting the evidence that led to thermonuclear war becoming unthinkable may be too remote a benefit. Perhaps even an illusory benefit. Certainly an inconsequential one to the government official whose prime interest in external media is whether or not these outsiders are supporting current internal policies.

So also with the cultural question. In a world of so many uncertainties, nations wish to preserve their cultures and to remedy any apparent threat even before thoughtful analysis. But, in fact, the appearance of transnational media spells not the end of nationality but the creation of ever more dualisms, which are arrangements by which both the desire to cling to national identity and the necessity for global organization are accommodated.

And the pressures to accommodate have become many and powerful. We have entered an age, as Professor Isaacs has written, when "the fundamental and decisive conflicts grow ever sharper over the hard stuff of wealth, access to sources of energy and other raw materials, over production, food, trade and military power." He believes that "these are the conflicts that will decide the fate of the world and its peoples." There hardly can be doubt about that. Nor should there be a failure to appreciate that these conflicts will be, again to quote Professor Isaacs, "ribbed and shaped and fleshed by the soft stuff . . . that are matters of skin color and other physical characteristics, names and language, history and origins, religion and nationality."[7]

Obviously, dualisms are not the only resolution to the paradox of a world with two tiers of culture, one a set of national diversities, the other of global homogeneity. History suggests that once again a new system can be created, but in the nuclear age dare we again try the traditional means of bringing that about: the sword? And, if not by brute power, by what other means? Socialism? Maoism? But is either a universal model that men everywhere will come to accept? The former has not passed that test, the latter still is being tested locally.

Meanwhile the old nation-state system has to adapt itself to a world in which the modernization process has made the earth so small that without radical reformation the duality phenomenon is mandatory. And with it comes the demand for transnational information flows, a demand American mass media merchants have been able to exploit more fully than any others.

In an international system opened up by U.S. political power, American foreign media operations got underway because U.S. media had a commercial incentive to do so, backed up by domestic experiences that proved useful abroad. At home the American media merchants had a solid domestic base, where they had refined their marketing skills, acquired a taste for innovation in order to achieve competitive advantages, and had perfected a content formula that offered broadly appealing material to heterogeneous audiences.

This simplified dissection of what in combination has been an effective system for international distribution of information and entertainment media suggests a fundamental question of whether something more than an organizational arrangement has been created in America and then marketed around the world like so many handbooks on how to play basketball. We have seen that the efficiency, or call it style, of the system has been widely accepted abroad. And we know that more global inter-connectedness results from it. But does this system offer anything much more substantive than prefaded denim or other even shorter-lived pseudocultures? Here, unfortunately, the available evidence is insufficient to do better than speculate a bit.

The one hypothesis that seems ripe for examination is that a strong link exists between American transnational media and the universal demand of groups in every society for a reasonable level of equitable status. It seems inconceivable that, for example, *Time* magazine was not a bridge between the feminist movement in the United States and the subsequent United Nations decision to proclaim an International Women's Year intended to improve the status of females. To be sure, neither that magazine nor other American media played anything approaching an exclusive role. In China, for instance, the subject had been placed on that country's agenda from within. Still, American media certainly have made a contribution of new information that helped some foreign audiences to contemplate the status of women. But the extent to which these media facilitated placing the issue on the international agenda on the U.N. can only be guessed at.

Speculation about whether these media foster the concept of equity around the world leads, in turn, to ask whether they themselves practice what has been suggested they may be preaching? Is the system of commercial American transnational mass media one in which there are fair benefits to both the communicators and their audiences? The question really concerns the latter, for the former either gain financially or opt out.

My own conclusion, already revealed, is that the benefits are fair to both groups, although I do not contend that the parties share the same rewards. My reasoning begins with a fundamental aspect of communications, namely that the attainment of communications depends upon mutually achieved access. By this is meant that without access to other countries being sought by transnational media and granted by foreign audiences there obviously is only potential, not consummated, communications. The motivations of each party to enter into an "access agreement" are their separate expectations of "rewarding effects."

Without such expectations, neither side would commit itself to the necessary agreement. Even if the agreement is concluded and communications established, it does not necessarily follow that both or even one party's experience will be realized. Furthermore, the agreement need not be a deliberate, conscious act, but, be it de facto or de jure, inadvertent or arranged, an access agreement must precede any communication, whether it's a two-person conversation or a mass medium reaching for a large international audience. The concept that he who talks seeks access to be heard and he who hears gives access to him who talks can be extended to any level of communications. In all cases, however, the parties expect rewards for their participation.

A review of *Newsweek International*'s development illustrates this process. Originally, the newsmagazine concentrated on trying to saturate the American domestic market, its exports were small and inconsequential, the corporate assumption being that Americans living abroad were the prime consumers of unessential random circulation. *Newsweek* then discovered that non-Americans were the principal readers of U.S. newsmagazines abroad. These readers belonged to what was termed earlier an international information elite who looked to some American publications for sources of information that were valuable in examining international reality (their expected rewarding effect). *Newsweek*, hopeful of new sources of revenues (its expected rewarding effect) launched an international edition to increase its access to a burgeoning foreign market.

The media merchant actually must conclude two access agreements, one of which—the market—is taken for granted domestically. Transnational media must first gain entry to a foreign country (perhaps a license is required from the host government) before it is possible to achieve personal access agreements with end-users, that is, in the *Newsweek* case, foreign readers.

The access agreement concept means that total inequality is impossible because neither party is capable of achieving and maintaining an access agreement independent of the other. This should not be taken to imply that absolute equity prevails at all times, but over the long haul there is equity, otherwise one party would disengage from the communications process. The notion of giant mass media monopolies victimizing small, hapless consumers is David and Goliath imagery that forgets about David's slingshot. The maligned consumers have a not-so-secret weapon of their own to employ when their rewarding expectations are inadequately fulfilled: they may threaten to or actually adjust or terminate the access agreement which is absolutely vital for any communications.

Media merchants naturally want assured access; host governments and consumers therefore have a strong bargaining position because they offer access in return for their expectations being rewarded. The merchants are fully conscious of the bargaining process, but the receivers often have less awareness unless their positions deteriorate. Inequity threatens if a merchant successfully attempts to assure access through monopoly or privilege. The result might be that audiences will no longer be able to indulge their preferences among competitors, but will have to resort to other weapons—bans, quotas, censorship, boycotts—in the bargaining process.

The open marketplace therefore affords the foreign audience leverage in bargaining with transnational media merchants. Nonetheless, let the buyer beware, for the rules of this game provide that when a buyer obviously wants something a seller has to sell, then the results must be presumed equitable if a contract is concluded.

The advantage of the marketplace system is that it permits the greatest amount of individual choice and enhances the prospects for the free flow of information to be genuinely free. In the end, this book contends that the free flow of information remains an honorable principle, worthy of being upheld in the interests of humankind.

Restatements of traditional liberalisms were not in fashion when this book was being written, for then the tragic misadventure of America in Vietnam was coming to a close and at the same time the poor countries of the world, cheered by a new-found power being wielded by Arab oil sheiks, were demanding transformation of the U.S.-organized global economic order. So suspect, so criticized, so deplored had internationalism American-style become by the outset of the final quarter of the twentieth century that every opportunity, appropriate or otherwise, was seized, especially by militant Third World leaders but others too, to automatically hurl hostile challenges, even expressions of contempt, at whatever America stood for.

Freedom of information has been so remorselessly abandoned around the world that free flow of information no longer is an endangered international principle; it is dead.

But to those who would like to bury instead of revive it, let them first be mindful that abandonment of this freedom undercuts democracy and that in a world "of sin and woe," to quote Winston Churchill, "no one pretends that democracy is perfect or all-wise." Indeed, Churchill told the House of Commons, "it has been said that democracy is the worst form of government except for all those other forms. . . ."[8]

NOTES

CHAPTER 1

1. Figure includes U.S. readers.

2. Statistics supplied to the author by the U.S., Department of Commerce, in a letter dated 27 November 1974.

3. When applying the term merchant more broadly, difficulties arise as in the case of some U.S. magazines in Europe. Six American magazines having strong appeal among businessmen circulate there: *Business Week* (23,000 European circulation), *International Management* (43,000), *Fortune* (25,000), *U.S. News & World Report* (18,000), *Newsweek* (140,000), and *Time* (340,000). All six reach influential readers. European advertising is sought by all but one—*U.S. News* which, because it neither attempts to exploit its foreign distribution nor promote it, fails to meet the finance criteria. So five of the six have some degree of influence and are financially involved in Europe. But only two—*Time* and *Newsweek*—have sizable circulation. In fact, the combined European circulation of *Business Week, International Management, Fortune,* and *U.S. News* (109,000) is nearly a third less than *Newsweek*'s, three times smaller than *Time*'s, and not even as high as the *International Herald Tribune*'s (120,000), which reaches the fewest number of persons of any mass media organization on the list. Therefore, *Time* and *Newsweek* are included but the other four magazines are not.

4. Nonprofit mass media organizations are considered to be in a separate category. Their importance, however, should not be underestimated because in terms of size and influence there are several giants. Among these are international broadcast stations that the U.S. government operates (Voice of America) or finances (Radio Free Europe and Radio Liberty); the Armed Forces Radio and Television Service that accompanies American military personnel abroad and in so doing attracts large so-called foreign eavesdropping audiences, and the National Geographic Society whose magazine has a foreign circulation of more than two million.

5. See Thomas H. Guback, "Film as International Business," *Journal of Communications* 24, no. 1 (Winter 1974): 89–117.

6. United Press merged with the International News Service, which was more international in coverage than distribution, in 1958.

7. Terry Ramsaye, *A Million and One Nights* (New York: Simon and Schuster, 1926), p. 822.

8. UNESCO, *News Agencies* (Paris: UNESCO, 1953), p. 59.

9. Eric Johnson (President, Motion Picture Association of America), "Hollywood Still Best U.S. Ambassador Despite Some Contrary Opinions," *Variety*, 7 January 1953.

10. U.S., Congress, Senate, Committee on Foreign Relations, *U.S. Information Agency Appropriations Authorization Act of 1973*, Report 93-168, 93rd Cong., 1st sess., 22 May 1973, p. 3.

11. James Keogh, "Information, Culture and Modern Diplomacy," *Foreign Service Journal*, July 1974.

12. See Ben H. Bagdikian, *The Information Machines* (New York: Harper and Row, 1971).

13. Statistics from *United Nations Statistical Yearbook, 1971* (New York: Statistical Office of the United Nations, 1972), pp. 477–91, 785–810.

14. See *UPI Progress Report*, 23 April 1973, New York.

15. See Daniel Bell, *The Coming of Post-Industrial Society* (New York: Basic Books, 1973), for an examination of this concept.

16. Peter Janicki, "The Nature of USIA Audiences and How Best to Reach Them," U.S. Information Agency document provided to the author, 1973.

17. Ibid.

18. Figure provided by *Time* to the author.

19. Elihu Katz, "The Two-Step Flow of Communications," *Public Opinion Quarterly* 21, no. 1 (Spring 1957): 69–78.

20. Janicki, "The Nature of USIA Audiences."

21. Taken from "A Profile of Subscribers and Newsstand Buyers: The International Editions of *Time*—1973." (New York: Time Inc., September 1973).

22. Figures from the *1973 COMSAT Annual Report to the President and the Congress*, (Washington, D. C.: Communications Satellite Corporation, 31 July 1973), p. 3.

23. Travel statistics reported by the U.S. Department of State in "International Educational and Cultural Exchange," U.S., Department of State Publication 8757, March 1974, p. 2.

24. Quoted from a speech by Peter Dunham (Senior vice-president, J. Walter Thompson Company), to the International Advertising Association, 11 December 1973, Princeton Club, New York City.

25. U.S., Department of State Publication 8757, p. 1.

26. The definition is from *The Random House Dictionary of the English Language*, College Edition (New York: Random House, 1968).

27. "*Reader's Digest* Multinational Fact Sheet, 1972," provided to author by *Reader's Digest*.

28. Tapio Varis, *International Inventory of Television Programme Structure and the Flow of TV Programmes Between Nations* (Tampere, Finland: University of Tampere, No. 20/1973), p. 31.

CHAPTER 2

1. Tapio Varis, *International Inventory of Television Programme Structure and the Flow of TV Programmes Between Nations* (Tampere, Finland: University of Tampere, No. 20/1973), p. 197.

2. *Viacom International Inc. 1972 Annual Report* (New York: Viacom, 1973), p. 7.

3. *TV Guide*, 29 April 1972.

4. Tapio Varis, "Global Traffic in Television," *Journal of Communications* 24, no. 1 (Winter 1974): 107.

5. The one instance of 100 percent imports involves a station in Saudi Arabia built by the Aramco consortium of American oil companies for the benefit of their employees in that country.

6. Information provided to the author by the Motion Picture Export Association of America, 31 January 1974. The largest drop, in 1966, occurred as a result of problems that year between American exporters and Australian buyers. The largest increase, 1973, was due to a combination of inflation, a campaign to raise prices, and several major feature film sales.

7. *Variety*, 16 April 1975, p. 1.

8. Leo Bogart, *The Age of Television* (New York: Frederick Ungar Publishing Co., 1958), pp. 168–69.

9. Terry Ramsaye, "The Rise and Place of the Motion Picture," in Arthur F.

McClure, ed., *The Movies: An American Idiom* (Cranbury, New Jersey: Fairleigh Dickinson University Press, 1974), p. 44.

10. Foster Rhea Dulles, "The Role of Moving Pictures," in McClure, ed., *The Movies*, p. 26.

11. Richard Schickel, "Almost Purely Emotional," in McClure, ed., *The Movies*, p. 65.

12. Ibid., p. 66.

13. Ramsaye, "The Rise and Place of the Motion Picture," p. 49.

14. Schickel, "Almost Purely Emotional," p. 56.

15. Lewis Jacobs, "Films of the Postwar Decade," in McClure, ed., *The Movies*, p. 68.

16. Ibid., p. 83.

17. Dulles, "The Role of Moving Pictures," p. 29.

18. Louise Tanner, "The Celluloid Safety Valve," in McClure, ed., *The Movies*, p. 86.

19. Ibid., p. 85.

20. Lewis Jacobs, "World War II and the American Film," in McClure, ed., *The Movies*, p. 176.

21. Figures from *Variety*, 15 April 1959 and 29 April 1964.

22. Leo Bogart, "The Growth of Television," in Wilbur Schramm, ed., *Mass Communication* (Urbana: University of Illinois Press, 1960), p. 102.

23. *Variety*, 9 April 1958, p. 27.

24. Ben Hecht, "Elegy for Wonderland," *Esquire*, March 1959, pp. 56–60.

25. John Howard Lawson, "The Decline of Hollywood," in McClure, ed., *The Movies*, p. 208.

26. Jacobs, "World War II and the American Film," p. 159.

27. UNESCO data published in Schramm, ed., *Mass Communications*, p. 197.

28. Various estimates have been given on the amount of time American movies have played in foreign theaters. Exact measurements were never attempted. The estimate given here is from the lower range cited in various sources.

29. *Variety*, 9 April 1958 and 15 April 1959.

30. *Variety*, 26 April 1961, 2 May 1962, 9 April 1958, and 15 April 1959.

31. *Variety*, 20 April 1960.

32. *Variety*, 8 May 1963.

33. Ibid.

34. Japan was the odd man out of this situation, even though the large Japanese motion picture industry suffered the same problems inflicted by television. The 9 May 1963 issue of *Variety*, for instance, reported that Japanese film output fell sharply from 535 films in 1961 to 375 the next year. Except for monster pictures of the *Godzilla* type, Japanese film abroad never moved beyond the occasional masterpiece that played the American and European art theater circuits. It should be noted, however, that hundreds of Japanese movies were imported into the United States for screening in their original (neither dubbed nor subtitled) form at a few theaters that catered to Japanese-Americans, principally located in San Francisco and Hawaii. But these films, like other ethnic film imports, generated miniscule business and therefore were without any impact in the American industry. The only foreign language film imports to do sizable business in the United States were a hundred or so Mexican films a year. In 1959, for example, Mexican film revenues in the United States were $3.2 million, or about $2 million less than French films, which then featured Brigette Bardot. See *Variety*, 20 April 1960.

35. *Variety*, 4 May 1966.

36. See Harold Myer, "New One World of Film," *Variety*, 12 May 1965.

37. *Variety*, 7 May 1969.

38. *Variety*, 4 May 1966.

39. Ibid.

40. *Variety*, 29 April 1964.

41. *Variety*, 12 May 1965.

42. Thomas H. Guback, "Film as International Business," *Journal of Communications* 24, no. 1 (Winter 1974): 97–98.

43. *Variety*, 9 May 1973.

44. See *MGM Annual Report, 1972* (Los Angeles: MGM, 1973).

45. Advertisement in *Variety*, 12 May 1971.

46. *Variety*, 29 April 1970.

47. Ibid.

48. *Variety*, 12 May 1972.

49. Ibid.

50. Ibid., statement by Eitel Monaco, president of ANICA.

51. *Variety*, 9 May 1973.

52. *Variety*, 29 April 1970.

53. Richard Dyer MacCann, "The End of the Assembly Line," in McClure, ed., *The Movies*, p. 243.

54. Charles Champlin, "Can TV Save the Films?" *Saturday Review* 44, no. 52 (24 December 1966): 11–13.

55. *United Nations Statistical Yearbook, 1972* (New York: Statistical Office of the United Nations, 1973), pp. 67–94.

56. Bogart, "The Growth of Television," p. 8.

57. Ibid., p. 307.

58. Ibid., p. 11.

59. Initially American video tape could be sold in but a few countries abroad because the U.S. television system of 525 lines per picture was incompatible with the 625-line systems chosen by most countries. The BBC overcame that handicap by inventing a video tape converter that removed this technical barrier at a cost (about $1000 per taped hour) and made London a transshipment point for videotaped U.S. exports. A more durable restraint to the use of video tape for TV program exporting, however, has continued to be union payments. Historically, films made in Hollywood under agreements with the American Screen Actors Guild were considered to be for continuing world usage, while live TV programs (later to be videotaped as if live), produced under agreements with the American Federation of Television and Radio Artists, were restricted in their usage. In other words, foreign sales of Hollywood telefilms do not require additional payments to labor unions, while videotaped programs do. A final consideration has been that films traditionally are produced with a sense of timelessness, whereas taped programs, because they are the successors to live shows, tend to contain topical allusions.

60. According to the Nielsen demographic report for October/November 1968 American television viewers at 8:30 P.M. totaled 81,230,000.

61. Les Brown, *Television: The Business Behind the Box* (New York: Harcourt Brace Jovanovich, Inc., 1971), p. 98.

62. Ibid., p. 186.

63. Ibid., pp. 15–16.

64. *MCA 1973 Annual Report* (Los Angeles: MCA, 1974).

65. Ibid.

66. Martin Mayer, *About Television* (New York: Harper & Row, 1972), p. 50.

67. The U.S. Federal Communications Commission limits to five the number of VHF—which is preferable for technical and economic reasons to UHF—stations that can be owned by a single broadcaster.

68. Several quotations in this chapter are from personal interviews conducted by the author with individuals who either requested or otherwise indicated that certain or all of their comments could not be used with direct attribution.

69. See Clive Jenkins, *Power Behind the Screen* (London: MacGibbon & Kee, 1961), especially chaps. 1 and 8, pp. 17–52, 204–25.

70. Interviewed by the author, 22 February 1975.

71. Interviewed by the author, 20 February 1975.

72. Interviewed by the author, 26 February 1975.

73. *Variety*, 8 April 1970.

74. Interviewed by the author, 27 February 1975.

75. Excerpted from "This is the World of Viacom," *Viacom International Television Catalogue*, November 1973.

76. *Metromedia Inc. 1973 Annual Report* (New York: Metromedia, 1974), p. 14.

77. Interviewed by the author, 24 February 1975.

78. John J. O'Connor, "TV: When Reliance on Imports Has Its Rewards," *New York Times*, 14 March 1975.

79. The U.S. Federal Communications Commission has similar restraints on foreign investment in U.S. broadcast stations.

80. Roger Rosenblatt, "On Television," *New Republic*, 8 March 1975, p. 31.

81. Figures given to the author in a telephone interview with William H. Fineshriber, Jr., vice-president of the Motion Picture Export Association of America, January 1974.

CHAPTER 3

1. Based on information provided to the author by the *New York Times* and the *Washington Post* for restricted use.

2. Estimate by the author using published and privileged sources.

3. *World Service Signposts* (Associated Press internal publication), 10 August 1973.

4. Stanley M. Swinton, "AP Global Operations," the Associated Press, mimeographed, March 1974.

5. The survey was conducted by the Associated Press and the findings reported in a speech by Stanley M. Swinton at the U.S. Naval War College, Newport, Rhode Island, 1974.

6. Kent Cooper, *Barriers Down* (New York: J. J. Little and Ives Co., 1942), p. 324.

7. Ibid., p. v.

8. Kent Cooper, *Kent Cooper and The Associated Press: An Autobiography* (New York: Random House, 1959), p. 270.

9. Sources: *United Nations Statistical Yearbook, 1973* (New York: Statistical Office of the United Nations, 1974); *Political Handbook and Atlas of the World, 1970*, ed. Richard P. Stebbins and Alba Amoia (New York: Simon and Schuster, 1970); *World Service Signposts* (Associated Press internal publication), pp. 11–13.

10. *World Service Signposts*, pp. 2–6.

11. George A. Krimsky, "The Associated Press," in *The American Way* (New York: American Airlines, 1974).

12. List provided to the author by Keith Fuller, vice-president of the Associated Press, in a letter dated 16 November 1975.

13. Interview with the author, April 1975.

14. "Manila Accuses a U.S. Newsman," *New York Times*, 28 February 1974.

15. Swinton interview, April 1975.

16. Lawrence Gobright quoted in "The History of AP," mimeographed, p. 2.

17. "The Associated Press," mimeographed, p. 5.

18. A copy of the letter was given to the author by UPI.

19. The number of foreign subscribers of both UPI and AP are those figures provided to the author by each organization. It should be noted, however, that there apparently is not a uniform standard of calculation. In some instances, it appears that national agencies were counted as single subscribers; in other cases, the members or subscribers to foreign agencies through which the Americans distribute were counted individually.

20. "From United Press International," mimeographed.

21. Negley D. Cochran, *E. W. Scripps* (Westport, Connecticut: Greenwood Press Publishers, 1972), p. 92.

22. Stephen Vincent Benet, "The United Press," *Fortune*, May 1933, p. 70.

23. Joe Alex Morros, *Deadline Every Minute* (Garden City, N.Y.: Doubleday & Co., 1957), p. 103.

24. Ibid., p. 108.

25. Benet, "The United Press," p. 94.

26. Interview with the author, 30 April 1975.

27. Benet, "The United Press," p. 94, reported that UP had 340 foreign clients. The 1975 figure is from the *UPI Progress Report*, 31 March 1975.

28. Interview with the author, 2 May 1975.

29. Provided to the author by the circulation department of the *Christian Science Monitor*, 20 May 1975.

30. Provided to the author by Don Shoemaker, editor of the *Miami Herald*, in a letter dated 11 April 1975.

31. Circulation figure contained in "European Businessman Readership Survey," Research Services Limited, January 1973 (Commissioned by the *Financial Times* which made a copy available to the author).

32. James O. Goldsborough, "An American in Paris: *The International Herald Tribune*," *Columbia Journalism Review*, July/August 1974, p. 37.

33. Eric Hawkins with Robert N. Sturdevant, *Hawkins of the Paris Herald* (New York: Simon and Schuster, 1963), p. 13.

34. Goldsborough, "An American in Paris," p. 42.

35. "European Businessman Readership Survey," p. 6.

36. Hawkins, *Hawkins of the Paris Herald*, p. 267.

37. Goldsborough, "An American in Paris," p. 45.

38. It is a practice of newsmagazines that publishing deadlines and issue dates are a week apart, so the significant decisions affecting the 5 May 1975 issue were made toward the end of the week of 20 April 1975 with printing begun 27 April. An impression of freshness is subtly conveyed to both the American reader, whose copy may linger for several days when the U.S. postal system is not very efficient, and to the foreign reader, who may be at the end of a complex distribution system.

39. Publisher's statement, 31 December 1975, Audit Bureau of Circulations, Chicago, Ill.

40. Robert T. Elson, *Time Inc., 1923–1941* (New York: Atheneum, 1968), p. 453.

41. Robert T. Elson, *Time Inc., 1941–1960* (New York: Atheneum, 1973), p. 259.

42. Ibid., p. 321.

43. Ibid., p. 320.

44. *FYI* (Time Inc. employee publication), 12 March 1973.

45. Elson, *Time Inc., 1941–1960*, pp. 326–27.

46. The estimate was made by the author.

47. "Decisionmakers," *Time Marketing Research Report* no. 1689, January 1972, p. 5. See also "A New Look at the Men Who Run Business in Latin America," *Report* no. 1686 (undated), and "Asia: The Men in Charge," *Report* no. 1796 (1973).

48. *The Market Coverage of the Worldwide Editions of Time* (Time Inc., 1972), p. 1.

49. *FYI* (Time Inc. employee publication), 15 January 1972.

50. Ibid.

51. *Time* estimates that each copy of its magazine is read by an average of five persons.

52. Interview with the author.

53. *The Washington Post Company Annual Report 1973*, 11 February 1974, p. 7.

54. According to data made available to the author, *Newsweek's* international circulation as of 30 June 1971, was 338,055, an increase of 49.6 percent over the 225,823 of 30 June 1967.

55. The profile of the typical reader of *Newsweek International* was virtually identical to that of the *Time* reader abroad as described previously.

56. Interview with the author, 17 December 1973.

57. Ibid.

58. *Newsweek International* promotional material, undated.

59. In 1972, columns by Ball, Brzezinski, and Bundy were discontinued in all editions of *Newsweek*.

60. *The Washington Post Company 1974 Annual Report* (1975), pp. 3–4.

61. Ibid. Income from operations for magazine and books: 1971 $2.7 million; 1972 $5.6 million; 1973 $9.1 million, p. 8.

62. Statement by Adrian Berwick, senior editor, *Reader's Digest* International Editions. U.S., Congress, House of Representatives, Subcommittee on International Organizations and Movements, Committee on Foreign Affairs, 88th Cong., 1st sess., 11 September 1963, p. 543.

63. From data supplied to the author by *Reader's Digest*.

64. Ibid.

65. Some information about *Reader's Digest* was provided to the author on the understanding that the source would not be explicitly identified.

66. For a detailed history of *Reader's Digest* see James Playsted Wood, *Of Lasting Interest* (Garden City, N.Y.: Doubleday & Co., 1967). Circulation figures cited are found on pp. 41, 245.

67. Ibid., p. 37.

68. Ibid., p. 156.

69. Ibid., p. 157.

70. Ibid., p. 230.

71. Interview with Jane R. Personneni, International Advertising Research Manager, *Reader's Digest*, 19 August 1974.

72. *Reader's Digest* provided the author with "Multinational Fact Sheets" for each international edition.

73. Ibid.

74. Ibid.

75. "*Selecciones del Reader's Digest*, a Mail Survey of Subscribers and Newsstand Buyers," conducted by Erdos & Morgan, Inc., February 1972; "*Reader's Digest* in Key Cities Europe, A Mail Survey of Subscribers," conducted by Erdos & Morgan, Inc., May 1974. Both were made available to the author by *Reader's Digest*.

76. "*Reader's Digest* Multinational Fact Sheets."

CHAPTER 4

1. President Truman called for a great "Campaign of Truth" in a speech before the American Society of Newspaper Editors, January 1950.

2. U.S., Department of State Publication 8757, Foreword.

3. Nobutaka Shikanai, "The Fuji Sankei Group's Activities," unpublished paper, 30 September 1974.

4. The comment was made to the author during a conversation in Hong Kong, 1972.

5. Results of the survey by Newsclip Ltd., London were made available to the author by *Newsweek*.

6. I am indebted to Professor Tunstall for having shared with me a draft of his article, "The Media are American: Anglo-American Mass Media in the World" (London: Jeremy Tunstall, 1974).

7. See Raymond Vernon, *Sovereignty at Bay* (New York: Basic Books, 1971), pp. 65–77.

8. *New York Times,* 24 October 1974.

9. John Spicer Nichols, "LATIN—Latin American Regional News Agency," a paper presented to the International Communications Division, Association for Education in Journalism, San Diego, 18 August 1974.

10. Seymour Martin Lipset, "The Possible Political Effects of Student Activism," *Social Science Information* 8, no. 2 (April 1969): 12.

11. W. Phillips Davison, "News Media and International Negotiation," *Public Opinion Quarterly* 38, no. 2 (Spring 1974): 174.

12. The level of mass media standards set by UNESCO are that for every one hundred persons there should be at least ten newspapers, five radios, two movie seats, and two television sets.

13. Alex Inkeles, "The Emerging Social Structure of the World," a paper presented at the International Political Science Association meeting, Montreal, Canada, 20–23 August 1973, was a major resource in writing this section.

14. For a thoughtful discussion of cultural diversity in the world see "Reconstituting The Human Community," a report by the Hazen Foundation, New Haven, Connecticut, 1972.

15. The suggestion is made by Stanley Hoffmann in "International Organization and the International System," *International Organization* 24, no. 3 (Summer 1970): 389–413.

16. J. J. Servan-Schreiber, *The American Challenge* (New York: Atheneum, 1968), p. 101.

17. Robert O. Keohane and Joseph S. Nye, Jr., "Transnational Relations and World Politics: A Conclusion," in Robert O. Keohane and Joseph S. Nye, Jr., eds., *Transnational Relations and World Politics* (Cambridge, Massachusetts: Harvard University Press, 1970), p. 372. This book is a pioneering study of transnationalism.

18. Georgi Arbatov, *The War of Ideas in Contemporary International Relations* (Moscow: Progress Publishers, 1973), p. 200.

19. James Keogh, "Information, Culture and Modern Diplomacy," *Foreign Service Journal,* July 1974.

20. Ibid.

21. *New York Times,* 12 October 1974.

22. See Frederick S. Siebert, Theodore B. Peterson, and Wilbur L. Schramm, *Four Theories of the Press* (Urbana: University of Illinois Press, 1963).

23. Herbert I. Schiller, "Freedom from the 'Free Flow,'" *Journal of Communications* 24, no. 1 (Winter 1974): 116.

24. Ibid., p. 112.

25. Ibid., p. 111.

26. Ibid., p. 113.

27. See Joseph Scanlon, "Canada Sees the World Through U.S. Eyes," *The Canadian Forum,* September 1974, pp. 34–39.

28. Canadian Institute of Public Opinion, Poll no. 341 (1970).

29. As quoted in D. C. Thompson and R. F. Swanson, *Canadian Foreign Policy* (New York: Praeger, 1970), p. 138.

30. Kenneth McNaught, *The History of Canada* (New York: Praeger, 1970), p. 238.

31. Canadian Institute of Public Opinion, Polls nos. 291 (1961) and 318 (1966).

32. John H. Sigler and Dennis Goresky, "Public Opinion on Transnational United States-Canadian Relations," unpublished paper, Fall 1974.

33. *Mass Media Volume II,* Report of the Special Senate Committee on Mass Media (Ottawa: Information Canada, 1970).

34. See Proposals for a Communications Policy for Canada, a Position Paper of the Government of Canada (Ottawa: Information Canada, 1973).

35. See the *Annual Report of the Canadian Broadcasting Corporation 1972–73,* (Montreal: CBC, 1973).

36. *Mass Media Volume III,* Special Senate Committee on Mass Media (Ottawa: Information Canada, 1970).

37. Several small American professional journals also benefited by the tax provision.

38. Isaiah A. Litvak and Christopher J. Maule, "Interest Group Tactics and the Politics of Foreign Investment: The *Time-Reader's Digest* Case Study," *Canadian Journal of Political Science/Review* 8, no. 4 (December 1974): 617.

39. Ibid.

40. Ibid.

41. *Toronto Globe and Mail*, 1 February 1974.

42. Mordecai Richler, "Letter from Ottawa," *Harper's*, June 1975, p. 29.

43. Title of an article in *TV Guide*, 16 March 1974.

44. The first nonexperimental DBS system was being developed for Japan.

45. This review drew heavily on an unpublished paper, Ithiel de Sola Pool, "Satellite Broadcasting: A U.S. Dilemma in the U.N.," undated.

46. Paul F. Lazarsfeld and Robert K. Merton, "Mass Communications, Popular Taste and Organized Social Action," in Lyman Bryson, ed., *The Communications of Ideas* (New York: Institute for Religious and Social Studies, 1948), pp. 95–118.

CHAPTER 5

1. Paul F. Lazarsfeld and Robert K. Mertin, "Mass Communications, Popular Taste and Organized Social Action," in Lyman Bryson, ed., *The Communications of Ideas* (New York: Institute for Religious and Social Studies, 1948), pp. 95–118.

2. Harold D. Lasswell, "The Structure and Function of Communication in Society," in Lyman Bryson, ed., *The Communications of Ideas*, pp. 37–51.

3. Interview with the author.

4. Robert O. Keohane and Joseph S. Nye, Jr., "Transnational Relations and World Politics: A Conclusion," in Robert O. Keohane and Joseph S. Nye, Jr., eds., *Transnational Relations and World Politics* (Cambridge, Massachusetts: Harvard University Press, 1970), p. 372.

5. Harold R. Isaacs, "Nationality: 'End of the Road?'" *Foreign Affairs* 53, no. 2 (April 1975): 446.

6. Kjell Skjelsback, "The Growth of International Nongovernmental Organization in the Twentieth Century," in Keohane and Nye, eds., *Transnational Relations and World Politics*, p. 74.

7. Isaacs, "Nationality: 'End of the Road?'" p. 440.

8. Sir Winston Churchill, in remarks to the House of Commons, British Parliament, 11 November 1947.

INDEX

Library of Congress Cataloging in Publication Data

Read, William H.
  America's mass media merchants.

  Includes bibliographical references and index.
  1. Mass media—United States. 2. Intercultural
communication. I. Title.
P92.U5R4   301.16′1   76–17231
ISBN 0–8018–1851–6

In a book packed with provocative ideas, a seasoned newsman charts the rise of the American mass media and examines the implications of their global penetration. Mark Twain's humorous comment that "there are only two forces that carry light to all corners of the globe—the sun in the heavens, and the Associated Press down here" has indeed proved prophetic. In the year 1973, for example:

- 200 leading newspapers outside the USA subscribed to either the *New York Times* or the *Washington Post-Los Angeles Times* news services
- UPI stories were translated into 48 languages
- *Reader's Digest* had a foreign circulation of 12 million copies monthly
- Exports of American films and television programs amounted to $335 million
- *Time* magazine's world-wide readership was a 25 million information elite.

The fact that American mass media have established themselves as strong currents in the global transfer of information and entertainment is beyond dispute. What the man in the street in Bogotá or Bangkok learns about world news probably came from them. William H. Read documents in detail the transnational development of the Associated Press and United Press International, the *New York Times* and the *Washington Post-Los Angeles Times* news services, the *International Herald Tribune*, *Newsweek, Time,* and *Reader's Digest.* He describes their day-to-day operations, the principles guiding their editorial selection and coverage, and their financing and management.

The international distribution of American movies and television programs is also scrutinized. Read recalls his own experience in seeing a mixed East Asian audience held spellbound by the adventures of "Marcus Welby, M.D." But how the world came to love Lucy, or cliff-hang with "Kojak," represents to many countries—Third World,